GENDER IN THE MUSIC INDUSTRY

Gender in the Music Industry

Rock, Discourse and Girl Power

MARION LEONARD
University of Liverpool, UK

ASHGATE

Published by
Ashgate Publishing Limited
Wey Court East
Union Road
Farnham
Surrey, GU9 7PT
England

Ashgate Publishing Company
110 Cherry Street
Suite 3-1
Burlington, VT 05401-3818
USA

www.ashgate.com

British Library Cataloguing in Publication Data
Leonard, Marion
  Gender in the music industry : rock, discourse and girl power. – (Ashgate popular and folk music series)
  1. Women rock musicians 2. Rock music – History and criticism 3. Women in music
  4. Gender identity in music
  I. Title
  781.6'6'082

Library of Congress Cataloging-in-Publication Data
Leonard, Marion, 1970–
    Gender in the music industry : rock, discourse and girl power / Marion Leonard.
        p. cm. – (Ashgate popular and folk music series)
    Includes bibliographical references (p.   ) and discography (p.   ).
    ISBN-13: 978-0-7546-3861-2 (hardback : alk. paper)
    ISBN-13: 978-0-7546-3862-9 (pbk. : alk. paper)
    1. Alternative rock music – History and criticism. 2. Women rock musicians. 3. Riot grrrl movement. I. Title.

  ML3534.L456 2007
  781.66082–dc22

2006032262

ISBN 978-0-7546-3861-2 HBK
ISBN 978-0-7546-3862-9 PBK

Reprinted 2013

MIX
Paper from
responsible sources
FSC
www.fsc.org   FSC® C013985

Printed in the United Kingdom by Henry Ling Limited, at the Dorset Press, Dorchester, DT1 1HD

Contents

List of figures

General Editor's preface

The upheaval that occurred in musicology during the last two decades of the twentieth century has created a new urgency for the study of popular music alongside the development of new critical and theoretical models. A relativistic outlook has replaced the universal perspective of modernism (the international ambitions of the 12-note style); the grand narrative of the evolution and dissolution of tonality has been challenged, and emphasis has shifted to cultural context, reception and subject position. Together, these have conspired to eat away at the status of canonical composers and categories of high and low in music. A need has arisen, also, to recognize and address the emergence of crossovers, mixed and new genres, to engage in debates concerning the vexed problem of what constitutes authenticity in music and to offer a critique of musical practice as the product of free, individual expression.

Popular musicology is now a vital and exciting area of scholarship, and the *Ashgate Popular and Folk Music Series* aims to present the best research in the field. Authors will be concerned with locating musical practices, values and meanings in cultural context, and may draw upon methodologies and theories developed in cultural studies, semiotics, poststructuralism, psychology and sociology. The series will focus on popular musics of the twentieth and twenty-first centuries. It is designed to embrace the world's popular musics from Acid Jazz to Zydeco, whether high tech or low tech, commercial or non-commercial, contemporary or traditional.

Professor Derek B. Scott
Chair of Music
University of Salford

Acknowledgements

This book is based on my PhD thesis, which I completed at the Institute of Popular Music, University of Liverpool, under the guidance of Sara Cohen. I would like to thank Sara for her suggestions, constructive criticism and support over the years. Throughout the writing of both the thesis and the book, the Institute of Popular Music proved to be an enormously supportive environment thanks to the encouragement and friendship of colleagues including Sara, David Horn, Mike Jones, Jason Toynbee, Mike Brocken, Holly Tessler, Debbie Ellery and Natasha Davies. Thanks also go to my external examiner John Shepherd, who provided invaluable feedback. Many thanks to the editorial team at Ashgate, in particular Heidi May, Derek Scott and Anne Keirby.

Sincere thanks go to all the musicians, riot grrrls and people involved with Ladyfest who so generously gave up their time to share their thoughts and insights. Special thanks go to Louise Hanman for extended conversations, Red Chidgey and Sakura for providing photographs and to the numerous other people, including Lisa, Maria and Marion, who provided me with contacts and mailed me with ideas. I also owe a debt of gratitude to others who helped me during the research process: Lori Taylor who went out of her way to generously provide access to difficult to find zines and press accounts of riot grrrl, the staff of Women in Music for providing materials from their archive, Kay Dickinson for providing stimulating company and a roof over my head during Ladyfest London, and the numerous venue and tour managers who facilitated interviews with touring musicians.

The ideas that were to make up this book were presented at seminars and conferences, occasions that always provided challenging and stimulating feedback. I would especially like to thank friends and colleagues from the International Association for the Study of Popular Music, including Dave Laing, Eamonn Forde, Paul Hodkinson, Keith Kahn-Harris and Dave Hesmondhalgh.

An early version of Chapter 5 appeared as '"Rebel girl, you are the queen of my world": feminism, "subculture" and grrrl power', in Sheila Whiteley (ed.), *Sexing the Groove: Popular Music and Gender*, London: Routledge. Parts of Chapter 6 appeared as 'Paper planes: travelling the new grrrl geographies', in Tracey Skelton and Gill Valentine (eds), *Cool Places: Geographies of Youth Cultures*, London: Routledge. I would like to thank the editors of these books for their enthusiastic response to my research.

I would like to thank the many friends who have provided encouragement throughout the process, especially Suzanne Roberts and Emma Latham (who also patiently read over drafts of the original thesis), Chloë Mullett and Laura Kinsey. I am especially indebted to my parents, Ellen and John, who have been untiringly supportive throughout. Finally, heartfelt thanks go to my partner Rob Strachan for his continual encouragement, support, friendship and patience in the process of writing this book.

Introduction

This book is about gender, rock music and the music industry. Over the past 20 years analysis of gender and rock has often begun with the premise that rock is created and performed by men or that it exemplifies a masculinist culture (Rodnitzky, 1975; Chapple and Garofalo, 1978: 269–96; Harding and Nett, 1984; Frith and McRobbie, 1990). This book explores this topic further, examining different representations of masculinity offered by, and performed through, rock music, and how female rock performers negotiate the gendering of rock as masculine. The central concern is not specifically with men or women performing rock but with how notions of gender affect the everyday experiences of all rock musicians within the context of the music industry. Feminist theory has distinguished between the biological categories of sex (male and female) and the socially constructed categories of gender (e.g. masculinity and femininity). This separation of biological sex from modes of gender socialisation has allowed critics to question apparently 'natural' modes of social behaviour and challenge gender distinctions that support systems of inequality between men and women. Contemporary debate has broadened the scope of gender studies from a focus on women to analysis of institutions and related discourses of masculinity and femininity, and it has problematised even the apparent epistemological surety of the categorisation of sex (Butler, 1990: 6f.). Gender identities and discourses are not to be understood as static but as dynamic, changing over time and relating to the particular contexts of their production. As Butler states: 'it becomes impossible to separate out "gender" from the political and cultural intersections in which it is invariably produced and maintained' (1990: 3). This book examines how gender is 'produced and maintained' by discourses, institutions, groups and individuals operating within the music industry.

Throughout the following discussion a broad definition of the music industry is adopted, which includes institutions such as record companies and studios, and individuals such as musicians, promoters and record company staff. The book examines the interaction between a range of such music industry representatives, considering the way in which professional and artistic relationships, as well as managerial and financial decisions, are influenced by conceptions of gender. The intention is not to offer a broad overview of every facet of the industry but to concentrate attention on a range of practitioners and to examine their working practices. Much of the following analysis is specifically concerned with how musicians (whether amateur or experienced professionals) negotiate the music industry. For this reason particular attention has been given to those music industry professionals with whom rock musicians have most frequent contact, such as journalists, sound engineers, promoters, photographers and A&R (artist and repertoire) staff. The book draws on interview material with musicians to consider how they discuss, relate to and are positioned by these other industry workers. It examines how musicians operate within the music industry, the interaction they experience with other music industry workers and how those musicians are presented to the public via promotion and publicity strategies.

Core questions about gender, rock and the music industry will be addressed using a case study of musicians within a specific music genre and time frame: UK and US 'female-centred' bands performing so-called 'indie rock' from the early 1990s to the present. The term female-centred is used here to refer to bands that predominantly comprise female members who control the majority of the bands' creative output. I have avoided the term 'female rock groups' in order to allow for the inclusion of bands that contain men and women in their line up.[1] I have not focused on solo rock vocalists as my interest lies in considering how gender affects the professional lives of rock bands. Thus, male-dominated bands with a female singer, or solo female vocal artists, are generally not included. This criteria is consistent with Mary Ann Clawson's study of gender and instrument playing in rock bands. Clawson omits vocalists from her study on the basis that 'ensemble instrument playing is both the principal site of musical authority in rock music and the activity from which women have been most fully excluded'(Clawson, 1999a: 99). While a rock group comprising female instrumentalists *and* vocalists challenges certain associations between rock and masculinity, a male band with a female vocalist does not.[2]

The decision to use female-centred bands as a case study should not be understood as an assumption that studies of gender are necessarily studies of women. Rather, through the analysis of these bands, this book will discuss gendered discourses and practices, examining key areas of music industry practice in which gendered identities are presented and negotiated, such as in music performance, through media discourse surrounding music, and within music networks and scenes. In relation to these areas, a detailed analysis will be offered of riot grrrl, a feminist network promoted by female musicians, which emerged in the early 1990s. Riot grrrl developed within indie rock scenes in the US and UK, and encouraged and facilitated the participation of girls and women within indie rock practice. The book will also consider the organisation and staging of numerous international Ladyfests, a network of festivals organised by women and inspired by the earlier riot grrrl initiative. In focusing on female-centred indie bands I do not wish to peculiarise the position of these groups as somehow significant or different because of the sex of the musicians. Indeed, all too often journalistic articles and populist books focusing on 'women in rock' serve to differentiate female musicians from 'regular' male rock performers and thus to ghettoise their work (Katz, 1978; Thomson, 1982). Instead, I wish to investigate how these musicians experience working within this industrial context and to what extent notions of gender are significant within their work environment. While the concern of this book is with popular music production and mediation, its emphasis on understanding the significance of gender within a professional context places it within a tradition of gender – and indeed feminist – studies, which seek to understand how perceptions of gender impact on social and cultural environments. Although discussion will centre around the discourses and professional practices of the music industry, it should be remembered that the gendered character of the music industry and rock music generally both reflects and serves to constitute the gendered character of wider social and cultural realities and structures.

The book focuses on 'indie' in order to consider how gendered understandings and representations operate within a particular subgenre of rock music, and in order to avoid discussing rock music as if it were a composite whole with singular or clear defining characteristics. Certainly rock has many common characteristics, from its tendency to employ particular instrumentation (electric guitars, drums and electric bass) and styles of performance,[3] to the existence of common song structures.[4] However, even basic definitions and histories of rock give rise to complications and dispute. One attempt to define or explain rock, for example, describes the emergence of rock 'n' roll in 1955 and the elements of 'European music (harmony, poetic narrative) ... [and also] driving rhythm, call-and-response shouts and scales with dissonant notes, known as "blue notes"' (Roberts *et al.*, 1998: 364). As Richard Middleton argues, even at that time rock contained not only 'boogie rhythms, rough sound, blues shouts and physical involvement but also sentimental ballad melodies and forms, "angelic" backing vocal effects and "novelty" gimmicks' (Middleton, 1993: 18). The subsequent development of rock over almost half a century has resulted in a proliferation of experiments with the form, and the establishment of distinct subgenres such as death metal, industrial and post-rock. Each of these subgenres can be described not only in musicological terms but also by other codes of practice such as performance style, associated fashions, record sleeve design, and the cultural practices of those who listen to and engage with them (whether at gigs, in record shops or in clubs).

The focus on indie rock allows for an in-depth discussion of music, performance and discursive practices within a more specific generic frame of reference. Indie (sometimes referred to interchangeably as alternative rock) is a particularly interesting case study as it has popularly been understood as being more open to female participation than other rock forms. As Holly Kruse comments, 'alternative rock has provided women with a place where they are freer to write songs, play instruments, form bands, and produce records than has traditionally been the case' (Kruse, 1999: 92). While the participation of women within indie rock will be discussed later, it may reasonably be asserted that indie is not associated with an overt masculinist agenda or with hostility to female participation. There has been a tendency in studies of women in popular music to collect together pieces of information on performers and practitioners across a range of occupations, and from diverse and distinct music genres such as pop, soul, rap and jazz (Thomson, 1982; Steward and Garratt, 1985; O'Dair, 1997). These studies presuppose a comparability of experience based on the premise that all the subjects under discussion are women. While such an approach may offer a snapshot of activity and participation, it ignores differences between women, assumes that they share common experiences, and fails to acknowledge that different music genres carry with them distinct histories, performance practices and discourses that affect how gender is constructed and experienced.

Discussion within this book is chiefly concerned with the day-to-day experiences of musicians performing and producing indie rock, and the related activities of those involved in the production, promotion and mediation of this music. While individual songs, albums and performances will be discussed, detailed musicological or lyrical analysis will not be offered. Analysis of the sonic and lyrical content of music performed by female-centred bands would certainly have produced rich research results, however this type of detailed textual analysis is not the central concern of this book. Discussion will centre on how the culture of the music industry, with specific attention to indie rock, is produced as a *gendered culture* that affects those who work within it. A number of the female-centred bands discussed in this book, particularly those identified with riot grrrl, have written songs that comment on issues of gender and sexuality as related to indie music scenes or to the wider social sphere. However, the concern here is not so much with how artists have commented on gender through their work (although this will be discussed to some extent) as with how they experience gendered attitudes within their working environment.

It has been argued that the sonic characteristics of rock music themselves constitute material grounds that militate in favour of the creation and reproduction of certain gender identities and against the reproduction of others. For example, in a discussion of the overtly masculine performance conventions of 'cock rock', Frith and McRobbie (1990: 374) have observed that 'the music is loud, rhythmically insistent, built around techniques of aroUSl and climax; the lyrics are assertive and arrogant, though the exact words are less significant than the vocal styles involved, the shouting and screaming'. This type of analysis tends to map between an understanding that loud and harsh guitar and vocal sounds signify strength and potency, and that such characteristics are associated with masculinity. This book is less concerned with how rock music might lend itself to be naturalised as masculine than with how the notion of rock as masculine is reproduced, sustained and promoted within rock culture and the wider music industry.

As the central case study is on 'indie' rock bands, it is necessary to establish a working definition of this term. The term 'indie' is somewhat problematic as its exact definition and its boundaries are open to dispute. Indeed, the term encompasses a wide range of musical expression, which may in turn be broken down into particular subgenres and subgroups. Indie music is associated with certain local and translocal 'scenes' or cultures,[5] with independent record labels, distributors and retailers, and with particular (though diverse) stylistic characteristics drawing influence from an eclectic range of sources including electronica, 1960s psychedelia and punk (see Straw, 1991). In the early 1980s there appeared to be a 'fit' with the musical style of indie bands and their industrial means of promotion via independent record and distribution companies. However, as Hesmondhalgh has described, the concept of 'indie' has changed over time such that it has emerged 'as a genre, rather than as an economic category' (Hesmondhalgh, 1996: 131). The investment by a number of major record companies in bands and performers whose music is categorised as 'indie' or 'alternative' has distanced this music from a tie with independent record labels and systems of distribution. As Hesmondhalgh has more recently argued, indie can now be viewed as a genre that 'has become part of the "mainstream" of British pop' (Hesmondhalgh, 1999: 34). There are now a large number of bands released on major labels and not identified with underground subcultures who are nevertheless categorised by retailers, DJs, journalists and consumers as 'indie' due to the musical, aesthetic and discursive codes that they tap into. Partly because of its historical association with independent record companies, distributors and promoters, indie has also been tied in to certain notions of artistic autonomy and of opposition to mainstream values and trends. This association has led some supporters of indie rock to suggest that it represents an authentic form of underground music (see, for example, Fairchild, 1995). However, such arguments construct notions of authenticity in particular and problematic ways. Trying to mark out the musical boundaries of indie is fraught with difficulties as the genre exhibits a 'circumscribed pluralism' (Straw, 1991: 380), which borrows stylistic influence from a broad set of references, and those borders are open to revision and debate. Moreover, as Hibbett has observed, definitions of indie are often 'problematically subjective' as 'particular notions of "what is indie" are closely bound to personal experience, as well as age and social class' (Hibbett, 2005: 59).

This book employs a very broad understanding of indie rock. The musicians discussed within it include those involved with indie music at a grass-roots level, such as those involved in the riot grrrl network, who described themselves using a language of opposition and resistance. Some of these musicians are signed to micro independent labels that distribute via DIY networks. However, I also discuss the experience of the members of bands signed to major record companies, such as Pooka (UK) and Kenickie (UK), whose music may be described as 'indie-folk' and 'pure pop' respectively. The reason for including bands who are signed to small independent labels, and who value the notion of the underground, will be self-evident as it is bound up with indie discourse. However, I have also included artists who are not connected to underground labels but whose music, attitudes and image work to categorise them as indie performers. These artists form part of an indie field of reference. They are discussed in music magazines and papers with a bias towards indie and underground music, featured in indie music fanzines and played on indie radio shows and at specialist indie club nights.

A considerable amount of space within the book is bound up with the analysis of 'discourses' within the field of rock music. By 'discourse' I refer in part to types of speech or expression in common parlance within the music industry, paying some attention to the forms of language employed by musicians and commentators. But, my main employment of the term draws on the work of Michel Foucault (1990) as it is concerned with how systems of expression and knowledge hold and imbue power. This analysis of indie rock will consider how written music histories are established and disseminated, how aesthetic conventions are talked about and defended, and how musical performance is discussed and valued. It will explore how these discourses offer an account of the nature of 'indie' music, and will argue that 'common sense' notions of a music genre often serve to conceal underlying systems of evaluation and appraisal. An analysis of such discourses aids the understanding of how certain gendered conceptions of music practice and consumption are reproduced and supported. Admittedly, practices and processes wider than those of discourse and canon formation may well be at play in constituting the gendered character of the music industry and rock music generally. However, in focusing on the discursive practices and processes through which rock music is produced, valued and historicised this book will consider central ways in which gendered notions of rock music and the culture of the music industry are maintained and reproduced.

The concerns of this book can be expressed as a number of key questions: why, despite the number of high-profile female rock musicians, does rock continue to be understood as masculine? To what extent do constructions of gender affect the everyday working relationships between a musician and other music industry workers, such as producers, promoters and sound engineers? In what way do written accounts (such as press coverage and rock histories) produce a gendered rock discourse? Do notions of gender affect professional decision making by personnel within the music industry, such as record company A&R staff and promotions officers? These questions will be addressed within the book by focusing on particular themes and issues including rock press discourse, media representation, marketing and performance strategies. In addition, the everyday working lives of musicians will be discussed through a detailed focus on the experiences of specific performers in indie rock bands.

Commentators have cited the male domination of the music industry as a reason for a lack of female role models and for the perpetuation of a masculine culture (Steward and Garratt, 1985; Frith and McRobbie, 1990; Cameron, 2003). In this respect, the music industry can be linked to a range of other areas of professional practice that are male dominated such as, for example, journalism or law. With respect to journalism, for instance, Aldridge (1998) has commented on how the 'prescribed behaviour is quintessentially macho, involving any permutation of drinking too much, smoking too much, working too much, turbulent personal relationships and bodily excess' (1998: 116). This working environment can certainly be cited as an example of a pervasive masculine culture and, significantly, there are few female journalists in key positions within the UK press. Aldridge notes that, by 1998, no woman had worked as editor of a UK national daily newspaper and that the women who had gone on to edit Sunday papers were judged 'as qualifying for the position by their ability to match the lads' behaviour' (1998: 116). Cameron's (2003) article, looking into the role and functioning of women within the music industry, similarly identifies instances of where the progress of women within their careers appears to hit a glass ceiling and falls below parity with men. He reflects that 'the position in classical music is analogous to that in the corporate sector ... whereby female prevalence thins out as we progress up the hierarchy' (Cameron, 2003: 915). This book will discuss how the gendering of rock as masculinist has been established and re-established through the intersection of conventions of rock performance and interaction, and through discourses particular to the rock genre. It will examine assumptions about the natural association of rock with masculinity and analyse how they affect female rock performers. Focusing on women performing in rock bands, consideration will be given to how the performance, marketing and consumption of rock music are bound up with a gendered discourse. The book will also discuss how particular modes of behaviour within rock music are informed by a culture of masculinity and how this affects everyday interactions and professional relationships within the music industry.

In researching this book I have drawn on numerous studies (including Walser, 1993; Reynolds and Press, 1995; Whiteley, 1997; Kennedy, 2002; Auslander, 2004) that address how masculinity and sexuality are represented in rock performance, both musically and visually. A number of these studies use examples of 'cock rock' (Frith and McRobbie, 1990; Shepherd, 1991: 152–73) or heavy metal (Walser, 1993) as these musical styles present clear examples of male display, employing macho poses and rasping vocals. The traditional notions and rather narrow images of male heterosexual identity and representation within such music have been usefully examined and questioned by scholars such as Gill (1995), Bradby (1993) and Wise (1990). Further useful studies have considered the gendering of rock instrumentation (Bayton, 1997; Clawson, 1999b; Waksman, 1999), discussions about gender and music on the internet (Coates, 1998) and the way in which music technology is targeted at a male audience (Thebérge, 1991; Keightley, 1996). I will discuss these texts in the course of this book, highlighting their relevance to an analysis of gender and rock discourse.

Often detailed analyses of the operation of the music industry have been gender blind or have given only brief attention to the subject of gender (Bennett, 1980; Hesmondhalgh, 1996; Jones, 1997). There are some exceptions, such as Cameron's (2003) article on the political economy of gender disparity in music markets and Dickerson's (1998) book, which considers the practices of the recording industry from a historical perspective by examining the careers of notable female performers over a 40-year period. Other studies have analysed gender in relation to select roles or occupations within the music industry (e.g. Steward and Garratt, 1985; Negus, 1992; Smaill, 2005). Keith Negus, for example, has discussed how few women are employed as A&R scouts within record companies and how women fulfil the supporting role of secretarial 'handmaidens' within A&R departments (Negus, 1992: 57–8). Negus also remarks that while there are few female sound engineers, producers or music journalists (1992: 85, 118–19), women tend to find employment as publicity officers and public relations staff, which 'involves the employment of skills which have traditionally been associated with women rather than men' (1992: 115). These women are responsible for 'looking after sensitive artists, maintaining personal relationships, providing support, and acting as a matchmaker by bringing people with similar dispositions together' (1992: 115). The fact that Negus discusses the issue of gender in connection with publicity officers and public relations staff is suggestive of the view that gender studies are most appropriately applied to studies of women in particular gendered occupations.

Studies that focus *solely* upon women musicians or female music industry workers have, by contrast, often paid little attention to the broader structure and operation of the music industry. Discussions of female musicians have often focused on the male domination of the music industry and have presented the achievements of high-profile female performers as a 'long hard climb' (Chapple and Garofalo, 1978: 269) 'against all odds' (Katz, 1978: 1), and as an attempt to rip 'up the infrastructure of male rock tradition' (Evans, 1994: v). I do not wish to oversimplify the work published on female performers but to highlight the way that this work has often been framed. Such texts seldom discuss how the difficulties encountered by female performers relate to those encountered by all musicians, regardless of their sex, such as difficulties regarding contracts, artistic freedom and career opportunities. Indeed, as Holly Kruse has stated, 'two crucial elements have been painfully lacking from most feminist critiques of popular music: analyses of popular music institutions and economics, and analyses of practice' (Kruse, 1999: 85).

It is noteworthy that the voices of musicians have frequently been absent from studies of the music industry (see Negus, 1992; Hesmondhalgh, 1996; Peterson and Berger, 1975) and so this book addresses the need for further research with musicians,[6] which is contextualised within an understanding of the music industry. Thus it contributes to the small but growing number of academic studies concerned with gender and popular music that draw on field research with musicians. Notable examples of such work are Mary Ann Clawson's (1999a; 1999b) research with male and female bass players, Groce and Cooper's (1990) research with local-level female rock musicians, Helen Reddington's (2003) research on female punk instrumentalists, Leslie Gourse's (1995) book, which draws on interviews with female jazz performers, and Sherrie Tucker's (2000) history of 'all-girl' jazz and swing bands of the 1940s. The doctoral work of Mavis Bayton (1989) represents a detailed academic account of the experiences of women performing in all-female rock bands in the UK. Bayton's thesis is a sociological study concerned with the careers of female musicians, which draws on in-depth interviews with performers at various stages of their careers. Bayton (1998) later updated this work, building in further ethnographic research with female musicians conducted from 1995–96. Bayton is crucially concerned with 'how women become rock musicians' and so offers a discussion of entry routes into musicianship, the constraints experienced by women, and various stages in the careers of female rock performers. Also noteworthy is the work of Carson, Lewis and Shaw (2004), which presents a historical and feminist analysis of women rock musicians over the past 50 years and includes original interview material with US musicians. As the authors explain, they 'privilege their words because their stories are so compellingly told and because they have so seldom been asked about their own music' (Carson *et al.*, 2004: xvi).

There are a considerable number of books and articles that do focus upon and examine the work of female musicians. Whiteley (2000), for example, has explored the changing role of women musicians from the 1960s to the 1990s through a case-study approach, which considers acclaimed performers in the genres of pop, folk and rock. While some studies have examined the work of female-centred bands (O'Meara, 2003) more often academic attention has focused on female solo performers, especially high-profile artists such as Madonna (Kaplan, 1987; McClary, 1991: 148–66; Paglia, 1992: 3–13; hooks, 1995: 318–25; Vernallis: 1998; Fouz-Hernández and Jarman-Ivens, 2004). In addition to this an identifiable body of work has developed that documents, revisits and reclaims histories of female performance. This includes texts that attempt to present a chronological account of the contribution of women to popular music (Gaar, 1993; O'Brien, 1995b; Hirshey, 2001), books that focus on female musicians performing in a particular geographical location (Dreyfus, 1999) and within particular music genres (Kent, 1983; Dahl, 1984; Placksin, 1985; Greig, 1989). These texts may be understood as part of the feminist project to write 'forgotten' women back into history, thus offering more complete documents of female participation in and contribution to particular fields of activity.[7] The texts address the fact that the work of female performers has often been marginalised within written histories of popular music. Admittedly some of these accounts have tended to be celebratory rather than critical analyses of the careers of female performers. Moreover, due to the broad scope of many of these books, they are able only to touch upon the work of some musicians and eras rather than offer in-depth analyses.

Some work has been conducted on women performing or participating in the culture of indie rock, such as Milioto's (1998) account of women in Japanese popular music, which compares Japanese pop (j-pop) performers with contemporary female punk, hardcore and indie musicians. In the past decade, considerable academic attention has been given to the emergence and significance of riot grrrl. Some of this work has considered the beginnings and development of this feminist network (e.g. Taylor, 1993; Gottlieb and Wald, 1994; Cateforis and Humphreys, 1997; Kearney, 1997; Rosenberg and Garofalo, 1998; Anderson and Jenkins, 2001). A number of studies have been concerned with the ways in which riot grrrl was promoted via the mainstream media (Davies, 2001) and through the micro-media networks of zines (Schilt, 2003b). Intersecting with these studies of the mediation of riot grrrl, some critics have traced the incorporation of certain riot grrrl ideas within mainstream culture (Jacques, 2001) and examined how the feminist rhetoric of this network has been repackaged and sold by media industries (Riordan, 2001). Particular attention has been given to the use and impact of the phrase 'girl power' by the British pop group the Spice Girls in the late 1990s, a phrase that had previously been promoted within riot grrrl zines (Treagus, 1998; Davies, 1999; Dibben, 1999; Driscoll, 1999; Hopkins, 1999; Whiteley, 2000; Lemish, 2003; Schilt, 2003a; Fritzsche, 2004; Taft, 2004). The insights afforded by this material have provided useful comparative material to my own research on riot grrrl, which is discussed in detail in Chapters 5 and 6. These chapters update my earlier work (Leonard, 1997, 1998) examining zine networks, and draw on interview material from the early 1990s to the present day in order to consider how riot grrrl has developed over time.

Other studies (Reynolds and Press, 1995; Nehring, 1997) that discuss gender and contemporary rock generally have also been useful in research for this book as they have included interesting analysis of female indie performers and of riot grrrl. In addition, interview material with female indie performers is included in a number of edited books focusing more generally on women in music (Evans, 1994; Raphael, 1995; O'Dair, 1997; Post, 1997; Woodworth, 1998), while further interview material is found in texts specifically focused on indie music (Juno, 1996). These books present the experiences of female popular music performers (including indie rock musicians) in terms of personal histories, making use of transcribed interviews in order to let the musicians 'speak for themselves'.[8] Such texts offer an insight into the way that contemporary female musicians discuss their music and think about gender and, as such, they have provided useful data with which to compare my own research findings.

A number of other studies (e.g. Jensen, 1993; Berry, 1994; Cooper, 1995) that focus on the participation and representation of women in a particular music genre have also provided useful insights for the writing of this book. While I have not directly cited such studies or followed their methodologies, I have nevertheless found them informative in their examinations of the operation of gender stereotypes in popular music. Beverley Skeggs (1993), for instance, has examined the work of a number of female rappers who have confronted and ridiculed misogyny in gangsta rap. Skeggs describes how female rap performers challenge music conventions while working within their boundaries. Hazel Carby's (1990) study of female blues singers from the 1920s and 1930s also considers spaces of resistance in song, examining how some vocalists use songs to express ideas about female sexuality, frustration and relationships. The close readings by Lori Burns and Mélisse Lafrance (2002) of lyrics by four female musicians from the 1990s, two of whom feature within the analysis of this book, explore the disruptive potential of popular song and also consider how songs can challenge discourses of sex, gender and race. While this book does not employ such lyric analysis, it does consider sites of resistance and the way women work within and against genre specific conventions. Other useful studies (Steward and Garratt, 1985; O'Dair, 1997) have highlighted and discussed the predominance of men within particular music genres as well as problematising gendered practices within a given genre (Johnson, 2000). An example can be taken of the 1998 national survey of women and jazz (Huxley and English, 1998), which investigated why fewer women than men involved themselves in jazz performance, education and events, and sought to uncover how this disparity might be redressed. The study considered how a lack of female representation within the field had become a barrier within itself.

In developing a workable theory of riot grrrl I have also surveyed a range of academic work concerned with youth subcultures. Various articles (Lull, 1987; Willis, 1990; Wilson and Atkinson, 2005; Williams, 2006), books (Mungham and Pearson, 1976; Hebdige, 1979; Brake, 1980; Cohen, 1980; Thornton, 1995) and edited collections (Gelder and Thornton, 1997; Skelton and Valentine, 1998; Muggleton and Weinzierl, 2003; Bennett and Kahn-Harris, 2004) have provided useful background reading on the ways in which youth subcultures have been theorised. Holly Kruse's (1993) work on identity in alternative music culture and Will Straw's (1991) analysis of communities and scenes are worth highlighting because of the close relation between their topics and the indie music culture under examination in this book. These works have been useful in helping me to consider notions of difference and resistance in relation to youth and gender. However, as McRobbie (1990) has argued, most studies of subcultures deal with 'male youth cultural forms' (1990: 66) and ignore issues of gender. McRobbie's critique emphasises that unless gender relationships are taken into account, 'youth culture will continue to "mean" in uncritically masculine terms' (1990: 68). Recent work, such as Schippers' (2002) ethnographic study of a rock music subculture in Chicago, has begun to take account of the politics of gender and sexuality. The study of riot grrrl offered in Chapters 5 and 6 contributes to the limited, but growing, body of work concerned with gender and female involvement in music subcultures and scenes such as punk (Roman, 1988; Leblanc, 1999; Reddington, 2004), new wave (Blackman, 1998), rock (Mäki-Kulmala, 1995), goth (Wilkins, 2004) and heavy metal (Krenske and McKay, 2000).

Finally, articles that discuss the sociology (Frith, 1981), ideology (Stratton, 1982), everyday practice (Sullivan, 1995), discourse (Davies, 2001; McLeod, 2001, 2002; Railton, 2001; Johnson-Grau, 2002; Kruse, 2002; Feigenbaum, 2005) and industrial context of music journalism (Forde, 2001) have been useful in developing an understanding of the institution of the music press. Studies of audiences and fans (e.g. Lewis, 1992), which have contested and discussed notions of teenage fandom, have also proved helpful in developing a consideration of how meanings are produced by music consumers. Among these, feminist accounts that contemplate their author's teenage years as a music fan (Garratt, 1990; Wise, 1990; Roberts, 1994) have provided useful background reading, highlighting the fact that the responses of music fans are varied and complex.

This book draws on a broad range of scholarship in order to examine the importance of gender within the practice, aesthetics and discourse of rock music and the music industry. Scholarly analysis of the music industry and studies concerned with popular music practice and consumption are discussed in its chapters, with a particular focus on current academic work concerned with gender and music. As I have mentioned, the central discussion of gender and rock is explored using the case study of female-centred indie rock bands. This selected case study builds upon Bayton's (1998) study of women rock performers, not by focusing on how the experience of female musicians differs from that of their male contemporaries, but by examining more generally how gender affects rock practice. The case study of female-centred bands complements literature focused on women musicians, offering a record of grass-roots music making and transient girl cultures. Moreover, the examination of the feminist culture of riot grrrl contributes to contemporary theories of youth subcultures by documenting riot grrrl's ideological agenda, the modes of involvement of its participants and its reception in the media. However, the aim of this study is not to construct a history but to analyse particular aspects of musical practice and discourse. My concern here is to progress from feminist scholarship that has documented and explored the experience of female musicians, to present an analytic discussion of gender and the music industry.

Methodology

In researching the subject of female-centred bands I have used methodological approaches drawn from the fields of Popular Music Studies, Women's Studies, Media Studies, Cultural Studies and Sociology. My research methods are discussed in more detail below.

Textual sources

In focusing on indie music I have drawn not only upon the academic studies discussed above but also on audio recordings, promotional videos, press releases, magazines, web discussion lists, guide books to indie music (Larkin, 1992; Cross, 1995; Daly and Wice, 1995; Weisbard and Marks, 1995; Thompson, 2000), compendiums (Schinder, 1996), journalistic accounts (Felder, 1993; Arnold, 1998) and anthologies (McDonnell and Powers, 1995; Becker, 1998). These sources provided illustrations of how indie rock has been presented, discussed and valued. In compiling studies of the media representation of particular performers I have also drawn on biographical material. For example, in developing a study of Courtney Love (discussed in Chapter 3), singer and guitarist with the US female-centred band Hole, background reading included a cut-and-paste biography by Nick Wise (1995), a more detailed biographical account by Poppy Z Brite (1998) as well as a fictional novel based upon Courtney Love's life (Hornburg, 1995). These accounts helped me to map how

Courtney Love was represented in the public domain. More generally, in researching rock discourse I have analysed a range of popular books (George-Warren and Dahl, 1994), encyclopaedias (Hardy and Laing, 1976a, 1976b, 1976c, 1995; Logan and Wooffinden, 1982; Stambler, 1989; Roberts *et al.*, 1998; Larkin, 2000; George-Warren and Romanowski, 2001), anthologies of rock writing (Heylin, 1993; Kent, 1994; McDonnell and Powers, 1995; Jones, 1996; Evans, 1997; Hornby and Schafer, 2001; Hoskyns, 2003) and biographies (Bowler and Dray, 1996).

My research on riot grrrl has examined how girls discuss and present themselves within self-published 'zines'. As Schilt (2003b) points out, zines are particularly valuable as a research tool as they represent a unique insight into the personal thoughts of girls that may not be accessed in traditional interview situations as 'examining girls' writings in zines is an unobtrusive method that captures how girls choose to represent their lives in writing rather than how they describe their lives to researchers' (Schilt, 2003b: 73). The term 'zine' is used here in preference to fanzine as the content of zines generally departs from the staple fanzine format of music reviews, rants and interviews. Instead zines are often devoted to discussions on gender politics, sexuality, personal reflections, ambitions and relationships.[9] I have consulted a wide range of the literature concerned with zine culture (Duncombe, 1997) and girl publications (Green and Taormino, 1997; Robbins, 1999; Eichhorn, 2001; Schilt, 2003b), as well as books that collect together interviews with zine writers and independent publishers (Vale, 1996, 1997). My interest in the communication networks of riot grrrl is concerned not only with paper-based zines but also the emergence and content of online e-zines. Therefore I have also drawn on academic work concerned with online zines (Smith, 1999), especially that which has centred on the emergence and significance of grrrl zines on the web (Cresser *et al.*, 2001; Harris, A., 2003). My investigation into Ladyfest, presented in Chapter 7, also draws on materials gathered from current and archived Ladyfest websites, online articles and discussion lists. During the course of this research I have collected 162 paper zines published in the UK and the US. The majority of these are directly concerned with riot grrrl although a number of publications collected at Ladyfest events are also included. Most of the zines were published between 1992 and 1994 and were produced as stapled booklets of photocopied leaves. A complete list of all the zines collected, including date of publication and place of issue, can be found at the end of the book in Appendix 1.

In order to examine how female-centred bands are discussed and represented across a broad range of written media I have also consulted a variety of newspapers and magazines. These include national and regional newspapers in the UK (such as *The Daily Star*, *The Guardian*, *The Independent* and *The Evening Standard*) and the US (including *The New York Times*, *LA Weekly*, *US Today* and the *Washington Post*), and monthly glossy magazines targeted particularly at women, such as *Elle* (UK) and *Vogue* (UK). They also include lesbian-targeted publications such as *Girlfriends* (US), *Shebang* (UK) and *LIP* (UK), and free magazines such as *Ms London* (UK) and *Girl About Town* (UK), which were distributed at London Underground train stations. Naturally, most of the journalistic coverage of female-centred bands is found in dedicated music publications and I have made use of a variety of pop and rock magazines, including *Select* (UK), *Raw* (UK) and *Rolling*

Stone (US), as well as accounts taken from publications specifically devoted to 'underground' or indie music like *Scrawl* (US), *Puncture* (US) and *Lime Lizard* (UK). I have paid particular attention to the writing about female rock performers that appeared in the UK weekly music press (*New Musical Express* and *Melody Maker*) in the 1990s.

Interview material

In addition to these textual sources, the book draws on personal interviews conducted with 88 people either directly involved with the field of indie rock or active within riot grrrl or Ladyfest networks. Almost all of the interviews were with women but the sample does include interviews with four male respondents. Sixty-three of the respondents were musicians, ranging from the amateur to the professional. Some had only recently formed bands, while others were internationally acclaimed artists who had released a number of albums and toured extensively. Many of the musicians interviewed also participated in indie rock in additional ways such as by writing zines, working in studio production, running record labels, working as record label press officers, promoting gigs and managing bands. A large number of these respondents were, or had been, involved with riot grrrl and some had performed at Ladyfest events. The remaining interviews were conducted with festival organisers, zine writers, journalists, a broadcaster and a spoken word performer. Almost all of these respondents were either involved with riot grrrl or with the production of Ladyfest events. The majority of respondents were either from the UK or the US. However, the sample does include performers from Canada, Ireland, Sweden, Germany and the Netherlands. The discussion of riot grrrl in Chapters 5 and 6 includes the reflections of participants from the UK, Canada, Ireland and the US. Interview material with women involved in Ladyfest covers a wider geographic terrain, reflecting the worldwide spread of these events. This material includes comments from women involved with events in Amsterdam, Brighton, Halifax (Canada), Istanbul, London, Madrid, Manchester (UK), Melbourne, Philadelphia, New York and Texas.

A complete list of interviewees, together with date and place of interview, appears at the end of this book in Appendix 2. This interview material is used to discuss specific issues concerning music business practice and enables a detailed focus on selected performers. The material also contributes to a discussion of rock discourse, which includes analyses of how female performers are represented within the written media. Interviewees have offered insight into common journalistic practice as well as disclosing information about the record industry that is generally absent from press interviews. This approach steers away from generalised models of the music industry, which ignore discrepancies within the industry and ossify industry relationships. By their nature, general overviews tend to present static models of the industry where industry roles are clearly defined and relationships between various industry agencies are concisely mapped. In contrast, case material on individual musicians reveals shifting relationships and balances of power between artists and industry bodies as the career of a band develops.

While not all of those interviewed revealed their age, the bulk of respondents ranged from late teenage years to those in their early thirties. Almost all of those interviewed were white, which is not to ignore non-white participation but reflects the predominance of white people in indie music production and its associated subcultures. This point should not be lost, for while this book is primarily concerned with the interweaving discourses of rock and gender, success and achievement are also mediated through discourses of race and ethnicity.[10] The 'whiteness' of riot grrrl and Ladyfest is discussed in Chapters 6 and 7.

In all the interviews respondents were asked to answer a series of open questions relating to their involvement with indie rock music. The method and place of interview, however, tended to vary depending on the accessibility of the respondents. All the interviews with established musicians[11] were conducted or arranged while the artists were playing a one-off gig or engaged in a scheduled tour of UK venues. Contact with musicians was generally established through a venue or tour manager, through a personal contact of my own or by direct communication with the artist themselves. Interviews often took place backstage at a venue, offering an insight into the working environment of a touring musician. All of these interviews were semi-structured, with a common set of key questions and issues addressed in each case. Conversational threads and divergences developed from these questions, allowing for anecdotes, reflections and discussion by the musicians around central themes of record deals, working environments, musical training and the lived experience of a rock performer. Interviews were recorded on cassette or minidisc and later transcribed. Over the course of this research some questions were refined, or additional questions incorporated, in order to reflect emphases and issues highlighted in interviews that had already been conducted. In three instances, arrangements had been made to conduct face-to-face interviews but due to various difficulties encountered these were rearranged as email interviews.

Reflections and comments by girls and women involved in riot grrrl were largely collected through postal questionnaires. Respondents were first approached and asked if they would assist with this research. These initial introductions were made either personally (at a gig, riot grrrl event or other social gathering) or by post (on the recommendation of a friend or previous interviewee). If the response was positive, a list of questions was then sent to the respondent. A core list of questions was used but some variations were made to the questions for riot grrrls living in the UK/US and for those whose background and musical involvement were already known to me. All of these questions demanded a detailed response by the respondent rather than a simple negative or positive reply. The intention was to discover the nature of the respondent's involvement in riot grrrl and their feelings and reflections on it. The respondents were encouraged to add their own comments or suggestions as they felt appropriate.

The majority of replies to the postal questionnaires were handwritten but six respondents recorded their answers onto cassette tapes that I had posted to them. This method of recording responses was particularly successful as it allowed for fuller replies, chatty asides and detailed reflections. Some of the respondents included recordings of their own songs on the returned tapes. This method of postal contact seemed highly appropriate given the nature of the riot grrrl network and the fact that many of the respondents produced zines and were thus in regular postal correspondence with other riot grrrls, zine writers and readers. Schilt (2003b) adopted a corresponding methodology of mail interviews in her work with riot grrrl zine writers, commenting that many 'mentioned in their zines that they felt uncomfortable talking to others in person or on the phone. Thus, written interviews seem to be the best option for making the respondents comfortable' (Schilt, 2003b: 74). This method allowed me to contact a broad range of people involved in riot grrrl internationally, including girls who were too young to attend gigs due to licensing laws. Many contacts were made through this method, as names and addresses of other potential respondents were suggested by interviewees. This 'snowballing' effect allowed me to follow the friendship chains of particular riot grrrls as, notably, often the same chains of connection were suggested by girls in different parts of the country.

Interviews with women involved in organising or participating in Ladyfests worldwide were collected between 2003 and 2005. The majority of these interviews were conducted via email. I considered the medium of email to be appropriate for this research as those involved in Ladyfest used electronic communication in order to organise and promote events and to network with others. I initially contacted people using email details available on Ladyfest websites and requested their help with my research. Those that responded positively were sent a questionnaire with around 20 open questions. Not all the people who consented to an interview eventually returned the questionnaire, however the responses I did receive were very useful in building a picture of the committee structures, organisation and rationale behind different Ladyfest events. In addition to this I attended Ladyfests in London in 2002 and Manchester in 2003, and conducted face-to-face interviews with a number of women at the Manchester event.

The relationship between researcher and respondent

During the course of my research for this book I was frequently asked questions, by friends and interested parties, concerning any difficulties I might have encountered in accessing well-known musicians and concerning the nature of their replies. It was commonly supposed that established musicians are both difficult to contact and liable to give stock answers in interviews. Certainly, securing an interview was not always a straightforward process. It often required persistence, travel, numerous telephone calls and extended periods of waiting at music venues. Sometimes requests were met with postponements or refUSls. I anticipated that established professional musicians might be more guarded in their responses than amateur music makers, due to their familiarity with the interview process and their experience of journalistic practice. The concern that musicians might not offer academic scholars frank accounts of their working lives has been expressed by others. David Hesmondhalgh, for example, restricted the number of interviews conducted with musicians for his doctoral work on the premise that 'information about contracts, deals and personal relationships would be extremely difficult for an academic researcher to access, and would result in futile quests for controversial material' (Hesmondhalgh, 1996: 273).

However, while in some cases these concerns proved to be justified, I found that many established musicians were remarkably candid in sharing their experiences and insights. The majority of interviewees greeted my research with curiosity and interest, and appeared happy to contribute to the project. The interviews allowed for detailed discussion of topics that are not generally recorded in newspaper, magazine or television reports. Topics discussed included the everyday working relationships between an artist and their record company representatives, the experience of gender discrimination in spaces of musical production, the logistics of promotion and the staging of a press interview. Interviewees variously discussed the process of gaining a deal, the details of their record contract, the difficulties in finding a good band manager and negotiations with record companies for better record promotion. While not all of this material has been directly referenced in this book, the insights gained into the working lives of female musicians have informed its development. Where, in some cases, respondents resisted certain lines of enquiry or gave predictable answers, I have considered how their answers reflect or reinforce notions of themselves as artists. The interview material is understood here not as a testimony of the 'the way it really is' but as individual and revealing responses by musicians in female-centred bands. In addition, interviewees involved with riot grrrl are presented as providing personal responses to this feminist network rather than as spokespeople for the 'riot grrrl movement'.

In reflecting on the process of this research it is important to consider my own identity in relation to this subject area and how this affected the responses from and interactions with research respondents. I had the benefit of being able to draw on a certain amount of 'insider' knowledge as I have been a participant within indie music networks since I was a teenager. I have attended dedicated clubs, gigs and festivals, regularly listened to indie music radio and television shows, been a keen consumer of the music press, collected many zines and performed in three bands. My experience of performing in two female-centred bands that released records through UK and US micro independent labels has given me a useful insight into the working practices and systems of promotion within indie music scenes. This background, together with my age and sex, enabled me during the fieldwork to be more readily accepted by respondents, with whom I shared some music tastes and an understanding of cultural codes. As Hodkinson pointed out in a reflection on his research into the goth scene: 'holding some degree of insider status can offer important additional benefits and possibilities, most notably with respect to generating of a relaxed atmosphere conducive to open conversation and a willingness to disclose' (Hodkinson, 2005: 139). However, in outlining my participation within indie rock networks I am not attempting to claim the position of a 'true insider'. While I have collected zines and attended numerous gigs by bands associated with riot grrrl, I did not name myself as a riot grrrl or become actively involved in its promotion. Similarly, my communication with those involved with Ladyfest (which I discuss in Chapter 7) has been as an interested researcher not as a fellow organiser. Thus, while I often shared a certain set of musical and cultural reference points with respondents I do not intend to present myself as offering an insider perspective.

As I have mentioned and will discuss in detail in Chapters 5 and 6, the material in riot grrrl zines often departs from the traditional fanzine content of music reviews and information, dealing instead with issues such as personal relationships, eating disorders, sexual discrimination and abuse. In many cases these issues are dealt with on a personal level, with the zine writer disclosing personal experiences or feelings, or narrating events that have occurred within a close circle of friends. This tone of intimacy was also a feature of much of the interview correspondence with zine writers. While I was personally unknown to the women who answered my queries, they invested a considerable degree of trust in me, as illustrated by the nature of their replies. For example, some of the respondents discussed issues surrounding their personal relationships, while others disclosed information about their lives and personal experiences. While I have not referenced any of this material or identified any of these respondents, such replies focus attention on the relationship between researcher and respondent, and on issues of anonymity and confidentiality.

However, my interviews with zine writers and those involved in riot grrrl also raised other issues relating to the relationship between researcher and respondent. Not least of these were the questions of authority and interpretation. Those active within riot grrrl were vocal about the need to keep control of the ways in which their activities were reported and understood. I was acutely aware in my role as researcher that I did not want to impose an authoritative 'reading' of this network but to reflect upon the activities and impact of riot grrrl through consultation with those involved. A number of respondents were university educated or conversant with academic frameworks and categories. For example, at the close of each interview I asked respondents to tell me a few details about themselves so that I could better gauge the range of respondents in my sample. One respondent replied: 'I think I would probably be lower middle/upper working (yes, I've done Sociology and it told me that if your mum is a secretary and your father a social worker you fall about there within our beautiful class structure' (personal communication). Indeed, one respondent actually framed his reply within popular music scholarship. In a discussion on the independent music scene he commented: 'The way that DIY/ underground culture works is based on what Sarah Thornton would call "subcultural capital".' He went on to explain that access to the indie music scene was made easier if one displayed one's knowledge about it through the referencing of record labels, groups, venues and participants (personal communication, 10 November 1999). While such a response does not pre-empt any further analysis, it does register a considerable level of reflexivity and self-awareness by the interviewee. These respondents were participants who engaged with the academic discourse used to describe them, and challenged and worked with the academic labels used to name them.

During the research for this book I developed an awareness of the impact of myself as a researcher on my field of study. An illustration of this can be taken from my research with various riot grrrls. While many respondents were relatively widely geographically dispersed, they were also part of an informal communication network. My interviews and enquiries quite understandably became a source of discussion. A letter sent to me by one respondent (with whom I was acquainted through a mutual friend) alerted me to this fact. She explained that she had recently attended a birthday party of one riot grrrl friend who had also invited quite a number of people that were on the contact list she had passed to me. She commented that my research topic had become a source of conversation. A comparison can be made with the experience of Lori Taylor who, when researching riot grrrl in the US, found herself valorised within a grrrl zine and a subject of discussion within riot grrrl circles. While I can relate to Taylor's embarrassment 'to have been noticed at all' (Taylor, 1993: 14), these instances highlight the dynamics of researching a living culture and testify to the fact that research is part of a process of involvement rather than objective study.

In conducting this research I found that while many involved in riot grrrl expressed a distrust of the media and, as will I discuss in Chapter 5, actually refused to engage with the mainstream press, they were receptive to my enquiries. Clearly, they understood my objectives to be distinct from those of a journalist and offered their insights with a view to building a more detailed picture of riot grrrl than a short press piece might be able to reflect. Their decision to trust me as a researcher also entrusted me with a responsibility to produce an account that accurately reflected their activities and reflected on their concerns. The young women involved in riot grrrl actively sought to control media attention and used their zines as forums in which to discuss and dispute media accounts; they thus presented a very proactive image of riot grrrls as engaged with the management of their own representation. As Anita Harris reflects in her research on grrrl zine culture: 'The act of refUSl to speak to unworthy listeners re-positions young women from an accessible and often vulnerable population to autonomous agents entitled to accountability, self-representation and informed participation' (Harris, A., 2003: 53).

Book structure

I have organised my analysis of gender, rock and the music industry into seven chapters. Chapter 1 discusses the association between rock and masculinity, and explores how the concept of rock as a masculinist tradition is produced and re-established. Rock is discussed here in a broad sense, without division into distinct subgenres. The chapter is concerned with the ways in which the notion of rock as 'male' or masculine is maintained despite the increasing numbers of women performing rock. Gender is discussed in relation to particular rock aesthetics, tropes, histories, canons and sites of celebration. The aims of this chapter concur with Holly Kruse's argument that:

> The important questions to ask now are not merely about whether rock/pop songs are sexist or what characterises male rock/pop versus female rock/pop. Instead, we need to ask how, in very specific ways, popular music helps to construct gendered identities and gendered understandings through both its systems of signification and situated practices. (Kruse, 1999: 100)

By considering the broad rock context the chapter is able to highlight the broad frames of reference and cultural terrain within which indie is situated. Chapter 2 then narrows the discussion by examining the case of indie rock music, which presents certain nuances and divergences from 'classic' rock performances, while also offering certain idiosyncrasies of its own. This chapter examines the popular notion that indie music is a more accessible form of rock for female practitioners. Drawing on personal interviews with members of female-centred bands, the chapter discusses the everyday experiences of female performers within musical 'spaces' such as the tour bus, recording studio and musical instrument shop.

Chapter 3 examines the representation of rock performers in the written media, analysing how journalists employ a gendered language in the construction of performer profiles. Music publications have a clear importance within the music industry as a platform from which to launch new acts, advertise gigs and new music releases, and develop band images. Specialist music publications operate as a key publicity tool for many of the indie rock performers discussed as they attempt to guide and educate the music-buying reader (see Toynbee, 1993). While some niche publications have a relatively small readership, they are strategically important in breaking new acts, defining and influencing taste cultures and conferring cultural kudos. Taking a selection of male and female indie rock performers this chapter examines how performer images are constructed in a range of UK publications including niche rock music magazines (such as *Raw* and *Puncture*), tabloid newspapers and broadsheet coverage. The chapter discusses in particular how journalists work with common narratives and reference points concerning notions of madness and genius.

Chapter 4 focuses attention on the subject of performance. Studies of performance have often attended to particular performance moments such as a promotional video or concert appearance.[12] For example, with regard to work on gender and performance, analysis of particular performed texts has been undertaken, such as the examination of particular song structures and musical materials (Bradby, 1990; Dibben, 2002) and critiques of the performance of gender within promotional videos (Roberts, 1990; Vernallis, 1998; Andsager and Roe, 1999). This chapter will also draw on a series of examples and instances of particular performances, however the emphasis is placed on performance contexts rather than on specific texts. A selection of performance contexts are considered including the stage (of a live music venue) and the screen (for the production of a promotional music video). The chapter explores how performances are presented and understood across these performance contexts. A broad understanding of the term performance will be employed, discussing not only live gigs and video shoots but also other situations where musicians are active in conveying or staging a public personae. The chapter considers, for example, how activities such as conducting an interview or participating in a photo shoot, may be understood as performances as they are methods through which a musician communicates ideas about their image and identity. This stretching of the notion of performance is comparable with Butler's (1990) discussion of gender as a performed identity. These latter activities may more traditionally be thought of as social interactions rather than as performances. However, by conceptualising the press interview and photo shoot as performances I aim to draw attention to the ways in which performer identities are constructed and played out within the media.

Chapters 5 and 6 examine riot grrrl, a feminist initiative that was first promoted by female-centred indie bands in the US and UK during the early 1990s. Chapter 5 charts the emergence and nature of riot grrrl and its publicity in micro, niche and mass media. It considers the gender politics of riot grrrl and addresses how such politics may adequately be theorised within subcultural theory. Chapter 6 concentrates analysis on 'zines', discussing the cultural importance and articulations of these texts in relation to riot grrrl. The chapter reflects on the development of riot grrrl as a network, from its establishment in 1991 to activities organised in the present day. The conclusion of this chapter considers how the riot grrrl slogan 'girl power' was adopted as the catchphrase of the British pop group, the Spice Girls. The discussion considers how this phrase was presented and given meaning through its promotion by this multi-million-selling act.

Chapter 7 documents and examines the numerous festivals that have been held worldwide under the banner of Ladyfest. Drawing on comments from organisers and participants this chapter traces the growth of Ladyfest and examines the extent to which these events continue the work of riot grrrl by operating with a feminist agenda and creating a receptive space in which to showcase female musicians and artists. It considers how these events act as a resource for female performers and audience members, enabling networking and confidence building, but also discusses the limited reach of these events.

The conclusion to this book draws upon the key points of all seven chapters to make some general observations on gender, the practice of rock and the music industry. Moreover, it assesses the importance of the book's findings in relation to the body of academic work on gender and music.

Notes

1   Examples of such bands discussed in the book are Hole (US) and Huggy Bear (UK).

2   This is not to ignore the impact of female rock vocalists such as Janis Joplin or Patti Smith but rather to clarify the focus of this study. A brief discussion of how these artists have been understood can be found in Chapter 1.

3   Rock is associated with certain performance conventions ranging from the gestures and mannerisms used by musicians in live performance, videos and promotional photographs to particular uses of instrumental sounds such as distorted guitar and harsh vocal timbres.

4   Rock songs commonly follow the structure of verse-chorus-verse-chorus-middle eight/instrumental solo-chorus-end. This structure is so commonly used that rock music that has diverged from this orthodoxy has often been categorised within distinct subgenre categories. The names of these categories (such as art rock, progressive rock and experimental rock) draw attention to differences in structural composition that distinguish them from 'classic' rock.

5   Illustrations may be taken of the 'Seattle scene' of the early 1990s, which was identified as the hub of the 'grunge' rock movement (see Daly and Wice, 1995: 96–7, 219) or the 1980s rock 'n' roll scene of Austin, Texas (see Shank, 1994).

6   A good example of such work is the doctoral thesis of Michael Jones (1997).

7   The anthologies of female rock journalism edited by McDonnell and Powers (1995) and Evans (1997) may be cited as further examples of attempts to reclaim ignored histories. As McDonnell and Powers state in the preface to the collection, 'Both of us felt such a project was a feminist act in itself: a way of breaking into the canon and restoring the women who belong there to their rightful place' (1995: 1).

8   Karen O'Brien's (1995) book on women musicians is another example of this style of book, although it is not concerned with indie rock performers.

9   A detailed discussion of riot grrrl zines is presented in Chapter 6.

10   A discussion of issues of race and gender in popular music is offered by Gayle Wald, who argues that: 'the gender transgressions of white rock performers in the 1990s ... signal the emergence of new cultural modes of expressing, displaying, and performing whiteness ...' (1997: 152). She concludes by arguing that a racialised critique of contemporary white female rock performers reveals that while 'membership in the "boy's club" has its difficulties ... [it] also has its privileges' (1997: 165).

11   'Established musicians' can be understood here as musicians who are either professional (whose main paid occupation is the production and promotion of their music) or those who have played and performed music for a number of years and seek to become professional. All these respondents had either produced a record or stated that release of a record was pending. The majority of these respondents were signed to a record label, had released at least one album and had completed national or international promotional tours.

12   This is not to overlook notable studies that examine different contexts of popular music performance, such as Finnegan's (1989) work on music making in Milton Keynes, Shank's (1994) study of the rock 'n' roll scene in Austin, Texas, and Berger's (1999) ethnographic research on the rock and jazz scenes in north-eastern Ohio.

Chapter 1

Rock and masculinity

I know it's a sexist thing to say, but women aren't as good at making music as men – like they're not as good as men at football. A girl in a dress with a guitar looks weird. Like a dog riding a bicycle. Very odd. Hard to get past it. (Julie Burchill, reply to a request to be interviewed for *Never Mind The Bollocks*, cited in Raphael, 1995: xi)

The purpose of this chapter is to unpack the gendered associations and definitions of rock. Rock encompasses many subgenres, such as heavy metal, punk, grunge and post-rock, each of which has particular associated codes of conduct and display, offering and encouraging separate gendered responses. Indeed, the distinctions between these categories is so marked that, as Johan Fornas states, 'rock actually seems to be more of a family of genres than a homogeneous category' (Fornas, 1995: 112). As the focus of this book is female-centred bands performing 'indie rock', there is a critical need to consider how gender is performed and negotiated within this musical style and practice.

Before discussion can move on to the subgenre of indie, however, it needs first to examine and assess the associations and presentations of the broad category of rock. The aim of this chapter is to explore the factors that prompt academics to pronounce 'rock music ... is probably the most blatantly misogynistic and aggressive form of music currently listened to' (Harding and Nett, 1984: 60) and, despite the rising number of successful female rock musicians, that 'the ongoing tradition of rock is still deeply masculinist' (Gottlieb and Wald, 1994: 252). The concern is to uncover how this gendering of rock is articulated, with particular attention to how a masculinist tradition is established, reproduced and maintained, and to highlight the implications of this tradition for female performers and music enthusiasts.

In particular, this chapter will consider how the masculinist 'tradition' of rock is, to use Foucault's (1990) phrase, 'put into discourse'. It will analyse how rock 'is spoken about, to discover who does the speaking, the positions and viewpoints from which they speak, the institutions which prompt people to speak about it and which store and distribute the things that are said' (Foucault, 1990: 11). Rock has variously been described as a male form, male-run, masculine and misogynist. Distinctions between these descriptions clearly need to be drawn in order to allow for a systematic analysis. However, consideration also needs to be given to whether there is overlap between these descriptions. For example, has the observation that 'rock is male-run' afforded the conclusion that it is therefore 'masculine', or has the association of rock and masculinity been generated from other factors. This chapter will take account of the pronouncements and interpretations of rock on the part of academics, journalists, fans, musicians and listeners.

Control and production

Frith and McRobbie's article 'Rock and Sexuality' (1990), first published in 1978, is an early endeavour to understand how rock is understood as expressive of male sexuality and explain how it exerts control. They begin this exercise by stating, 'in terms of control and production, rock is a male form. The music business is male-run; popular musicians, writers, creators, technicians, engineers and producers are mostly men. Female creative roles are limited and mediated through male notions of female ability' (Frith and McRobbie, 1990: 373). Undoubtedly the predominance of men working in the industry has created problems of access and opportunity for women wishing to work in the music business. These problems have been considered by a number of critics. Sandstrom (2000) and Smaill (2005), for example, have discussed issues related to sound engineering as a gendered field, while Steward and Garratt (1985: 60–81) have documented the experiences of various women working within the music industry, including managers, sound technicians and producers, who have had to deal with sexism as part of their working lives.

However, conceding that the rock industry has historically been male dominated does not solve the core of the problem, for this explains only why rock may be thought of as a traditionally male career path. It does not distinguish rock from any other profession that has had a predominance of male workers. It does not explain why rock has been essentialised as a male form. When we talk of rock we are not only speaking of a community of musicians, engineers, producers and promoters; as Frith and McRobbie point out, 'rock' refers to a musical genre, an audience, 'a form of production and artistic ideology' (Frith and McRobbie, 1990: 373). Given this, the statement that rock is produced and controlled (mainly) by men is all the more unsatisfactory as an explanation of why rock signifies as male. The production of a cultural product by a male or female does not explain why it might be understood as intrinsically gendered. Of course, Frith and McRobbie do not propose that rock is seen as a male form simply because the music business is male-run. Instead, they argue that this fact is a natural entry point for their analysis. I, in turn, wish to use their comments as the springboard for this chapter. Their article, albeit problematic, is an important attempt to explain the masculinity of rock. In tracing the arguments put forward, and their attendant complications, I can perhaps better understand how the discourse of masculinity operates within this genre.

The gender of genre

Frith and McRobbie explore meaning within rock by examining the overtly macho subgenre 'cock rock' in comparison with the music labelled as 'teenybop', which is targeted at a young female audience. By choosing to study 'cock rock' and 'teenybop' Frith and McRobbie use two neat and polarised examples from which they can construct their arguments. Or rather, perhaps, they construct these styles as clear, identifiable opposites. Cock rock performers are defined as 'aggressive, dominating and boastful … Women, in their eyes, are either sexually aggressive and therefore doomed and unhappy, or else sexually repressed and therefore in need of male servicing' (Frith and McRobbie, 1990: 374). One may take issue with this representation of rock. Such a clear definition rests on a cock rock archetype, thus ignoring songs by representative performers that do not fall neatly into this category (such as ballads) or rock artists who do not conform to the archetype. Moreover, by assuming that the rock performer is male they erase the history of female practitioners while also failing to acknowledge the popularity of 'cock rock' among girls and women. While Frith and McRobbie do mention that there are 'overlaps and contradictions' (Ibid.: 375) they do not work these theoretical complications into the body of their work, choosing instead to trade on easily identifiable tropes. Yet this is to do a disservice to the complexity of the 'cock rock' subgenre and, in a sense, to remake it for academic ease.

However, arguing that it is necessary to be attendant to the complexities of rock music practice and consumption does not deny the existence of the attitudes that Frith and McRobbie outline. Examination of music magazines and books produced for the 'hard rock' or 'heavy rock' market reveals that the characterisation presented by Frith and McRobbie in 1978 still has currency. A 1996 biography of Iron Maiden quotes lead singer Bruce Dickinson explaining his understanding of heavy metal. The quote appears in a section discussing Iron Maiden's 1990 album *No Prayer For The Dying*, which includes such titles as 'Hooks In You' and 'Bring Your Daughter … To The Slaughter'. Dickinson states: 'Metal hasn't got the soft, round, flowing rhythms women tend to like. It's too fast, not at all smoochy, the quick release after the pent up moment. … At the root of it, heavy metal is somehow quintessentially male, the equivalent of the female "not a dry seat in the house". What happens in the concerts is almost ceremonial' (Bowler and Dray, 1996: 118). Such gendered attitudes can be found not only in the discourse of heavy rock performers but also in the social codes of heavy metal scenes. As Krenske and McKay's (2002) ethnographic study of a heavy metal music club in Brisbane, Australia, revealed, the attitudes and behaviours of people within the club were highly gendered and women 'perpetually "did" gender on men's terms' (2002: 301). They found that women's 'access to, and experiences of, the subculture were determined by unequal relationships with men – women "participated" in male-defined terms or not at all' (Krenske and McKay, 2002: 301). Thus some aspects of rock music do replicate the macho attitudes outlined by Frith and McRobbie, and so testify to the masculinist nature of the genre. However, my concern is also to understand how rock music is perceived as masculinist even when such overtly macho statements are absent.

Frith and McRobbie's stylisation of the teenybop image as 'based on self-pity, vulnerability, and need' should also be problematised. One may take the example of the US indie rock band Nirvana, the proponents of 'grunge rock', whose *Nevermind* album sold ten million copies worldwide. The music produced by the group was loud, guitar-heavy rock with a raw vocal style often shouted over the instrumentation. However, the public image of lead singer and songwriter Kurt Cobain was of a vulnerable and sensitive individual. *Rolling Stone* journalist Chris Mundy has commented that, 'Cobain was notoriously quiet. He was moody and introspective, and the actions swirling around him often spoke louder than he did' (George-Warren and Dahl, 1994: 110). Cobain's public persona is an example of how the archetypes that Frith and McRobbie outline often bleed into one another.

This seems to throw into question Frith and McRobbie's (1990: 376) suggestion that 'the contrast between cock rock and teenybop is clearly something general in rock, applicable to other genres'. Had they selected other subgenres within rock they would perhaps have been faced with a more difficult task for analysis.

A question of sexuality

The work carried out by so-called 'Queer Studies' scholars on popular music (Bradby, 1993; Brett et al., 1994; Gill, 1995; Smith, R., 1995; Kearney, 1997) challenges the assumption that rock should naturally be interpreted as heterosexual. While Frith and McRobbie's article discusses sexuality, it frames 'cock rock' as both presenting and appealing to an aggressive form of heterosexuality. The article explains that 'cock rock' links performers such as Elvis Presley, Mick Jagger, Roger Daltrey and Robert Plant (Frith and McRobbie, 1990: 374). Elvis is a pertinent example, for Gill argues that the period of his ascension in the 1950s was when 'rock 'n' roll acquired its reputation as a rampantly macho and masculinist art form' (Gill, 1995: 85). However, Gill points out that Elvis's status as 'the ultimate heterosexual male' was a perception promoted by 'the heterosexual males who wrote the articles and books that said he was' (1995: 85). Admittedly, a male homosexual reading would still strengthen the position that rock expresses male sexuality, although it would offer an alternative reading of how that sexuality might be characterised. Sue Wise's article (Wise, 1990: 390–8) challenges the traditional construction of Elvis by recounting how he held meaning for her as an adolescent who was developing a sense of herself as a lesbian. Her description of Elvis as 'teddy bear' rather than 'butch god' illustrates how fans produce meanings rather than consume set images. While a male performer may display a certain type of masculinity or sexual identity, the person listening to his records or attending his concert is active in making sense of that performance and may create a personal understanding of it that is at odds with the musician's original intention.

My intention is not to criticise Frith and McRobbie for any shortcomings in their article. Indeed, Frith's 'Afterthoughts' (1990: 419–24) address what he considers to be some of the confusions in the original paper. He comments, 'our account of how music carries sexual meaning now seems awfully dated. We rejected rock naturalism but we retained the suggestion that sexuality has some sort of autonomous form which is expressed or controlled by cultural practice' (Frith, 1990: 420). Frith and McRobbie's attempt to explain and analyse particular styles shows the difficulty in trying to isolate and understand musical texts and contexts. It demonstrates that meanings are not fixed but are open to negotiation. Moreover, despite the contradictions inherent within rock we are still left with the problem of understanding why rock is understood as a masculinist discourse.

Constructing histories and policing conversations

Analysis of the ways in which male rock performers are discussed and presented in music journalism and by record companies helps us to understand how the masculinity of rock is established, maintained and reinforced. In a discussion of rock and gender on the internet, Norma Coates comments, 'The gender of rock may appear stable, but it is "stabilised" through a constant process of reiteration and the performance of "masculinity", which act to keep that which is unrepresentable within it firmly outside' (Coates, 1998: 79). Like Coates, I am interested in understanding how this impression of stability is achieved and what strategies are employed to keep women musicians 'firmly outside'. The following discussion will consider how musicians are presented to fans and consumers in the written media and by the record industry, and will explore how worth and prestige are allocated to individual performers. My aim is to examine whether these processes of presentation can be said to be gendered.

Norma Coates (1998) has pointed to a rock discourse that seeks to give the impression of an archetypal (and male) rock performer. Yet, it is not only the gender of the rock performer that is in a constant process of reiteration but the very history of rock itself. Because of the commercial nature of music production, the industry continually seeks to present music product as understandable (placing all new releases within recognisable genres and categories) and accessible. The establishment of a canon of 'important' recording artists plays a part within this process, as it offers a list of performers who can be considered culturally worthy. This aids record companies in attempts to capitalise on old product, as it enables them to promote selected recordings as 'classics' or 'seminal'. Music canons act both to guide the consumer and also to help record companies to narrow the mass of old recordings into a manageable and saleable quota of back catalogue artists.[1] I do not want to suggest, however, that the process of canonisation is purely driven by a commercial imperative. Popular music canons are formed through aesthetic judgements made by musicians and critics such as biographers, journalists and historians, who are informed by, often tacitly agreed, notions of value, taste and worth. Certainly, the commercial success of recordings and their appeal to the listening public also informs this process but, as the canon includes artists whose albums were commercial failures at the time of the first release, it does not dictate the artists deemed for inclusion. Through this process a large number of musical texts that have been variously promoted by record labels and music journalists over the past few decades can be given an aura of stability by the selection of particular performers as 'greats'. This process is advantageous not only to record companies but also to music journalists who can then reference these 'established' artists as points of comparison in record reviews and as antecedents to new musical movements. As Marcia Citron comments, 'the canon creates a narrative of the past and a template for the future' (Citron, 1993: 1).

These rock and pop canons are produced by various sections of the music industry. Record companies, publishing houses, radio stations, music and style magazines, and music papers regularly produce lists of hallowed artists. These are sometimes presented as definitive guides to a music genre or era, or they may take the form of a detailed retrospective of a particular year or performer. Although there is a degree of variance in the artists selected for inclusion, a number of performers are regularly cited as 'important'. Once artists have become established as canonical, magazine and book publishers may focus on them to create other celebratory texts that both trade off their status and reinforce it. Collections of rock writing about these stars are an example of how this process of reiteration operates. However, artists do not become canonised through one linear process of record company promotion, chart success, music press acclaim, inclusion in rock encyclopaedias and collected editions. Rather, one can think of these as several elements of different processes, which may occur in synergy and that feed into one another and support the canonic process. The fact that rock anthologies and encyclopaedias are often compiled by journalists working for the music press is illustrative of the crossover between these processes.

Yet, while these canons seek to make rock history intelligible, they also serve to characterise and reify it. These texts communicate a particular conception of rock history that works to 'stabilise' gender. Examination of a number of rock guides and encyclopaedias illustrates how rock lists and canons commonly privilege male performers. To ascertain the level of gender bias within these publications a sample of ten encyclopaedias and guides published between 1977 and 2001 was analysed.[2] The number of entries devoted to female solo artists and bands with one or more female vocalist or musician was compared with the total number of entries in each publication. It was found that between 8 and 22 per cent of entries included a female artist or band with one or more female member, while all other entries were made up of male artists or bands with exclusively male membership. A large percentage of the featured female performers were either vocalists or singer-songwriters with very few entries for female-centred bands.[3] While I do not wish to denigrate the contribution of female vocalists, it might be noted that the role of vocalist has traditionally been perceived as an acceptable feminine occupation.

A similar bias towards male performers can be noted within the 'definitive' rock guides and listings regularly published in the music press and magazines, as well as in book form.[4] For example *VH1's 100 Greatest Albums* (Hoye, 2003) lists only 16 entries related to releases by female solo artists or bands that feature at least one female musician, while *Rolling Stone*'s (2005) special issue dedicated to 'The Immortals: 100 Greatest Artists of All Time' included just 11 such entries. Comparison of the content of these various music press charts reveals that, while each listing is decidedly different, there are a core number of artists who frequently feature within many of these charts. Strachan (2003) offers an investigation of 31 critical polls published between 1974 and 2000 in a range of rock publications published in seven different countries. He comments that, of 'the total of 3375 entries recorded in the study, 60 per cent related to just 50 artists. … and just three were women' (Strachan, 2003: 227). Thus while the percentage of entries given to female artists within music press polls is relatively small, the number of such artists included within the reiterated canon of popular music artists is even more restricted.

As Sarah Thornton argues, it is difficult to place 'popular culture' within a historical frame because of its 'heterogeneous, informal and unofficial character' (Thornton, 1990: 87). Historians of popular culture consequently have to employ certain criteria for attributing historical importance, such as 'sales figures, biographical interest, critical acclaim or amount of media attention' (1990: 87). This process of charting the history of rock can be thought of as a sifting of the mass of recorded music released. According to Hirsh's model of Cultural Industry Systems (Hirsh, 1990), the music industry creates an excess of product to account for the unpredictability of 'hit' songs. The process of list making and canonising may be viewed as an opposite process whereby the large number of past releases are sifted into a knowable and clearly identifiable collection. This process of sifting operates in stages. For example, an end-of-year poll might include the biggest sellers, most critically acclaimed artists and the brightest hopes of that year. A further sifting of these artists will take place for a retrospective on a particular decade. Obviously, the fact that the latter chart aims to review a larger time span necessitates the omission of many artists who appeared in earlier polls, but it is also apparent that it encourages a particular selection of these artists. Only artists who achieved great commercial success or were well received by critics tend to appear. The chart becomes more 'stable' and more predictable.

It is arguable that this process also favours male artists, as female artists are less likely to have been granted cultural importance by music critics. In a sense there is a circularity to this process as, once the rock canon has become established as male, future male performers can be judged against celebrated artists and fitted into a tradition. Anthologies of rock writing may be used as examples of this sifting process. These collected works contain journalistic articles about celebrated artists who have enjoyed sustained critical acclaim or commercial success. It is notable that these collections contain proportionally less female artists than the broader rock listings books. In Dylan Jones' collection of *Classic Rock and Pop Writing from Elvis to Oasis* (Jones, 1996) only two of the 40 entries focused on female performers: Annie Lennox and Madonna. *The Penguin Book of Rock and Roll Writing* (Heylin, 1993) is only slightly more inclusive, with seven of the 82 articles concerned with female performers or female-centred bands, and two additional articles featuring bands that have a female member. Nick Kent's *Selected Writings* (Kent, 1994) present a poorer picture, with none of the 18 articles included dedicated to female performers.

It is not only through the selection of articles about male subjects that the music press transmits the notion that rock is a predominantly male practice. Within the numerous volumes of collected music journalism the majority of writers included tend to be male, a point that may lead readers to assume that the deficit of female rock performers is also echoed by a scarcity of female rock journalists. For example, Dylan Jones (1996) included only five articles written by women out of the 40 entries in his anthology. Similarly, Hoskyns (2003) included three female contributors in his collection of 30 articles celebrating *40 Years of Classic Rock Journalism*; Hornby and Schafer (2001) included four female journalists among the 29 contributors to the *Da Capo Best Music Writing 2001* collection, while *The Penguin Book of Rock and Roll Writing* (Heylin, 1993), included only six pieces penned by women out of a total of 82 articles. The book *Rock She Wrote*, by Evelyn McDonnell and Ann Powers (1995), aims to correct the idea that women have been absent in rock journalism by collecting articles by over 60 female journalists, fans and artists from the 1960s to the 1990s. In the preface to their collection they list 93 other female writers who they regretfully did not have room to include. Liz Evans' (1997) collection, *Girls Will Be Boys*, has a similar project and includes 21 articles written by (mainly British) established female journalists.

Female music critics have sought to correct the gender bias within rock music histories by writing about the contributions made by female musicians. Gillian Gaar

(1993), Lucy O'Brien (1995b) and Gerri Hirshey (2001) have constructed histories of women in popular music, while a number of other female writers (Evans, 1994; O'Brien, K., 1995; Raphael, 1995; Juno, 1996; Post, 1997; Woodworth, 1998) have published lengthy interviews with contemporary musicians. However, these texts seem to register as alternative histories that are supplementary to established canons rather than necessary corrections to outdated lists. Thus, while such texts may certainly raise awareness of the achievements and works of female performers, this does not ensure any alteration to the way histories or lists supposedly reflecting 'rock music' are compiled.

Rock: the vote

An illustration of the way in which the work of female musicians is separated out from 'general' rock lists may be noted in the US magazine *Rolling Stone*'s 30th anniversary issue dedicated to 'Women of Rock' (1997). The issue contains 28 interviews with women musicians and a 30,000-word history of female performers. The editor, Jann S. Wenner, states 'the major music story of 1997 was the rise of women artists', and suggests that women's contribution to music is fully appreciated by *Rolling Stone* in his comment that, 'women have never been considered insiders in music. Now, they're not only controlling their lives but also their artistic destinies and careers' (1997: 31). However, this rhetoric rings quite hollow when one turns to the final page of the edition, which has a printed ballot for the 1997 *Rolling Stone* readers' poll. Of the 60 suggested artists only nine were women, a fact that seems to suggest that female musicians are still considered outsiders to rock music. The UK magazine *Q* (December 2001, issue 185) ran a similar set of features in 2001 under the title 'Sirens! 100 Women Who Rock Your World', which included articles on seven high-profile female artists and a top 100 readers' poll. Nevertheless, despite appearing in the same themed issue, the critics' guide to the '50 Best Albums of 2001' featured only eight albums by female artists or bands with one or more female musician.

The suggestions put forward by the *Rolling Stone* writers for the best and most influential artists of the year will not necessarily be the choices made by their readers in the end-of-year poll. However, while readers' polls give the illusion of independence, there are several factors that may influence the outcome. The suggestions made by the writers communicate to the readership the types of artists and music genres the magazine deems worthy. Readers may feel pressured to choose within these selections in order for their vote to 'count' in the final poll. Readers may understandably select artists whom they think might win rather than attempting to reflect their own personal taste on the entry form. Often the results reflect the artists and works that have been most heavily featured in the particular magazine or publication. While these selections may not be a true reflection of the diversity of readers' tastes, they serve to reinforce the canon established by the publication and give credibility to the choices made by staff writers.

It may be argued that these factors influenced the results of the UK 'Music of the Millennium' album chart announced in January 1998. The chart was compiled from the votes of readers of the *Guardian* newspaper, Channel 4 television viewers and customers of the music store HMV, and was promoted as 'the definitive list of music of our time'.[5] Of the 100 albums in the chart, only eight were by female solo artists or female groups. Four other bands included one or two female performers, however the rest of the list comprised exclusively male bands or artists.[6] The majority of the artists featured were those commonly included in polls compiled by the music press and music magazines.[7] The 'Music of the Millennium' results raise the point that readers' polls are perhaps less 'independent' than they might appear. This seems to reinforce the concern that Sarah Thornton voiced in her study on popular music histories, that 'if aesthetic/political radicalism and particular kinds of sustained media attention determine inclusion in histories, then the cultural experiences of large parts of the population – not in tune with the tastes of music critics or not already represented in the music press – will be lost' (Thornton, 1990: 89).

Having established then, to some extent, that rock has been characterised historically as male, there is a need to understand how this perception is maintained. Consideration of music charts and polls illustrates how male rock performers are constantly re-presented as typical of the genre. Norma Coates' (1998) analysis of the internet discussion group 'Rocklist' illustrates that such re-presentations are common and may be found not only in the music press or music magazines but also on the internet and in academic debate. Coates argues that Rocklist, which describes itself as an online 'academic discussion of popular music', exemplifies the masculinist discourse of rock and 'replicates the social dynamics currently operative in nascent cyberspace' (Coates, 1998: 81). Coates describes how Rocklist assumes a male gendering of rock and how most contributors do not consider debates about gender to be a natural part of rock discourse. In 1995 Coates posted a comment to Rocklist that reflected on the nature of the online debate. She commented that, 'when questions about gender and rock (and women and this list) are posed, they are generally either: (a) answered by a male "expert"; (b) trivialised; or (c) just plain ignored' (Coates, 1998: 83). This discussion group, Coates argues, not only speaks from a male perspective, but also, through its choice of topics and mode of debate, 'performs' the masculinity of rock.

Documenting women in rock

This chapter has so far considered the absences and biases in rock writing and rock canons. It has problematised how rock is often characterised as male and heterosexual. Yet while female performers are not usually included in rock canons, neither are they absent from media coverage. In the next section I shall consider the ways in which female-centred bands and female rock musicians are given coverage in the written media. My focus will be on local and national newspapers in the UK, style and fashion magazines, and the music press. I will consider whether media coverage focusing specifically on female performers offers different gender problematics.

The coverage of female rock musicians in the print media accounts for a broad range of writing from in-depth interviews in music magazines, such as the UK publications *Q* and *Mojo*, to live reviews in the weekly music press and daily newspapers, and brief mentions in the news sections of women's magazines. As one would expect, the content of the articles often echoes the coverage of male music performers by reflecting the tastes, biases and access to information of the journalists. Indeed, as Toynbee argues, often the journalistic mode of address is 'didactic and, perhaps more tellingly, correctional' (Toynbee, 1993: 296). Toynbee's analysis of music journalism is useful for he presents the music press not simply as a provider of information or mirror of people's tastes but as a 'carrier of a critical technology, a means of knowing what music is like' (Toynbee, 1993: 299). The aim of this section is to consider whether the popular media display any common approaches to artists because of their gender. I will argue that, while journalistic articles undoubtedly show a great amount of variance, there is some similarity in the way that female musicians are presented, which helps to re-establish rock as a masculine discourse.

The very phrase 'women in rock', which features in a great number of articles focusing on female musicians, is itself problematic. Rather than simply pointing to the activity of female musicians within a particular music genre, the phrase usually works to peculiarise the presence of women rock performers. This point is reinforced by the fact that journalistic accounts often describe female musicians by this phrase, rather than referencing them just as 'rock performers'. Rock discourse thus normalises the male performer and so deems the activity of women in this field as worthy of note. Moreover, as Kearney comments, the phrase 'women in rock' acts as a barrier to the possible normalisation of women within the music industry: 'Since rock has been constructed as a naturally masculine sphere in which women, because of their sex and gender, can never be fully incorporated, "women in rock" implies the contingency and incompleteness of female performers, as well as their inauthenticity in comparison with male artists' (Kearney, 1997: 211).

The notion of authenticity is certainly a feature of this debate due to its importance in the ideological construction of rock music and practice. While, since the 1960s, pop has been constructed as commercial and disposable music, rock has alternatively been judged as a 'genuine' music form. As Railton (2001) reasons, the distinction between rock and pop articulated within rock discourse is not based purely upon sound but upon the values that these music forms are understood to embody. The rationale for distinguishing rock from pop supports a construction of these forms as gendered whereby pop was allied with femininity and rock presented as an articulation of masculinity. As Railton (2001: 324) argues, rock 'distanced itself from the "low" [mass-produced, commercial, popular music] ... by masculinising itself, and by introducing a particular way of enjoying music that eschewed the feminine, emotional and physical response of early 1960s pop fans in favour of cool, laid-back and thoughtful appreciation of the music'. In order to substantiate rock's claim to authenticity, critics have argued that it is part of a folk art tradition and accordingly reflects its musical roots in blues and country music. Moreover, rock has been perceived as a vehicle for genuine emotional outpourings, which, because of their authentic nature, are not sullied by their dissemination through a capitalist industry. Thus, the concept of authenticity is articulated not just in the music form or text but also in the body of the performer, who is understood to communicate directly to their audience.

Yet this claim to authenticity is in itself a construction. As Jon Stratton (1982: 267–85) argues, this concept of the 'real' is a useful idea for journalists and musicians to invest in as it helps to mystify the criteria by which a musical text may be judged worthy. Thus rock writers and performers employ a language of emotion in order to hide their dependency on commercial concerns. Instead of mentioning market placing and record sales, reviewers can recommend a band by describing them as 'an incredibly involving experience … it's close to spiritual' (Knowles: 1998: 21). However, my concern here is not to dismantle rock's claim to authenticity, but to consider how it is articulated. The pervasiveness of the concept of authenticity within rock discourse invites analysis and my interest is in whether this concept may be understood to be gendered.

News and views

In September 1992 the British weekly music paper *Melody Maker* ran a three-page feature (Joy *et al.*, 1992: 44–6) assessing the visibility of women rock performers. The feature comprised a number of articles by staff writers and acted as a lead-up to the *Melody Maker* 'discovery' of the so-called 'riot grrrl phenomenon' in October 1992. As such it created interest in and discussion about gender issues, and so created a discursive space within which riot grrrl could be debated. It seems reasonable to suggest that, as this feature was designed to evoke a response, the articles were intended to be contentious. However, the issues that the feature raised and the way in which the writers framed their views, illustrate how rock has been naturalised by the weekly music press as a male form, practice and ideology.

While the introductory paragraph to the piece comments on the high profile of a number of female musicians, the writer is careful not to integrate these performers into the (male) history of rock 'n' roll. Instead, the journalist points to the possibility 'that wimmin have finally won the right to rock *on their own terms*' (Joy *et al.*, 1992: 44, my emphasis). Yet even this cultural gain is immediately brought into question as the feature proposes to 'examine the fate of the new femme rockers' and question 'whether the revolution is just an illusion' (1992: 44). Arguments forwarded in the article distort and simplify the work of women in the music industry while disempowering female rock performers. Sally Margaret Joy suggests that possible ways to become 'a rock 'n' roll starlet' are to come from 'a musical middle-class family', to 'lig like mad' or to find favour by changing your hair colour to blonde (Joy *et al.*, 1992: 44–5). These suggestions (even if laden with irony) deprive female musicians of agency, position them as dependent on familial support or male admiration, and deny the existence of performers who have found success through musical ability.

However, Everett True's article (1992: 46), entitled 'Why Women Can't Rock', which was published in the same issue, presents a bleaker prediction for the future of women rock performers. True presents readers with his résumé of rock history, arguing that women performers are always presented as outsiders. While True states that the marginalisation of women in music is unjust, he also argues that this situation does not have the potential to change: 'rock is a firmly patriarchal form of expression, all the way down the line: the fans, the critics, the money-holders, the musicians. It's too far gone now for any change' (1992: 46). True's article dismisses the ways in which women have been active within rock throughout its history and represents rock as wholly masculine. While True describes how rock has a gender bias, his article does not challenge or aim to correct this. Instead, this piece can be read as an example of the music press in didactic mode, where True explains to his readers that 'women can't rock. The rules don't allow it' (1992: 46). True's summation of the intractability of rock's masculinist discourse serves to reinforce its authority. His argument thus aids the normalisation and perpetuation of certain gendered representations.

It's a girl!

The documentation of the work of female rock musicians in the niche music press and popular print media is crucial to the publicly perceived presence of women working within this field. However, the nature of this coverage often reinforces the notion that it is rare and novel for female musicians to produce rock music. In order to make an article appear newsworthy reporters often describe female artists as groundbreaking practitioners in a male field. While the article may refer back to a small number of female-centred bands who have previously been visible within this field (often cited are The Go-Gos, Blondie and The Pretenders), the implication is that a current group of female musicians has now emerged to offer a fresh challenge to a masculine discourse. Liz Evans' (1993b: 35–41) article, 'Rebel Yell', published in the women's magazine *Elle*, is an example of this. Evans, focusing on the female-centred indie bands Voodoo Queens, Lovecraft, Sidi Bou Said and Chia Pet, declares, 'a generation of female musicians has arrived, women and girls who are not content with taking a back seat to their leather-clad, ego-touting brothers. To prove it, they're picking up guitars and drumsticks and raising a particularly female kind of hell' (1993b: 36–7). While such coverage is certainly helpful in raising the profile of a musician or group, the way in which this is presented makes the history of women within popular music, or – more specifically – rock music, appear stilted and discontinuous.

The exposé-style coverage often afforded to female rock performers tends to erase the history of women who have spent many years working in the music industry as practising musicians. The periodic articles on 'women in rock' in the music press present female performers as both notable and a topic for debate. In 1992 *Melody Maker* presented a discussion between female musicians, journalists and music industry workers that aimed to examine 'the hopes, the fears, the past and the future of Women In Rock' (*Melody Maker*, 1992a: 26). While such debates may raise the profile of female music workers they also re-identify rock as a male preserve. The creation of a debate or question around 'women in rock' is common practice in the music press and music magazines. *Melody Maker*'s 1992 debate echoes a similar discussion staged by the paper in 1973 (Partridge, 1973: 1, 36). The 1973 '*Melody Maker* Special on Women in Rock' similarly featured debate between female industry workers, journalists and musicians, including artists Marsha Hunt, Elkie Brooks and Maddy Prior. Notably perhaps, the debate was chaired not by a female journalist but by the male staff writer Robert Partridge. A similar feature appeared in the *NME* in 1980 when the front and centre pages were devoted to the subject (Pearson, 1980: 1, 27–30, 51). The article explored the attitudes of 11 women working in the rock industry and questioned 'Did they feel the market and opportunities for women in rock had opened out? Was it easier for women? Or, as they are still outnumbered by men, is it an uphill struggle?' (Pearson, 1980: 27). In 1997 *Select* ran a front cover declaring 'The Future is Female' and offering readers 'a 20-page fem-centric spectacular' (*Select*, 1997: front page). The issue contained a feature on the indie band Sleeper, an obituary to 'lad culture' and interviews with (among others) female journalists, musicians and visual artists. Comparable features have appeared in other UK and US music publications, including *Spin* (1997) and the *NME* (2002).

Neither is this approach restricted to the music press. For example, in 1995 *Everywoman* magazine ran a feature entitled 'Babes in Boyland', which queried 'are women finally carving a place for themselves in the rock world?' (O'Brien, 1995a: 10). Ten years later, an article in the UK daily paper *The Independent* declared with gushing enthusiasm: 'Hold on to your fretboards – the women's rock revolution is here. Electric guitars, once the preserve of sweaty lads in leather jackets, are now cluttering up female bedrooms too' (Barnes, 2005). Singer and guitarist Kim Deal has commented on the frequency with which such articles are written: 'Since the Pixies started I've been doing interviews since about 1986 … This is the question I hate: "What about the resurgence of women in rock now?" I get asked that about every six months, or not even every six months, about every three months I get asked about the resurgence of women in rock' (personal communication, 5 September 1995). Such articles, which regularly 'rediscover' women performers, work against the normalisation of women working within rock.[8]

Fads and fashions

Intense media scrutiny also carries the danger that women rock performers may be viewed as a passing fashion rather than a sustained presence. Examination of a group of articles published in 1980[9] illustrates this point. The *NME* refers to 'the current vogue for lady singers' (Edmands, 1980), *The Guardian* declares that 'girl singers are at long last in fashion in Britain' (Denselow, R., 1980b) and the British Sunday supplement the *Observer Magazine* comments that, 'it's a happy fact that female rock 'n' rollers are becoming increasingly fashionable and successful' (Denselow, A., 1980). A later *Observer* article credits the success of Debbie Harry and Blondie as opening 'the floodgates for girls in rock' (Sky, 1980). However, by staging female performers as a fashion, journalists ensure media invisibility of these subjects once the 'fad' is understood to have passed. As Toynbee argues, once the music press detect that a music scene is on the wane, 'journalists move quickly to initiate collapse, by roundly condemning previously paradigmatic artists/texts, and at the same time disciplining recalcitrant readers who cleave to the old order' (Toynbee, 1993: 297). The comments of *Guardian* critic Robin Denselow illustrate how the press 'manage' news stories by referencing a conceptual time frame of public interest. The journalist predicts a decline of interest in female performers by music buyers brought about by too much record company investment in these artists: 'The craze for girl singers is in danger of becoming self-defeating ... it would be silly if girl rock then faded from fashion like fold rock [*sic*] or glam-rock. But record companies hammer a saleable commodity to death, once they see one, and this is the year for finding female singers by the dozen' (Denselow, R., 1980a). By treating female musicians as a popular music fad this journalist argues that record companies are saturating the market, a strategy that can only result in fewer women gaining record deals in the long term.

By periodically grouping female artists together as a fad, journalists both marginalise and reduce the historical importance of these music makers. One may consider the example of a 2003 music review by John Harris of new albums by the artists Peaches and Dido. Written in a rather weary style, Harris uses the theme of 'women in rock' as a framing device to tie together the reviews of these two very divergent music makers. Aware of the cliché of grouping dissimilar artists together under the label 'women in rock' Harris derides journalists' use of this term in the early 1990s while simultaneously employing the phrase as a pivot to his article. He comments:

> Back around 1993 ... an agenda-cum-project-cum-string of clichés briefly took hold of music commentary in both the UK and America. ... its concerns were usually grouped under the prosaic phrase 'Women in Rock'. ... Their central point was something like this: it was surely only a matter of minutes before females – led by the likes of Polly Harvey, Courtney Love and Sonic Youth's Kim Gordon – would nudge the last traces of rock music's once-unvanquishable sexism into touch, and assume their rightful place alongside the boys. (Harris, J., 2003: 99)

While highlighting the limitations of the phrase 'women in rock', Harris does not so much set out to critique masculinist rock discourse but to confirm it. He explains that the earlier championing of female musicians was naively celebratory as:

> Unfortunately more mainstream cultural currents quickly squashed such dreams. ... the umbilically linked forces of both Britpop and lad culture enshrined the idea that music was best played by lager-slurping males ... men are still in charge, and the brief era of the female-fronted band – Elastica, Sleeper, Echobelly – seems very distant indeed.' (Harris, J., 2003: 99)

Harris's article thus reclaims rock as a male preserve and distances the success of a number of female rock performers as a peculiar phase within the history of rock music motivated by feminist whimsy.

Not all media articles treat female performers as faddish commodities. However, often the way in which they discuss these musicians works to peculiarise or distance them from male performers. It is commonplace for journalists to describe the music of female artists by referencing only other female acts. As a member of the Canadian all-female indie band Jale commented, 'we get compared to, almost exclusively, all women bands. I mean, we get compared to L7 which is absurd. We've even been compared to The Bangles and The Go-Gos!' (personal communication, 23 June 1994). By placing these artists in a purely female lineage writers create a distinction from canonised (male) musicians. This practice can be very frustrating for performers and misleading to music press readers seeking out new music to purchase. As Lauren

Laverne commented when she was vocalist with female-centred band Kenickie: 'one of the most irritating things [is] being compared to people we sound nothing like maybe because we look like them or maybe there is three of us and there is three of them. I mean, we sound fuck all like The Ronnettes. No-one would ever dream of saying anything about Roxy Music or The Stooges in reference to us and that's what we like' (personal communication, 9 May 1997).

Yet gender problematics also occur when female artists are referenced within the established male rock lineage. While potentially this may be understood as an inclusive approach to women rock performers, sometimes this results in an erasure of their female identity. Both Patti Smith and Janis Joplin are included in most rock canons and often viewed in comparison to their male contemporaries. They are regularly cited in popular and academic work as important figures in the history of women rock performers. However, while these performers are granted critical cachet, they are usually figured as adoptees to rock's masculinity. In the editorial to *Rolling Stone*'s 'Women of Rock' edition, Jann S. Wenner describes Patti Smith as 'a seminal figure who modelled her life on the great men of rock – and even wanted to be one' (*Rolling Stone*, 1997: 31). This depiction of Patti Smith as tomboy is commonplace and has been noted by a number of critics (Reynolds and Press, 1995: 236f.; Coates, 1998: 79). In this respect Smith's public persona has much in common with that of Joplin, who is frequently described in similar terms (see Archer and Simmonds, 1986: 180–93; Gaar, 1993: 101–8; O'Brien, 1995b: 99–105). The successful careers of these women do not pose a threat to the masculinity of rock if they are understood in rock history as female performers who were 'one of the boys'.

Nevertheless, while Joplin may be described as 'one of the boys', she was still judged as a woman in a man's world. Joplin's rock 'n' roll persona and physicality in performance has been understood as a performative masculinity, an enacting of male codes of behaviour. Yet not all aspects of Joplin's public life have been understood in the same way as those of her male contemporaries. Joplin's promiscuous behaviour and reliance on drugs and alcohol have been popularly understood as elements in the tragic decline of an insecure and unattractive woman. While there are numerous books, articles and television programmes dedicated to artists who 'died too young',[10] Joplin's story is often described in terms of personal frailty rather than rock 'n' roll heroics. As Simon Reynolds and Joy Press comment, male musicians can draw on the 'tradition of adventurism … [where] bad behaviour is, if not exactly sanctioned, seen as a logical extension of masculinity' (Reynolds and Press, 1995: 272). Joplin is viewed as tragic as she is understood to have failed in terms of feminine conduct. The 1980 film *The Rose*,[11] which was loosely based on Joplin's life, contributes to the myth of her decline. The film features the female protagonist fleeing from her stadium concert to a childhood space of safety: her old school. The performer is then portrayed consuming pills and alcohol, and making a desperate phone call to her parents. The protagonist is not presented as a rock icon but as a casualty, someone who has failed to live up to the expectations of her management, fans and parents. In terms of rock history, then, Joplin is presented both as 'one of the boys' and also judged against accepted codes of feminine behaviour. The interpretation of rock history is not neutral but is informed by a masculinist conception of music practice, performance and personal conduct.

Specialist and exclusive

There is evidence, then, that rock discourse continues to exclude women as bona fide rock musicians through the treatment of female-centred bands as exceptional and faddish. Yet this process becomes more complex if consideration is given to how individual members of a female band are received within various music magazines, books and websites. This reveals intersecting gendered discourses concerning instrumentation. Specific coverage on female instrumentalists is often more scant than coverage of female solo artists or bands containing female musicians. While a female-centred band may receive a certain amount of favourable coverage, the skill of the individual members of the band is seldom isolated and celebrated in rock lists and books. For example, *Mojo*'s '100 Greatest Guitarists of All Time' (June 1996, issue 31) included only three women. A similar paucity of entries may be found in books celebrating instrumentalists. *Big Noises* by Geoff Nicholson (1991) will serve as an example, containing biographies and discographies of 37 guitarists and a list of 100 additional 'mighty guitar moments', each by a different artist. None of these entries concerns female musicians. Likewise a book compiled by *Guitar World* magazine identifying 113 'greatest guitarists of all time' and 'the 100 greatest solos of all time' includes no female musicians within its selection (Kitts and Tolinski, 2002). Moreover, the titles of the chapters within the book are indicative of its masculinist agenda as it categorises the musicians included under headings such as 'Founding Fathers', 'Country Gentlemen', 'Jazzmen' and 'Visionaries and Madmen'. While the comments of one woman, Nancy Wilson of Heart, are included within the book, it is notable that Wilson is subsumed in a chapter entitled 'Leading Men'.

Attention can also be given to the 'highly technical, consumer-orientated musicians' magazines' (Théberge, 1991: 272), which often focus on specific instruments. Examples of these specialist magazines are the titles *Electronic Musician*, *Total Guitar*, *Guitar Player* and *Modern Keyboard*. The internet site *Drummergirl* points to the absence of features on female drummers in specialist music magazines. To illustrate this, the site allows the browser to view the front covers of several recent editions of *Modern Drummer*, taken from the publisher's website. Each cover features a close-up shot of a celebrity male performer with their drum kit in view. Donna, a designer of the *Drummergirl* site, sarcastically comments that this has led 'to the conclusion that women drummers don't exist … And if they do exist, they can't play. If they could play, they would be featured more often, wouldn't they?'[12] *Drummergirl* attempts to increase public awareness of female percussionists by offering details on useful published material, information on international performers and event listings, as well as providing links to other related sites. The absence of cover stories on female musicians is not particular to magazines aimed at percussionists. Paul Théberge's analysis of these specialist magazines reveals similar editorial practices in other titles. He comments, 'by the end of 1989, after fifteen years of publishing (a total of over 160 issues), *Keyboard* had devoted its cover story to only a handful of select, female artists' (Théberge, 1991: 286).

Analysis of the content of musicians' magazines shows a clear predominance of features on male musicians. Mavis Bayton's study (1997) of magazines aimed at guitarists, based on research conducted in 1988, 1992 and 1996, reveals a similar absence of features, photographs and news items on female musicians. Bayton isolates one article from 1996 that, unusually, focuses on a female guitarist. She comments, however, that the text was written by a man, directed at a male readership and traded in the sexist clichés of rock 'n' roll. These observations also hold true for many of the advertisements carried in these publications. The promotional space in these magazines, constituting a high percentage of the content, is devoted to advertising musical instruments, equipment and accessories. The target market of aspiring musicians is suggested by the copy, which emphasises the need for professional equipment if musicians want to get picked from the rest, and sometimes features endorsements by successful (male) professional musicians. Historically advertisements in these magazines have used images of scantily clad women to connote ideas of sexual attraction, social status or empowerment. This strategy of targeting male readers is still in operation. For example, the front cover of the magazine *2001 Guitar Buyer's Guide*, published in June 2000, featured women wearing bikinis and high heels standing astride a guitar.

Publishers of these magazines have defended the gender bias in the adverts they carry by stating that they are targeted at a readership that is almost exclusively male. However, as Paula Bocciardi[13] has pointed out, there is a certain circularity to this argument, where the targeting of advertisements to men helps to exclude a female readership. Leaving aside the issue of readership, one can see how the content of these magazines reinforces the conception that rock practice is a male territory and technical musical knowledge a male preserve. Théberge argues that the decision by magazine editors to carry only music-related advertising, and the regular inclusion of musical tips and transcriptions, works to evoke a sense of community. However, while the text may speak to an imagined transnational community of connoisseurs, it is important to understand that this delineation excludes as well as embraces. By speaking in masculinist terms to a male readership about male performers these magazines work to create a community that excludes female performers and readers.

Conclusion

There are many aspects and illustrations of rock's masculinist tradition that I have not been able to cover in this chapter. I have not, for example, considered the semiotics of band logos or album cover design. Neither have I explored the codification and naturalisation of masculine performance styles. This is an area I shall explore in the next chapter, which relates these codes to female performers, and in Chapter 4, which explores strategies of performance. While I have touched upon the masculinist tone of many music journalists, I have not had room to consider the macho language and behaviour used by many male rock stars, which is both allowed for within rock and which actively 'speaks' rock as a masculinist tradition.[14] In Chapter 3, I will consider in more depth how gender affects the way that journalists construct rock musicians.

I have focused instead on discursive fields in rock, considering journalistic practice, types of publication, and the choices and selections made by book editors.

I have discussed how a rock canon has become established through various agencies in the music industry, and I have considered how this celebration of stars also works as a process of exclusion. I have considered also how categories, such as 'women in rock', can work as discursive tools to position performers and to exclude them from complete integration into rock culture. Moreover, I have illustrated how rock journalism often assumes a male audience and thus female readers are neither catered for nor addressed. My aim has been to illustrate and examine how the masculinity of rock is continually 'put into discourse' (Foucault, 1990: 11) by different agents and operations of the music industry. Rock cannot be *proved* to be an essentially male practice but when one considers the many presentations of rock performers by record companies and the media one notes how this idea is assumed and naturalised. The everyday practices of the music industry thus produce rock as a masculinist tradition.

Notes

1   Hirsh (1990) has noted, because of the uncertainty in predicting chart successes, the music industry has adopted a strategy of overproduction. He reflects, 'it is apparently more efficient to produce many "failures" for each success than to sponsor fewer items and pretest each on a massive scale to increase media coverage and consumer sales' (Hirsh, 1990: 135). Yet, one can further argue that once these successes have been achieved, to realise maximum financial return, record companies need to employ strategies for remarketing these old and arbitrary hits. The establishment of canons of hits and hitmakers involves a selection and filtering of these products and creates categories of marketable 'classics'

2   The following figures show the number of entries devoted to female solo artists and bands with one or more female musician or vocalist compared with the total number of entries in each text:

The Encyclopedia of Rock Volume One (Hardy and Laing, 1976a) contains 39 out of 460 entries (8 per cent), *The Encyclopedia of Rock Volume Two* (Hardy and Laing, 1976b) contains 64 out of 473 entries (14 per cent), *The Encyclopedia of Rock Volume Three* (Hardy and Laing, 1976c) contains 58 out of 455 entries (13 per cent), *The New Musical Express Book of Rock Number Two* (Logan and Woffinden, 1977) contains 65 out of 641 entries (10 per cent), *The Illustrated Encyclopedia of Rock* (Logan and Woffinden, 1982) contains 80 out of 674 entries (12 per cent), *The Encyclopedia of Pop, Rock and Soul* (Stambler, 1989) contains 86 out of 510 entries (17 per cent), *The Faber Companion to 20th-Century Popular Music* (Hardy and Laing, 1995) contains 272 out of 1750 entries (16 per cent), *The Virgin Encyclopedia of Nineties Music* (Larkin, 2000) contains 286 out of 1306 entries (22 per cent), *Guinness Rockopedia: The Ultimate A–Z of Rock and Pop* (Roberts *et al.*, 1998) listed 150 out of a total 750 artists, producers and DJs (20 per cent), *The Rolling Stone Encyclopedia of Rock and Roll* (3rd edn) (George-Warren and Romanowski, 2001) contains 351 out of 1625 entries (22 per cent).

3   Cameron has noted a similar gender bias within the jazz canon with less that 7 per cent of the *Guinness Who's Who of Jazz* (Larkin, 1995) given over to female artists. The majority of these entries are 'for singers in the "traditional" (i.e. verging on blues or cabaret) mould' (Cameron, 2003: 908).

4   Lists published in a number of UK music magazines can be used as illustration. The number of entries listed here are for female artists and bands with one or more female musician. In August 1995 *Mojo* (issue 21) published 'The 100 Greatest Albums Ever Made', compiled by its contributors, the list contained only nine entries. Overall only seven female

artists were represented as two of these artists featured twice. *Q* magazine featured eight such entries among its list of '50 Best Albums of 2001' although arguably this number increases to ten if compilation albums are included (*Q*, December 2001, issue 185). The '100 greatest singles of all time' (*Mojo*, August 1997, issue 45), voted for by songwriters, musicians and producers, contained 11 entries. *NME*'s '100 greatest British albums ever' (28 January 2006) included only nine entries.

5   Quoted from 'Music Of The Millennium' website (http://www.hmv.co.uk/uk/rockpop/main), accessed 12 March 1998.

6   Journalist Lucy O'Brien commented on the lack of female representation in the chart in a short broadcast on Channel 4 (27 January 1998). The transcript of the broadcast was published in *Women in Music* magazine (O'Brien, 1998: 1).

7   Other lists compiled by music press readers display a similar gender imbalance. The '100 Greatest Albums Ever Made' (*Mojo*, January 1996, issue 26) features 11 entries. The '100 Greatest Singles of All Time', voted by *Q* readers, features ten entries (*Q*, February 1999, issue 149).

8   See Brenda Johnson-Grau (2002) for a discussion of numerous other 'women in rock' articles, appearing chiefly in US publications from 1968 to 1999.

9   Taken from the Robert Shelton Archive, Institute of Popular Music, University of Liverpool.

10   See, for example, Sheinwold (1980), Archer and Simmonds (1986), Henderson and Johnson (1999) and the series of books published by Parragon Books, Bristol, in 1995 entitled *They Died Too Young*, which featured artists such as Kurt Cobain, Sid Vicious and Jim Morrison. Such artists have also been the subject of celebration within television programmes. For example, on 26 August 2000 Channel 4 broadcast an evening of television dedicated to 'Hellraisers' such as the late Keith Moon, drummer with The Who.

11   A list of all the films and documentaries cited in the book (including date of release and director) appears at the end of the References.

12   *Drummergirl* (http://www-personal.umich.edu/~ dichaw/ dgirl/ agenda.html), accessed 16 November 1997.

13   Paula Bocciardi, 'Female Drummers', first published in *Drum!* magazine, reprinted on *Drummergirl* website (http://www-personal.umich.edu/~ dichaw/ dgirl/ agenda.html), accessed 16 November 1997.

14   There are countless documented illustrations of this behaviour within the print media. Gina Morris's interview with Shaun Ryder (Morris, 1997) is one such example.

Chapter 2

Gender and indie rock music

The previous chapter considered the gendered associations and definitions within the broad category of rock music. It argued that the discourse of rock encyclopaedias, guides, anthologies and journalistic practice in the weekly music press and music magazines serves to establish, reproduce and maintain a masculinist rock tradition. This chapter narrows the focus and explores the significance and operation of gendered attitudes within indie rock music. Unlike the previous chapter, only brief mention will be made of music guides and the canonic processes of this subgenre. Analysis of the presentation of indie female-centred bands and artists in the written media will appear in the next chapter. This chapter will explore the professional practices of indie rock musicians, including the processes of recording, purchasing equipment, touring and negotiating with record company personnel. Drawing on personal interviews with a number of female performers, it will consider whether the indie scene is an accessible environment for female musicians. It will explore how music 'contexts', such as the tour bus, recording studio or musical instrument shop, can be understood as cultural sites in which particular codes of behaviour are normative. It will examine how these contexts of musical practice, performance and participation may be read in gendered ways. While indie rock musicians will be the focus of discussion it must be noted that, within the context of the recording studio or performance venue, musicians interact with music industry workers who may not restrict themselves to one music subgenre. A tour manager or lighting technician, for example, will be hired by a band for the duration of a tour and so may work for a variety of music performers. Thus indie musicians are engaged with, and are participants in, a wider community of music industry professionals, some of whom specialise in indie rock music (e.g. promoters and sound engineers), while others may work within a broader spectrum of popular music production (e.g. marketing staff at record companies).

Gender and indie music

The discussion of rock and masculinity in Chapter 1 considered how rock guides and encyclopaedias privilege male performers, observing that such definitive guides (whether published in book form or presented as 'essential' lists in the music press) offer readers a canon of notable rock performers. The predominance of male musicians in these guides has suggested an absence of female rock performers and has served to re-establish rock as a male practice. Examination of ten rock guides and encyclopaedias revealed that female solo artists, female-centred bands, bands with one or more female musicians and bands with female vocalists accounted for between 8 and 22 per cent of the total number of entries in each text. This low percentage, calculated using the broadest possible criteria, demonstrates how male dominated these guides were. If one considers the overall number of musicians included in these guides (i.e. counting individual members of each band) then a very small number of female musicians are represented when compared with the number of male performers.

Examination of a number of indie and alternative rock guides, using the same defining criteria, provides a useful comparison as it offers a gauge of the number of female musicians esteemed within indie/alternative rock culture. While there are fewer guides to indie music than there are general rock volumes, analysis of a selection of texts indicates an increased inclusion of female musicians. *The Guinness Who's Who of Indie and New Wave Music* (Larkin, 1992) contains 216 entries for female solo artists and bands with at least one female member out of a total of 841 entries (26 per cent), the *Spin Alternative Record Guide* (Weisbard and Marks, 1995) contains 100 out of 379 entries (26 per cent) while *Alternative Rock* (Thompson, 2000) contains 78 out of a collection of 361 entries (22 per cent) for bands and artists who had 'made the greatest contributions' (Thompson, 2000: viii) to alternative rock. In these texts female groups, artists and bands with at least one female musician accounted for between 22 and 26 per cent of the overall entries. *The Alternative Music Almanac* (Cross, 1995: 279–87) offers a similar proportion of bands with women performers in its list of 20 classic/essential alternative albums, with five out of the 20 listed groups containing at least one female member. The *NME Writers 100 Best Indie Singles Ever*, published on 25 July 1992, offers a slightly lower percentage (19 per cent), but still represents a greater inclusion of female musicians than many general rock lists published by the music press.[1] This suggests that the indie music scene may offer a cultural space that is more appealing or accessible to female performers and within which they are more likely to achieve success and prestige.

In order to gain an indication of any trends in the types of instruments that female musicians perform with in indie bands an analysis was undertaken of the entries within Thompson's (2000) book *Alternative Rock*. Within the 78 entries that included women performers Thompson listed 101 female solo artists or members of bands. Of those listed, 60 provided lead or accompanying vocals, 27 played guitar, 24 played bass and 13 were drummers or percussionists. Thus, within this guidebook, the majority of listed women performers were vocalists while approximately half were either bassists or guitarists. Obviously, this analysis cannot be understood as an overview of the roles and participation of female musicians in indie rock in general. Clawson's (1999b) research has suggested that women's participation in instrumental playing in alternative rock has been weighted towards bass playing: 'alternative continues to be a male-dominated musical genre, with the bass remaining a principle site for women's still limited access' (Clawson, 1999b: 196). Clawson (1999b) and Halberstam (2003) have argued that a reason for a higher percentage of female rock instrumentalists playing bass might be because the bass is seen as having less status than the guitar. As Halberstam comments, 'The bass can be read here as a "masculine" instrument in terms of its production of noise in the lower registers, but it can also be read as a stereotypically "female" instrument, given that many women in rock bands have been relegated to bass player because the "lead" guitar was presumed to be a male role' (Halberstam, 2003: 324).

The greater visibility of women in indie music has contributed to the popular notion that indie is a less masculinist musical tradition. As mentioned in the previous chapter, a number of critics have published edited interviews with contemporary female rock musicians,[2] which have offered oral histories of those musicians' experiences as performers and songwriters. The fact that many of the interviewees are indie rock performers is perhaps indicative of the greater presence of women within this genre. However, it is questionable whether one can use such a cause-and-effect model when discussing the success of female indie musicians. In her discussion of rock women, critic Nicole Arthur does not talk of the tolerant nature of alternative rock or its freedom from reactionary attitudes. Instead, she suggests that, 'the most mundane explanation for this surge of female musicians is probably the most accurate. There were more women in the workplace than ever before, and the music business was no exception' (Arthur, 1995: 208). Arthur thus argues that the increased visibility of women in alternative rock is not due to the 'female-friendly' culture of this genre but is reflective of a general increase in the number of women in areas of paid employment.

The apparent liberalism of indie music culture may be a popular assumption rather than one evidenced by female musicians. This view was supported by Kim Gordon, bass player with Sonic Youth and member of the female-centred band Free Kitten: 'I think in general there's a preconception about indie rock, that it's not sexist and that it's very accepting of women, but I see the mainstream of it as pretty conservative, like college rock or something' (Gordon, quoted in Evans, 1994: 175). Holly Kruse also observed, in a study of 'alternative music' played on US college radio, that: 'Nothing about the social and economic organisation of alternative music necessarily seeks to subvert the white, patriarchal structures of the mainstream music establishment' (Kruse, 1993: 40). Ten years later this sentiment was reiterated in an interview with Brea, a radio DJ and Ladyfest organiser in Austin, Texas. Asked whether she considered indie rock to be more progressive in terms of gender politics than the larger rock context she comment that: 'I think a lot of people think it is because there are few indie rock bands that get a lot of attention with women in them, but turn on any college/indie rock station and see how many bands with women in them that you hear. It's not many' (personal communication, 2 September 2003). Louise Wener, the front person for the UK band Sleeper, who enjoyed some chart success in the mid-1990s, has similarly commented that her experience of and frustration with the maculinist culture of indie rock has remained unchanged over the past ten years: 'The truth is, the world of indie rock was then, and still is, a doggedly macho environment, notoriously unforgiving of female interlopers' (Wener, 2005: 6). As I will discuss in Chapters 5 and 6, in 1991 female musicians and zine writers in the US and Britain identified and challenged aspects of macho or sexist behaviour within indie music culture through the feminist riot grrrl initiative. The following discussion will consider how the culture of indie music is more generally experienced by contemporary female-centred bands. Drawing on interview material it will discuss how different attitudes towards gender affect the way that female musicians participate in and experience indie rock culture.

Connoisseurship and the culture of indie rock

Examination of a number of indie guides illustrates how a canon of notable indie rock performers has become established. The category of indie music as used in these guides is an umbrella term that covers a variety of sonically divergent groups and artists. Moreover, this canon is often expanded to include artists and groups whose music has shaped and influenced contemporary indie rock performers. The influence of artists such as The Velvet Underground, Big Star, Can and The Beach Boys is referenced in interviews, reviews and biographies. Periodically the music press publish articles or fact files on bands or albums that have become touchstones for contemporary indie music.[3] Indie music radio shows also frequently broadcast old 'important' tracks or recruit long-established or reformed groups to play a session for the show. The indie music enthusiast is encouraged by these media sources to seek out the musical lineage of indie rock and to engage in a discourse in which they construct themselves as cultural archivists and music experts. Hibbett (2005: 57) reflects that in this regard indie rock culture can be likened to the principles and politics associated with 'high art' as it privileges those with 'insider' knowledge, celebrates the obscure and excludes mainstream tastes. In a discussion of alternative rock, Will Straw argues that the desire to uncover prestigious, rare, alternative rock albums has come to be understood as a male trait: 'the cultivation of connoisseurship in rock culture – tracking down old albums, learning genealogical links between bands, and so on – has traditionally been one rite of passage through which the masculinism of rock-music culture has been perpetuated' (Straw, 1991: 378). In a later article Straw (1997) develops this argument concerning record collecting as a male practice by exploring how people become knowledgeable about records, how that knowledge is displayed or revealed to others and how the conception of the obsessive male collector has been likened to that of the 'intrepid explorer' who hunts down rare albums.[4]

In a song entitled 'His Indie World', the American singer-songwriter Mary Lou Lord satirises the exclusivity and obscurantist nature of the indie scene. The subject in the song laments the fact that her music tastes (Joni Mitchell, Nick Drake, Neil Young and Bob Dylan) do not fit in with those of her boyfriend, who favours contemporary US 'underground' indie bands such as Guided By Voices, Velocity Girl, Rocket From The Crypt and Built To Spill. The comic intent of the track is explicit, for while the subject of the song declares herself an 'outsider', the list of performers referenced demonstrates a clear knowledge of underground indie music and an understanding of how people are protective of musical boundaries. While the song explores ideas of exclusion, it does not suggest barriers to female musicians within the indie scene. Mary Lou Lord litters the song with references to female indie performers (including the female-centred bands Bikini Kill, Slant 6 and Huggy Bear, and the artists Kim Gordon and Kim Deal). The song instead concentrates on how the selectivity of musical reference points within the music scene and a tendency towards obscure, little-known artists act as a form of exclusion and elitism. Mary Lou Lord has commented that she was inspired to write the song by people within the indie scene who rejected any music that was outside of the indie canon: 'I was hanging out with these kids who were listening only to current indie music and I'd ask them if they'd heard Nick Drake. They'd say, "No." Then I'd ask if they listened to Joni Mitchell. They'd say, "No, and we don't want to listen to her."' (quoted in Woodworth, 1998: 106). The lyrics and comments of Mary Lou Lord illustrate how an exclusive indie rock canon has become established. As examination of a number of indie rock guides has revealed, this canon is dominated by male artists and the practice of collecting rare and 'important' tracks has, in turn, been understood as a male trait.

The image of a music enthusiast obsessed with researching record releases from small independent companies and collecting rare vinyl albums is linked with the image of the socially inhibited 'geek' or 'nerd'. Commentators have noted (Milano, 2003; Shuker, 2004) this image is a gendered one as the popular conception of the nerdy record collector is of a male character. As Straw comments: 'the nerdish homosociality of those who collect popular music artefacts is as fundamental to the masculinism of popular music as the general valorisation of technical prowess and performative intensity more typically seen to be at its core' (Straw, 1997: 15). The labels 'nerdy' and 'geeky' are also applied in relation to other social activities such as trainspotting, stamp collecting and science fiction fandom. However, while these labels have a rather negative association, which one might expect to see disputed, the persona of the nerd has often been celebrated or used self-referentially within indie music cultures to indicate knowledge of and dedication to music. This is evidenced in internet sites such as *Geekrock* and *Patheticore*[5] and zines entitled *Pathetic Life* and *Losers*.[6] The association between masculinity and nerdishness has not however been uncontested. The role of the outsider 'geek' has been appropriated by female musicians and website designers. This can be noted in websites launched since the mid-1990s, such as *Nrrdgrrl* and *Geekgirl*,[7] through to the current three-piece UK band Geekgirl. In these instances the notion of outsiderness and difference inherent in the definition of a geek is valorised while the stereotype of an insular, highly knowledgeable male figure[8] is also challenged. Nevertheless, the conception of the *male* indie nerd or connoisseur remains highly pervasive within indie rock culture.

As discussed earlier, the culture and performance of rock music has traditionally been understood as a display of masculine power, excess and overt (hetero) sexuality. Indie, while employing the musical conventions of rock, has frequently presented a softer, less macho articulation of masculinity or male experience. Sara Cohen's study of male indie rock groups in Liverpool documents how the lyrics and sounds produced by the bands convey the impression of 'a fragile masculinity' (Cohen, 1997: 29) while Tony Grajeda discusses how the aesthetics, production values and emphasis on home recording within US 'lo-fi' indie contribute to an understanding of this music as 'gendered feminine within the overall masculinist discourse of rock' (Grajeda, 2002: 238). Likewise Andy Bennett observes that indie guitar performance rejects the 'machoistic and overtly sexist performance traits' of other styles of rock and heavy metal, commenting that the 'use of the guitar in any form of on-stage posturing that even remotely resembles the thrusting movements of heavy metal players appears to be an unwritten taboo within indie-guitar circles' (Bennett, 2001: 55). In an earlier consideration of independent music in the 1980s, Simon Reynolds argues that indie culture opposes ideas of health and physicality associated with 'youth' and promoted through pop music. He comments that indie rejects the way in which dance, soul, disco and funk have sexualised the body through vocal delivery, dance and lyrical content. Reynolds comments that 'Indiepop *is* danced to, but strictly demands physical responses that contravene the norms of dance and sexual attraction, that involve a *sacrifice* of cool' (Reynolds, 1989: 246). This apparent 'sacrifice of cool' is simply the articulation of a different set of cultural values and conventions. Setting themselves apart from the 'slick' workings of the pop industry, indie performers and fans embrace alternative cultural symbols. For example, the 1986 indie fashion of wearing outmoded anoraks worked on one level as an anti-fashion statement but also as a symbol of subcultural identification or 'geek cool'. The image of the 'indie nerd' (introspective, insecure and self-deprecating) continues to be celebrated within some sectors of indie culture and articulated through affected mannerisms, lyrics and clothing. The 'loser' image (attached to a number of highly successful male performers in the 1990s)[9] further illustrates how indie music has continued to offer images of weak or vulnerable masculinity.

In an article entitled 'Velocity Girls: Indie, New Lads, Old Values', British journalist Laura Lee Davies (1995) discusses her initial attraction towards indie music in 1981 because of its sound, affordable style, and because 'on a superficial level, the artists (if not the indie media) had a *softer* gang mentality than the bikers, the mods' (Davies, 1995: 125, my emphasis). However, Davies goes on to discuss her belief that indie music has not really offered a new space to female performers, music enthusiasts or music press readers. While she notes 'the increasing female presence at gigs, in the press, and in bands' (1995: 134), Davies argues that the culture of indie music is white and male.[10] She comments that, 'despite the seemingly feminine, or certainly less macho nature of so much of indie music's lyrical content, almost all of the genre's leading "scenes" have, over the years, been quite male-dominated, if not laddish' (1995: 128). Bennett concurs with this, commenting that 'indie-guitar culture, as with many other rock and pop-based music cultures, remains a primarily male concern' (Bennett, 2001: 57). It may be argued that while the image associated with indie music is quite separate from the overt masculinism of many other rock subgenres (e.g. heavy rock and progressive rock), it nonetheless remains attached to a notion of masculinity. Indie music may be understood as offering an alternative articulation of masculinity rather than operating as a gender-neutral or pro-female category. Admittedly, indie music encompasses many different variants and so it is difficult to conceptualise all bands within this category. Indeed some bands, such as the UK all-male indie rock band Primal Scream, have offered alternating presentations of masculinity throughout their careers, from fey affectation to cock rock posturing. However, the image of the 'soft' or less aggressive male can be regarded as a predominant trope within indie music culture.

Putting indie music in context

The focus of this discussion will now turn to the different contexts in which indie rock music is produced (through the processes of recording, performance or music consumption) and to the particular personal and social dynamics involved. Particular contexts, such as the recording studio or backstage area, are often associated with strict gender codes. The following analysis considers whether these codes are stable or contested within indie rock music practice and questions whether contemporary female indie performers would agree with the comment that, 'the masculinist values underpinning the rock working environment make the life of a rock musician one which most women would not choose' (Bayton, 1989: 385). Some critics have commented that as rock music is male dominated and male identified, the success of female rock performers is the outcome of struggle and opposition.[11] Such an analysis reinforces the notion of female musicians as outsiders and suggests that male music industry workers impede the achievements of female performers, whether through intimidation, discrimination or lack of concern. I wish to avoid the suggestion that gender roles are fixed within a particular music genre, as this implies that the relationship between male and female musicians, engineers, producers and other music industry workers is both predictable and knowable. Drawing on interview material I will consider the complexity of working relationships in different spatial contexts and will argue that specific music contexts are culturally encoded. Through this approach I hope to avoid a blanket description of the operation of gender in indie rock music and offer an effective way of understanding the role that gender plays in the working life of a musician.

Within the various contexts inhabited by working musicians particular behaviours become established, legitimate and dominant. These behaviours can be read as 'performances' that reflect social or professional status and demonstrate degrees of privilege, power, knowledge and 'insiderness'. Often these performances also enact a particular set of gender roles.[12] One can consider music instrument retail outlets as an illustration. As critics (Cohen, 1997: 23; Bayton, 1998: 30–31) have discussed, a pervading masculinist atmosphere can be felt in many music instrument shops. Mavis Bayton comments that, 'young women … typically find trying out equipment a severe trial. They are scared of showing themselves up and being "put down" by the assistants. They are inhibited in what they perceive to be a "male" arena' (Bayton, 1998: 30–31). The music instrument shop is a context in which technical knowledge or 'expertise' is privileged. Certain behavioural codes have become established in music instrument shops. For example, one is not expected to demand swift attention from the staff or clearly displayed product information. Instead, the music shop is a context in which the consumer is expected to demonstrate their knowledge of product lines, instrumentation and gadgetry. Most often, when buying a piece of equipment one is not ushered quickly to a purchase point but is instead engaged in conversation by a shop assistant on the merits and uses of the item. Musicians 'trying out' an amp become performers in this context, where their skills can be assessed by other customers or shop workers.

A number of musicians commented to me that they have found musical instrument shops alienating. They explained that this was not because they were concerned about a personal lack of technical expertise, but because they have not wished to engage in a public display of their knowledge or offer a demonstration of their performance skills. Corin Tucker, vocalist and guitarist in the US all-female band Sleater Kinney, commented: 'I hate music stores in general. They are a weird male resort, the last of the geeky music guys, frustrated and overknowledgeable, playing some weird game with any man, woman or child who unwittingly steps in' (personal communication, 5 November 1998). Similarly Rina, a musician based in Melbourne, Australia, commented that when she was in music stores she tended to 'feel as though I'm getting ripped off, or considered stupid because I don't know what a XP100 – Gpeg is, or something like that. In other words, the men are quite competitive with their music knowledge, rather than supportive' (personal communication, 19 August 2003). The music instrument shop often works as a context in which the masculinist tradition of rock is reproduced and maintained. Miki Berenyi, who at the time of interview was vocalist and guitarist in the London-based indie band Lush, stated that she found this to be a frustrating element in her professional life as a musician:

> walking into a guitar shop and trying to buy a pedal you know and some fucking arsehole there thinks he just knows everything and it's like 'What? You want to buy a guitar?'... Denmark Street[13] is hell. ... I just used to go to one shop 'cos it's the only shop where they used to be nice to me and all the others were just really sexist. Where you were just like 'Yeah, all right love, yeah, be with you in a minute. Do you want a reed for your flute or something?' and you were like 'No, actually, I want a guitar amp' (personal communication, 20 January 1996)

Lisa Eriksson, who performed in the UK-based indie band Schulte/Eriksson, also recalled a number of incidents where retail assistants in music shops gave her inadequate assistance because she was a woman. She mentioned one occasion when she attempted to purchase strings for her guitar:

> I have been in [to a music shop] to buy strings, I say: 'I would like to buy ten strings for an electric guitar', and they go: 'Is that your boyfriend?', and they point to any guy who is in the store. And I said, 'No, I have never seen him before'. I ask, 'What has that got to do with buying strings?', and they said that they thought that I was buying them for him. ... You go up and ask [for guitar strings] and they say, 'Oh, do you want them for a violin?', and I say, 'No, *electric guitar* strings', and they go, 'Oh, for an acoustic guitar?', and you go, '*Electric* guitar! You sell them right there!' (personal communication, 20 March 1999)

Berenyi's and Eriksson's experiences highlight how the performance of particular instruments has become culturally gendered. The remarks by both musicians that the male retail assistants were resistant to the idea that they were electric guitar players indicates just how associated this instrument has become with masculinity (see Bayton, 1997; Waksman, 1999). It is clear that the ascription of gender codes to instruments has material affects and is integrated into patterns of socialisation often from an early age. A recent UK report detailing the playing of different instruments by schoolchildren found that many instruments were clearly gendered with 89 per cent of flute players being girls while 81 per cent of electric guitar and bass guitar players were boys (Hallam *et al.*, 2005). The attitudes of the retail assistants described by these musicians work to preserve the musical instrument shop as a male context as they inhibit female interaction and prioritise male customers. Eriksson commented that she felt male customers were given a more efficient service because she has frequently had, 'to wait really long because they think you are just the girlfriend. They don't go up to you and ask: "Can I help you?". It takes much longer.' She commented that she has now adopted a strategy 'to always laugh and to keep the stories' (personal communication, 20 March 1999).

Studios

As a number of critics have commented,[14] the technical environment of the studio has also often been naturalised as a masculine context. This is related to a culturally understood 'fit' between masculinity and the 'mastery' of 'complex' technologies (i.e. those that are not concerned with domestic work). Lucy Green (1997) and Sheryl Garratt (1985: 75) discuss how, from school age, girls are not encouraged or expected to experiment and engage with technology, except in the domestic sphere. Green's research on the attitudes of schoolteachers and pupils concerning music performance reveals how boys are perceived to have a greater interest in music technology and 'noisy' instruments such as the electric guitar and drums (Green, 1997: 175–82). Garratt observes that women have been so culturally distanced from recording technology that the manufacturers of the Solid State Logic computer desk included a program that flashes crude insults on a display panel in response to user errors. As Garratt reflects, the inclusion of this feature echoed the macho language often heard in studios and so could be understood as a form of exclusion of female workers (Garratt, 1985: 76). The work of Paul Théberge further illustrates how musicians' magazines and the manufacturers of musical technology, such as the 'home studio', speak to and target male consumers (Théberge, 1997: 122–5). Such targeting of male consumers is not a recent trend for, as Keir Keightley (1996) points out, manufacturers of 'hi-fi' equipment in the 1940s and 1950s directed their marketing specifically at a male audience.

The instances highlighted by the above critics demonstrate how the recording studio has become culturally constructed as a masculine context. Thus a female sound engineer or recording musician may be understood as working within a cultural context that is *already* gendered. This may seem somewhat bleak in its analysis but it does not close off the possibility of negotiation, disruption and a rearticulation of gender relationships. The issue is that this context has become popularly produced and understood as male. The naturalisation of studio work as a male occupation may also be found in popular music literature. In his description of a recording engineer, Mike Ross-Trevor remarks: 'A wise producer will always confide in *his* engineer. If an engineer feels that a producer needs guidance, *he* will be more than happy to extend *his* responsibilities' (Ross-Trevor, 1980: 118, my emphasis). Admittedly, numerous writers choose to use the term 'he' to refer to an active subject in their writing, but Ross-Trevor's unproblematised reference to a male recording engineer is perhaps indicative of popular assumptions concerning male-dominated professions. It is difficult to assess to what extent these attitudes concerning gender and technology have inhibited women from choosing to work in recording studios. Other factors, such as a lack of encouragement, opportunity and female mentors, may also help to account for the paucity of female studio workers. Andrea Odintz reveals how:

... a 1993 survey of music-related businesses, including recording studios, showed that less than 20 percent of all technical positions were held by women, less than 2 percent of those were 'first' or 'lead' positions. Compared to women rock performers, female recording technicians have moved more slowly, unlike, say, women in publicity, a thoroughly female-dominated music profession. (Odintz, 1997: 217)

Smaill's recent research report on women DJs and sound engineers working in the UK suggests similarly low levels of female involvement. Smaill interviewed 37 DJs and sound engineers at different career stages and of both sexes. The sound engineers 'typically estimated the percentage of sound engineers that are women to be between 2% and 5%, mostly concentrated in live sound engineering. The percentage of women DJs was usually estimated to be between 5% and 15%' (Smaill, 2005: 13). While this chapter is not primarily concerned with accounting for a lack of female engineers and producers, it does wish to assess the impact of this lack on how female musicians experience the process of recording.

It has been suggested that advances in recording technology might permit female artists to circumvent the (traditionally) male context of the recording studio, allowing them to control their own recording processes. Keith Negus reviews this argument, which suggests that 'these technologies have the potential to challenge the way in which the production of pop has been gendered' (Negus, 1992: 86). However, Negus balances this argument with the observation that 'it has tended to be boys rather than girls who have responded to the opportunities provided by new electronic instruments and recording equipment' (1992: 86). Yet undoubtedly some female artists have profited from the flexibility afforded by new recording opportunities. The female-centred band Pooka remarked in an interview that they felt comfortable with recording technology because they had a home studio. The indie music artist Helen Love, whose band bears the same name, has also commented on the usefulness of a home studio. Love explains that the band employ technology in the creative process of writing new material: 'We sort of do it backwards! We have a studio in the house and we work it all out on tape. Then we work out how we are going to play live' (Love, quoted in Kofman, 1997: 17). She commented that this practice of home recording has allowed her to avoid any potential gender conflicts she might experience in a professional studio: 'I suppose I don't get as much flak as a lot of other female artists would because I'm detached from it. I've got the studio here and we can just get on with it ourselves and not have to put up with that condescending attitude' (Love, quoted in Kofman, 1997: 17).

The experiences of female musicians are inevitably tied up with the possibilities open to them and the amount of control they have over the recording of their music. The different experiences of bands are reflective not only of attitudes towards gender but also of the status and experience of the performers and their personal interaction with the studio engineer or producer. The reflections of musicians in two different indie bands may be taken as an example. Two members of the female-centred band Coping Saw, based in Yorkshire, described their first experience of working in a 16-track recording studio in 1994. These musicians found the studio to be an alienating environment. The engineer indicated that the studio was his domain rather than an area in which the band were free to experiment:

Bela: [The engineer] wouldn't let us really get involved with even touching his [sound desk]. I was all eager at first and wanted to look around – 'Ooooh, what does this do and blah, blah, blah.' He wasn't protective but there was a definite atmosphere there.

Simone: It was his baby. His studio.

Bela: Like, I'm the sound engineer. This is my girlfriend. You are the band. I am going to make you wait for absolute ages and not even make you a cup of tea.
(personal communication, 9 February 1995)

This incident could be read as an example of male possession of technology. However, it is perhaps more illustrative of power dynamics between studio workers and musicians, and the intimidation of inexperienced performers. The comments made by members of the Swedish band Girlfrendo provide a contrast with those of Coping Saw. Vocalists Josephine and Safari described their experience of working in a small, inexpensive studio in Gothenburg, Sweden, as enjoyable and exciting:

Safari: I love recording. It's the best thing.

Josephine: It's so much fun because we are just playing around … I think it's great because no-one stops us from doing anything. If we want to press a button they let us … We produce it ourselves.
(personal communication, 19 June 1998)

The comparison between these two bands is interesting for Safari and Josephine did not view their inexperience of studio work as an impediment but as a reason to experiment with the available technology. Other, more experienced, musicians commented that their working practices had changed as their knowledge of studio work expanded. Melanie Woods, drummer and vocalist with the London-based all-female band Sidi Bou Said, reflected on a recording experience of the band: 'Looking back on it now, we would have done it differently but then we wouldn't have known that' (personal communication, 13 May 1995).

The process of working in a studio is one of artistic experimentation and decision making, and so the working relationship developed between a producer and the artist(s) they record can be crucial to the way in which these parties assess the success of the music produced. Mavis Bayton raises the issue of the power dynamic between musicians and producers: 'Producers engage in various manipulative strategies in order to gain more control. They may belittle musicians' skills. This is particularly relevant to women musicians who often lack confidence. A producer might wear band members down over a period of time by constantly asking them to re-do their parts' (Bayton, 1989: 219). The musicians interviewed for this book did not generally recount problems of intimidation by producers. They did, however, discuss the collaborative aspect of sound recording. Miki Berenyi reflected on how the status of a producer relies not only on technical ability in recording sound but also on reputation as a creative individual: 'people think that a producer is there to help you make your record but he is also there to do his own art or whatever it is. Quite often it becomes a battle' (personal communication, 20 January 1996). She recalled that, when recording one of Lush's records, a producer had refused to allow the group to use a particular guitar effect, explaining to them that he would not permit such a sound on *his* record.

In her discussion of the indie scene in Liverpool, Sara Cohen remarks that 'conversation within the scene's male networks ... is frequently "insider-ish", involving nicknames, in-jokes and jargon that discourage women newcomers from joining in' (Cohen, 1997: 22). Attempts have been made within indie rock circles to address this process of exclusion by demystifying technical language and encouraging participation. For example, *Rockrgrl*, a US feminist magazine devoted to women rock musicians, has periodically printed a section entitled 'Terms of Engearment', which explains technical language and the functions of musical equipment to its readership of 'gadgetgrls'. With a similar aim, those involved with riot grrrl organised workshop events that allowed girls and women to experiment with musical instruments in an encouraging and non-threatening environment. A number of other female musicians discussed in interview how they circumvented the problem of not being au fait with technical terms. Members of the band Kenickie (Figure 2.1) described how they used symbolism and descriptive words to communicate their ideas:

Lauren Laverne: X, who plays the drums is a really accomplished guitarist and musician so we describe how we want something. We'll go 'I want something that goes a bit weeegargh!'

Marie du Santiago: Or we'll go 'This guitar's a bit nylon. I want it to be more red velvet' and he'll go right, okay.
(personal communication, 9 May 1997)

Figure 2.1   Members of Kenickie pictured in Birmingham, May 1997. L–R: Emmy-Kate Montrose, Lauren Laverne and Marie du Santiago

An unfamiliarity with technical or musicological terminology was thus not a huge stumbling block but demanded the development of a bypass strategy. Admittedly, the use of descriptive language when recording (irrespective of the gender of the musicians) is very commonplace; so much so that Miki Berenyi referred to it as the universal language of the studio. As Thomas Porcello has pointed out, the language that sound engineers and musicians use in the studio to talk about sound refers to complex sonic textures and timbres so that 'talking about music, indispensable to the functioning of any recording studio, is heavily reliant on competence in managing a wide range of metaphoric discursive conventions' (Porcello, 2004: 739). However, it is noteworthy that female musicians mentioned this use of language as a way in which they could translate that which was unfamiliar into something with which they felt comfortable.

Members of Kenickie commented that their experience of sound recording and mixing in a studio was shaped not only by the studio engineers and producers they worked with but also by management and promotional staff working for their record company. Record company employees were responsible for booking Kenickie into the recording studio, agreeing a recording budget, establishing a time frame for sound recording and mixing, and organising the band's schedule for promotional work. Thus when examining gendered attitudes and behaviours within the context of the recording studio, consideration must be given not only to those directly working in the studio but also to the record company staff responsible for overseeing the recording process. It was the experience of Kenickie that attitudes towards gender difference affected the way in which their professional life was managed by their record company. Lead vocalist Lauren Laverne believed that record company staff expected her band to have different sensibilities to their male contemporaries and encouraged them to work on the promotion of their records rather than placing emphasis on the development and recording of new material. She stated that she felt that this emphasis centred around issues of gender: 'I think this is true of a lot of girls. They won't let them go into the studio because they won't expect you to experiment with your music. They don't expect you to value it' (personal communication, 9 May 1997). Moreover, Kenickie commented that they felt that their record company did not prioritise the band's attendance at the mixing of their album:

Lauren Laverne: If we were boys they would say, 'Well, you have got to be at the mixing of your record!' and would let us hang around the studio all day. But with us they'll say 'Yes, you can go to the mixing as much as you want. Now, you have this day's work to do.'

Marie du Santiago: They are like, 'Yes, go to the mixing. You have an interview at twelve. You will be finished at nine and then any mixing you want to do after that, in your own very tired time, enjoy!'

Lauren Laverne: We always do go to the mixing but they sort of don't let us by giving us things to do.
(personal communication, 9 May 1997).

Touring

This chapter has so far discussed how particular contexts in which indie music is produced, performed and traded (such as musical instrument shops and recording studios) have become associated with masculinity or, perhaps more accurately, masculinities. The touring experience of a band can also be conceptualised in terms of music contexts as the musicians occupy a definable set of privileged sites and spaces. While the stage is a public performance site, most of the spaces occupied by a band on tour may be thought of as 'private' or as areas of privilege, such as the backstage area, the dressing room, the hotel and the tour bus. Sites of public performance (such as the stage, promotional video and press interview) are discussed in Chapter 4. However, the discussion here is concerned with the meanings and codes of behaviour associated with these 'private' contexts. While the experience of indie musicians will be examined, the contexts under discussion are also common to other rock performers.

A number of rock mythologies have grown up around the image of musicians on tour. The music press and journalistic anthologies are littered with boastful tales from musicians of drunken hedonism, sexual adventure, the trashing of hotel rooms and the defenestration of television sets.[15] These mythologies may be read in gendered terms as narratives of (male) conquest, excess and freedom. Rock documentaries, such as Blur's *Starshaped* (1993), have further glamorised the lifestyle of a touring musician and presented images of excess as real segments of everyday life on the road. The familiar format of these documentaries is echoed in the spoof movie *Spinal Tap* (1984), which offers a window into the life of a fictitious, overtly sexist, heavy metal group. As Jonathan Romney argues (1995: 86), music documentaries 'offer us a fantasy "Access All Areas" pass', allowing viewers into the hidden world of the music business. PJ Harvey's documentary *Reeling With PJ Harvey* (1994) punctures the glamorous image of touring by recording banal sequences in the form of a video tour diary. At various points in the film the band are pictured asleep on the tour bus, waiting around to go on stage, asking the film-maker to move the camera set-up so that they can use the toilet facilities, and peering at a map to find their location in a new city. While this certainly remains a mediated account of life on the road, its sequences of mundane activities offer a contrast to mythologies of boisterous rock antics.

Romantic notions of rock musicians having extraordinary lifestyles of indulgence have been exaggerated and reinforced by rock documentaries and popular music films such as *Velvet Goldmine* (1998), *The Doors* (1991) and *Stardust* (1974). It is possible to argue that these cinematic accounts offer a double function, reinforcing popular mythologies and also operating as templates of 'authentic' and 'successful' rock careers. While tales of excess in film, biography and music journalism transmit a particular conception of rock stardom, they also establish and reflect a modus operandi for touring musicians. Miki Berenyi commented that she had met many male musicians who attempted to mimic a romanticised vision of life 'on the road'. She remarked:

A lot of people who go on tour do like to have this boys club thing. It's all lads together and they can all talk bollocks and absolute lies about how many women they shagged without someone like me going 'Oh yeah? ... no chance!' ... They want to live out this sort of rock and roll lifestyle – where it's groupies and God knows what. I mean it's a fantasy of theirs. (personal communication, 20 January 1996)

This raises the question of how female performers negotiate a working environment that has repeatedly been characterised in such masculinist terms. Ann Powers has argued that: 'women who love [indie guitar pop/rock] learn the art of transference ... that everybody in indie rock is a boy'.[16] This statement found reflection in some of the comments made by interviewees. Marijne Van Der Vlugt, lead vocalist with the indie band Salad, described herself in masculine terms when asked about her experience of being on tour: 'You get the occasional person who asks "How does it feel being in a band with three boys and to be on the road?" Well, it feels perfectly normal because I'm a tomboy. ... I'm a tomboy anyway and I like the company of men' (personal communication, 18 April 1997). Marjne's rationalisation for her participation in a predominantly male band rested upon the adoption of a masculine gender construction that allowed her to assimilate herself in male company. However, this description was not restricted to female performers in male-centred bands. Another interviewee, who performed in an all-female band, also described herself as a tomboy. These comments suggest that some female performers have adopted a policy of describing themselves in masculine terms in order to defend (or justify) their status as authentic rock musicians.

Sara Cohen's ethnographic study of rock culture in Liverpool in the 1980s considered the absence of women within this culture and highlighted ways in which women were understood by male musicians as intruders or as a threat (Cohen, 1991: 201–22). With reference to female musicians, Cohen found that, 'outside performances they were often *mistaken* for girlfriends of male band members' (1991: 206, my emphasis). Cohen reveals how women on the performance circuit were granted less status than their male contemporaries. The fact that female performers were 'mistaken for' (or understood within the role of) a 'girlfriend', illustrates how the figure of the touring musician is traditionally understood as male and women are often considered as appendages. The tendency to marginalise women in rock in this way has persisted over time. In 1978 Clem Gorman 'authoritatively' informed readers of his book *Back Stage Rock* that 'most of the women at backstage parties are wives or girlfriends of performers or roadies' (Gorman, 1978: 34). The comments made by members of the female-centred band Kenickie in the late 1990s illustrate how women occupying the backstage area are still often conceptualised in the limited (and negative) role of the 'groupie'. Guitarist Marie du Santiago and bassist Emmy-Kate Montrose related a story of how the band were expelled from a venue where they were playing as support to US all-male rock band The Ramones because they were 'mistaken' for groupies:

Marie: The Ramones' crew tried to throw us out for being groupies.

Emmy-Kate: We were locked out of our dressing room. This man came up the corridor and he kicked Marie and said get out of the corridor. One of The Ramones came and

apologised after. There were all these Japanese groupies hanging around for The Ramones. They must have thought we were the English ones.
(personal communication, 9 May 1997)

A similar event is detailed in Smaill's (2005: 16) research report on gender segregation in music technology by a live sound engineer who describes how she was barred from entering a venue because staff did not believe that a woman could be operating the sound desk. Smaill comments that other female engineers had reported similar experiences. Clearly these are not everyday occurrences and I do not want to suggest that all venue workers and road crew are unenlightened men. However, such illustrations may be understood as instances of confirmation, where the backstage area is re-established as a male space.

The interaction between touring musicians and sound engineers working for the venues in which they perform has been conceptualised by some critics and performers as a relationship of conflict. In her research with all-female bands in the 1980s Mavis Bayton found that: 'women's bands often experience P.A. engineers and their roadies as hostile, seeing women as unwelcome intruders on male terrain, and willing to exploit their ignorance and lack of confidence. They tend to assume that all women are technically incapable and that any man knows more than any woman' (Bayton, 1989: 366). Some of the musicians interviewed for this book reported that they had been treated differently by male sound engineers because they were women. Miki Berenyi took the instance of when she had requested alterations to the sound that she could hear through her on-stage monitor: 'I have a go at a monitor bloke and say "Look, can you just fucking sort it out". He'll go "God, she's such a bitch" because it's a woman telling him how to do his fucking job. If it was a bloke he'd go "Oh yeah, Iggy. Brilliant!"' (personal communication, 20 January 1996). Similarly, members of the British female-centred band We Start Fires commented that sound engineers in venues often treated them differently than male acts on the same bill and tried to 'catch them out' with technical terminology. Nikki, the bass player and backing vocalist in the band, commented: 'They just assume that because you are girls you do not have a clue about anything but then afterwards [after the soundcheck] they are like "Yeah, wow, you are actually good."' (personal communication, 10 September 2003). However, a number of interviewees commented that while they had experienced such discrimination this was not part of their daily lives. Corin Tucker, of the US all-female indie band Sleater Kinney, remarked: 'Usually, I would say no, we don't experience sexism, but we recently played a show in Boise, Idaho where we complained to the soundman and he called our drummer a "bitch" and proceeded to call us all bitches. We had him thrown out' (personal communication, 5 November 1998). Again, this may be read as an instance where the masculinism of the rock environment was confirmed. While this does not form part of everyday working relationships, the context of a rock tour does to some extent permit the exhibition of such masculinist behaviour. Corin Tucker's final remark, 'We had him thrown out', illustrates that the confidence and status of the band members was such that they could both challenge and address this instance of discrimination. Lois Maffeo, vocalist, guitarist and songwriter in the US indie band Lois, has commented that while she has also experienced a degree of difficulty in working with soundmen she has managed this very differently:

> I played acoustic, and all these guys would be like, 'Yeah, I know where to put the microphone so it'll sound the best.' And I would say, 'Go ahead. Put the microphone where you want.' Then they walk back to their sound place, the show starts, I put the microphone where I know it sounds best – 'cause I've done this a million times. I don't want to be in charge of educating this ape about feminism. I don't have time! (Maffeo, quoted in Juno, 1996: 127)

As with the experience of working in a studio, the interaction between band members and sound engineers working within live music venues is affected by a number of factors. While gender operates as one of these factors, other elements, such as experience, musicianship and professional codes of behaviour, also need to be taken into consideration. For example, the female-centred band Girlfrendo commented that they felt they were taken less seriously because of their playful attitude and lack of technical knowledge:

> Josephine: That's because of the way we behave. 'Cos we tend to be quite messy and childish.
>
> Safari: We don't know that much. We don't know anything about the machines and gear and that's why they don't listen to us. I don't think it's because we are women. (personal communication, 19 June 1998)

However, some female musicians commented that promoters and tour managers treated them differently because they were women. Lauren Laverne, vocalist with Kenickie, felt that tour managers held different expectations for her female-centred band as they did not expect them to engage in the excesses of rock 'n' roll. Lauren felt that Kenickie were expected to behave with greater efficiency than male artists when on tour as co-workers did not expect them to play out the role of the debauched rock icon. She commented:

> I think people expect more of you when you are a girl because they expect you to be an all round cabaret show act. If we were boys they would just expect us to turn up and if we were late they would think, 'Huh, they have slept in again. They are crap at keeping time'. Like, we're living out a Keith Moon rock dream and – 'Look at them throwing a TV out of a window. Isn't that cute!'. Whereas with us it's, 'Come on Spice Girls, up at eight thirty, here we go. Come on – do your dance'. So we have to do a lot more work than other bands. (personal communication, 9 May 1997)

Lori Barbero, drummer with the US all-female band Babes In Toyland, commented that rock promoters clearly viewed her band as different from 'regular' male rock bands. The conception of women rock performers as 'other' regularly accorded them different treatment and resulted in promoters using different selection criteria in booking support acts for their shows. She remarked:

> Like last night, both bands that we played with in Amsterdam were female bands. That is cool and all. The more female bands the better and then it won't be such an issue

and people might get over it. Just because we are playing they think they have to get any female band within a hundred mile distance. Even in small towns, they get a female band even if they have never played before. It is not even for the right reason. (personal communication, 10 July 1994)

The romantic notion of the rock musician, particularly the touring musician, is associated with a liberation from mundane life and domesticity. Few music press interviews engage with or contextualise rock musicians in relation to their family or domestic environment. Thus the conceptual sphere of rock music has been separated from and to some extent opposed to the context of 'home'. Cohen's ethnographic work with male bands in Merseyside found that 'marriage and fatherhood did not suit the image many bands wished to present. One said of a fellow band member that he didn't like people to know he had a wife and child and was embarrassed when they found out' (Cohen, 1991: 209). This raises the issue of how female musicians with young children organise their schedules. As Bayton discusses, it is difficult for female musicians to combine the occupations of a travelling musician and the parenting of a young child. Bayton points out that childcare is hampered by the lack of baby-changing facilities at rock venues and the absence of clean or safe environments. However, these organisational difficulties are regularly overcome by mothers on tour. When I interviewed Kim Gordon during her tour with Free Kitten, she was accompanied by her husband, Thurston Moore, who shared the responsibility of parenting their young daughter, Coco Hayley Gordon Moore. In a radio interview the vocalist and guitarist Kristen Hersh explained that her family accompanied her when on tour. She described this as a demanding decision in terms of logistics but a rewarding one as it offered a sense of normality to her when on tour:

> I have the six year old and the one year old. My husband is the tour manager. ... It's hard to travel with kids every day. You know – imagine a family vacation where you never stop. There is no Grand Canyon at the end. There's no Disney World. It's just mom making peanut-butter and jelly sandwiches and kids whining forever. I'm not making it sound very nice but it is. It's sweet. It's exactly what you want when you are on the road – a nice grounding influence and little cuddle monkeys.[17]

Industry relations

Interviews with female indie rock musicians reveal the operations of daily professional life within different music contexts and in relation to various music industry personnel. Examination of music contexts within indie rock must consider not only physical 'sites', such as the recording studio or tour bus, but also the overall business context of the music industry. Discussions with musicians about their experience of working with record companies challenged some of the ways in which the relationship between performers and the music industry have been conceptualised. Problems of access to accurate information are inevitable when interviewing public figures. The level of information disclosed in an interview is dependent on a number of factors, including the status of the performer, the relationship established with the interviewer and the amount of time available for a conversation to develop. When interviewing musicians for this book some questions required only simple replies, such as record release dates. Other enquiries, however, relating to industry practices, elicited more guarded responses. Thus, in this respect, caution must be taken in accepting certain replies without qualification. An illustration may be taken of an interview with a female musician performing in a well-known band who was questioned about the relationship between her band and their record company. At the time of interview the band were signed to a major record company, having previously released records on an independent label. She commented that by signing to a major record company the band had not suffered any loss of artistic control: 'We have never been told what to do … We still swear as much as we used to, we wear what we want to … They [the record company] are really great and a lot of women are there. They are so cool. I couldn't be much happier' (personal communication). However, at a live performance I had attended some months before, the band had made an announcement from the stage that they had not been informed by their record company of the release of a new album of their material. They requested that audience members should boycott its sale. When the musician was asked about this she admitted that the band had been unaware of the release of this album and explained that it had been put together quickly by their record company so that profit could be accrued from the publicity the band were receiving on a high-profile promotional tour. Part of the album was made up of tracks taken from one of the band's live shows. She commented that she was particularly annoyed that the record company had selected tracks from that performance for release as at the time of the show she was experiencing a major personal crisis. It seems that, in this instance, the record company did not think it important to either inform the band of the planned release or to take the personal feelings of the band members into consideration. The initial comments of the musician when describing the relationship with her record company illustrate how musicians feel it necessary to circulate positive images of themselves as creative musicians who enjoy artistic freedom. Uneasy with the suggestion that signing to a major record company has resulted in a reduction of control, the musician felt forced to both defend her own decision to sign *and* the practices of the company she was working with. Difficulties within her working relationship or instances where the company may have overridden her bands' artistic decision making were concealed in order to produce an image of artistic autonomy. In interviews with the media, musicians are encouraged to present their record company as an artistically sensitive institution so that their music is not interpreted as the product of cynical marketing strategies. The desire to be understood as an unfettered artist encourages performers to conceal the workings of the music industry.

In a 1982 article analysing the music press Jon Stratton considers the problem within the music industry of defining the realms of the 'aesthetic' and the 'commercial', and discusses how the music industry trades on these two concepts. Record companies and promoters are commonly understood to be concerned with the commercial worth of music product, whereas the music press and artists are understood to make choices and decisions based on aesthetic judgements. Stratton argues that this is a falsehood as both music journalists and music performers are dependent on the commercial success of the record industry. However, the concept of 'the artist' helps to mystify this dependency and give journalists and performers a palatable distance from capitalist economics. Stratton states that:

> the artist, the innovator, tends to see him/herself in opposition to the industry as a commercial enterprise which appears to be continually pressuring the artist to produce new marketable products. In this situation the artist protects him/herself by mystifying the creative process which is experienced as being distinct from the commercial, capitalist side of the industry which would prefer rational, analysable standardisation. (Stratton, 1982: 272)

However, in the interviews I carried out with female musicians, I found that they clearly saw themselves as positioned within a commercial industry and actively sought involvement in business decision making. The comments from the British band Pooka illustrate this point. Pooka were a band comprising female vocalists and lyricists, Natasha and Sharon, whose music was made up of the harmonising of vocal melodies to the accompaniment of an acoustic or electric guitar. When recording or performing live, Pooka expanded their line-up by employing other musicians to play drums, bass and additional guitar. The band's music was released through the labels Warner Bros and Rough Trade. At the time of interview they were signed to Trade 2/Island Records, a subsidiary of the major label Polygram. Throughout the interview Sharon and Natasha spoke confidently of their position within the music industry and their current drive to market their band. Rather than distancing themselves from marketing decisions, they expressed a desire to be involved in strategies for their promotion. However, Pooka commented that often managers and record companies did not welcome the involvement of musicians in business decisions. Sharon commented: 'They [record companies] like to see artists being all artistic and fey. They don't like the artist to be all assertive and thinking about business matters' (personal communication, 9 October 1997). Indeed, Pooka stated that during their career they had found that some record company employees had used the concept of 'the artist' to distance them from business decision making. Natasha commented:

> Because it's music they say, you know, 'You're the artist. You are having a good time. You're the one that goes and plays the music and gets all the beers at the end of the night. You're having a great time, you know. I'm doing all the hard work.' But they don't see it. We slog, we drive, we put all the gear into the van and lug it out again. We really work hard and so it's a bit frustrating. (personal communication, 9 October 1997)

In this instance, record company representatives used the mythology of rock stars on tour to legitimate a reduction in the band's control over their business matters. Thus, it is not only within the public realm of texts, such as documentaries, films, biographies and journalistic articles, that rock mythologies circulate. The concept of artistic temperament and behaviour patterns, and the split between creativity and commerce, form part of a rock discourse that pervades the industry and affects business practice. Indeed, Sharon from Pooka commented that she felt record company employees assumed it might offend them to hear the band discussed as 'a product'. Thus a female indie rock musician working within the music industry is regularly challenged not only by attitudes concerning prescribed gender roles but also by the need to negotiate other performance roles such as that of the creative artist or industry professional.

Conclusion

This chapter has considered the extent to which indie rock music contributes to the articulation of a masculinist rock discourse. The greater percentage of female performers within this genre has led to a perception that indie music offers greater accessibility to women. However, the view that indie music is somehow less patriarchal in its organisation and practice has been challenged by a number of critics and female musicians. As Chapter 5 and 6 discuss, those involved in riot grrrl have been most vociferous in their criticisms of how gender distinctions operate within indie music. This chapter has drawn on interview material to explore how attitudes concerning gender colour the working lives of female indie rock performers. The experiences of these artists illustrate how gender bias is articulated in the overt language of sexism but can also operate in more concealed ways – for example, where female performers are encouraged to concentrate on marketing and promotion rather than on creative development.

By choosing to examine identifiable social contexts of music practice and production this analysis has explored how particular behavioural modes operate within them. The adoption of these behavioural models, such as hedonistic display within the backstage area, allows musicians to participate in established rock conventions while simultaneously confirming their status as authentic rock performers. This illustrates how music professionals are encouraged to participate in particular social 'performances' and how, to some extent, their status is judged upon these enactments. Through a consideration of how these performances may be read in gendered terms, this chapter has explored how women are sometimes excluded or discouraged from full participation in rock music culture and how individual female performers have challenged established models of masculinist behaviour. Consideration has been given to how some women purposely distance themselves from the 'rock 'n' roll lifestyle' by bringing their family on tour as a 'grounding influence'. Interviews with female indie rock performers revealed that while sexual discrimination has not formed part of everyday working practice, every performer had encountered instances of gender bias throughout their career. I have argued that these instances work as moments where the practice of rock music is reconfirmed as masculine.

Notes

1 'NME Writers 100 Best Indie Singles Ever' (first published in *NME*, 25 July 1992), taken from the website (http://www.rocklistmusic.co.uk/nme_singles.htm#indie), accessed 29 April 2007.

2 See Evans (1994), Raphael (1995), O'Brien (1995), Post (1997), Woodworth (1998).

3   See, for example, the section 'Respect Overdue! Yesterday's Obscure Classics Revisited', regularly published in the *NME* in 1999.

4   For literary accounts exploring this issue see Nick Hornby (1995) and Giles Smith (1995).

5   *Geekrock* (http://www.geekrock.com), accessed 27 September 2000; *Patheticore* (http://www.ludd.luth.se/~burrito/), accessed June 1998.

6   For a further discussion of this in relation to zines see Duncombe (1997: 17f.).

7   *Nrrdgrrl* (http://www.winternet.com/~ameliaw/), accessed 27 August 1996,

Geekgirl (http://www.next.com.au/spyfood/geekgirl.html), accessed 27 August 1996.

8   The nature of these websites and their link with the musician-initiated riot grrrl network is discussed in Chapter 6 of this book.

9   For example: Kurt Cobain, lead singer and guitarist in Nirvana; Thom Yorke, lead singer in Radiohead; E, singer and guitarist with Eels; solo artist Beck.

10   For a further discussion of gender and race in rock music see Wald (1997).

11   See, for example, the chapter 'Long Hard Climb: Women in Rock', Chapple and Garofalo (1978: 269–96).

12   I will return to the subject of the 'performance' of gender roles in Chapter 4, discussing these codes of behaviour in relation to indie music performance on the stage, in promotional videos, press interviews and photo shoots.

13   A London street that is home to a number of music-related businesses, including publishers, management and musical equipment retailers.

14   See, for example, Cohen (1991), Negus (1992), Green (1997), Théberge (1997), Bayton (1989, 1998), Sandstrom (2000) and Smaill (2005).

15   See, for example, accounts in Jones (1996), Kent (1994) and Dellar (1995).

16   Ann Powers (3 March 1992: 8) 'A Shot of Testosterone', *Voice, Pazz and Jop*, cited in Kruse (1993: 40).

17   Interview with John Cavanagh on his 'Original Masters' programme, BBC Radio Scotland, February 1998.

Chapter 3

Meaning making in the press

Following the consideration of gender and indie rock in general in Chapter 2, this chapter will focus on media representations of indie rock performers. More specifically, it will examine how the written media frame the public and artistic personas of musicians. The discussion will draw mainly on journalistic accounts in British publications, examining articles in national daily papers, Sunday supplements, style magazines and the music press.[1] The analysis will be presented through an examination of the press coverage of a small number of musicians, considering how their work and personalities are represented. The aim is to consider how male and female performers are publicly constructed, to what extent these constructions rely on a narrow set of archetypes and how these public images are gendered. A focus on journalistic accounts offers particular benefits to an analysis of the media construction of gender roles. First, the examination of press accounts allows for detailed comparative analysis of gendered discourse in action. More generally, the music press is noteworthy because of the crucial role that it plays in the promotion of musicians and in the production of popular music discourses.

The role and significance of music journalism

Music journalism, particularly that which appears in dedicated music publications, has historically occupied a central role within the promotional strategies of the recording industry by promoting musicians and new music releases, as well as providing information about tour dates, work in progress and forthcoming releases. This has been particularly true of rock music, which emerged in the 1960s alongside a discernible rock press that served to ascribe aesthetic and ideological significance to the form. However, while journalists share a close relationship with music industry institutions and their representatives, press articles do not simply regurgitate information sent from the publicity departments of record companies. The role of journalists is to write about a *selection* of *interesting* new releases and offer an *interpretation* of those records to their readers. In order to establish and maintain credibility it is important that music journalists are perceived to have a critical distance from the music industry. This is often achieved by placing a heavy emphasis on the social importance of popular music while playing down its status as a product (Frith, 1981; Stratton, 1982). Such a need to create a 'sociology of rock' (Frith, 1978) has meant that the music press has been at the forefront of producing popular music discourse.

This is not to divorce the discursive from the industrial as these are intimately connected. Indeed, much critical work on the music press has started from the viewpoint of the industrial. Hirsh (1990) argues that journalists (along with other figures such as disc jockeys and film critics) take on the gatekeeping role of 'surrogate consumers', whose role it is to filter the large range of product released by the cultural industries. While this 'filter' metaphor is useful it is perhaps limited in that it does not account for the full complexities of the relationships between differing sectors of the cultural industries and suggests a rather linear unidirectional flow between industry, media and consumer. Later work (Negus, 1992; Lindberg *et al.*, 2000), which has applied Bourdieu's notion of cultural intermediaries to media organisations, has sought to give a more rounded picture of the relationships between differing organisations and how cultural and industrial judgements are affected by factors such as class, ethnicity and institutional context. Such a theorisation allows for the way in which the music press occupies an intermediary role, and has implications for both the recording industry and audiences. For instance, positive press reviews are highly sought after not only for their ability to launch an act to consumers but also because they can enable support for a new act within a record company or attendant media. As Negus comments, 'press coverage is often the first signal to personnel within the recording industry itself that a new artist exists, and can decisively affect the way an act is perceived and received by the media and consumers' (Negus, 1992: 116). Similarly, the importance of music journalists as cultural intermediaries and the historical centrality of the music press in the discursive framing of rock music affects how acts present themselves. As Chapter 4 argues, the way in which rock acts choose to represent themselves (or are represented by their record companies) within the press constitutes a 'performative' aspect of their public persona. Such performance is necessarily affected by the dominant discourses of the music press and may often be specifically guided by expectations of what the music press want or value at a particular time.

The intermediary status of music journalists also has significant implications for audiences. Writing in 1981, Frith argued that importance should be placed on a music journalist's opinions because of the journalist's ability to lead public taste. He commented that music papers 'are important even for those people who don't buy them – their readers act as opinion leaders, the rock interpreters, the ideological gatekeepers for everyone else' (Frith, 1981: 165).[2] Music journalists, then, do not simply describe sounds or provide information about popular music. Instead they offer ideological positions relating to music for an imagined readership. As Frith notes in his later work on music criticism: 'for most rock critics ... the issue in the end isn't so much representing music to the public ... as creating a knowing community, orchestrating a collusion between selected musicians and an equally select part of the public – select in its superiority to the ordinary, undiscriminating pop consumer' (Frith, 1996: 67). In this sense journalism within the specialist music press, or 'niche media', is quite distinct from that within national newspapers, whose brief when writing about popular music is to offer interpretations of that music to a broad base of readers. As *Guardian* critic Caroline Sullivan reflects: 'It's not necessary to be so cutting edge as in the music press, but I do have to monitor trends and be adaptable' (Sullivan, 1995: 141).[3] However, this distinction does not reduce the importance of the music press, whose copy is often used as source material for columnists in newspapers and other magazines. The music press operate to produce a discriminating readership by addressing their readers as 'informed' music enthusiasts, guiding them towards 'significant' new releases, publishing canonic lists of 'classic' albums, informing them of the new acts to watch and reviewing records by referring to 'good' tracks from rock's history. Chapter 2 discussed how female musicians are often absent from rock canons and journalistic points of reference. What follows examines the specificities of journalistic discourse in more detail by examining how reviews and features direct readers towards a gendered understanding of rock.

Music journalism can be understood to be informed by a culture of masculinity that is reproduced in a number of different ways. One influencing factor may be the male dominance of the field,[4] although I do not wish to argue that this alone determines the production of a discernible masculinist style of writing. Nevertheless, the fact that men have tended to dominate music writing and the editing of the music press should not go unacknowledged. McLeod (2002: 94) has noted the lack of female appointments to senior positions in music journalism so that by '1999, the number of female editors or senior writers at *Rolling Stone* hovered around a whopping 15 percent, [while] at *Spin* and *Raygun*, [it was] roughly 20 percent'. As discussed in Chapter 1, there are numerous ways in which a masculinist culture can be identified within music journalism, from the ways in which women musicians are written about (Railton, 2001; Johnson-Grau, 2002; Feigenbaum, 2005) to the targeting of a male audience by music magazines (Théberge, 1991; Kruse, 2002). As Kruse comments, 'popular rock and pop criticism has traditionally presented its subject matter in a way that assumes writer and reader coexist in a phallocentric world in which women are peripheral' (Kruse, 2002: 138). Furthermore, masculine mythologies within rock music have been supported by a number of high-profile male 'character' journalists whose writing has constructed not only their subjects but themselves as maverick dandies living life according to the clichéd mantra 'sex and drugs and rock 'n' roll'.[5] Admittedly these characterisations have been somewhat undermined by insider accounts by female rock journalists (Steward and Garratt, 1985: 87–93; Sullivan, 1995; Evans: 1997: xiii–xxii), which have humorously punctured the flamboyant myths that their male colleagues have created about themselves. Nevertheless such mythologies have retained a cultural power, endorsed by 'classic' rock writing, which has served to reproduce a gendered discourse of rock.

Recent research by Forde (2001) on the professional and organisational factors that inform music journalism has considered how publishing houses have increasingly placed emphasis on producing magazine titles with distinct corporate identities, which has had the effect of reducing 'personality journalism'. Forde points out that, in the pursuit of circulation buoyancy and in reaction to bureaucratic restructuring, contemporary music journalism very often follows a house style where journalists place more emphasis in their copy on representing the brand values of the music paper they are working for than developing a distinctive individual writing style. Rather than undermining it, this shift in music journalism 'from polyglottism to branding' (Forde, 2001) can be seen as favouring the continuance of a masculinist discourse. As most music papers (with the exception of some pop titles) are targeted primarily towards a male readership and editors are concerned with delivering that readership to advertisers, it is perhaps unsurprising that the prose style adopted within these publications is generally masculinist in tone, geared towards the idealised male reader. As Aldridge (2001) discusses (with respect to the increased competition between newspapers in Canada from the late 1990s) commercial pressures and demand for healthy circulation figures can lead to a working environment where the pursuit of gender equality is compromised. Aldridge found that 'masculinist behaviour was a side-effect of the management "cure" for the corporate illness of increased competition' (Aldridge, 2001: 619). In this work climate a new 'ruthlessness' prevailed that followed a particular logic whereby 'male colleagues were deferred to; "safe" editorial policies were pursued; and unreconstructed sexism had returned to the newsroom, the editorial meetings (conferences) and even into the news coverage' (Aldridge, 2001: 619). The factors of increased competition and workplace culture can help to explain why, despite an increase in the number of female contributors, the language of the music press has remained decidedly macho in tone. Davies (2001) suggests that female music journalists may feel pressurised to adopt this discursive style in order to be accepted by their male peers: 'Sexist remarks can therefore not be viewed as demonstrative of the prejudices of individual journalists, but as part of what is regarded as the only appropriate discourse for pop music writing' (Davies, 2001: 304).

Of course, the dominance of men working within journalism and the production of a masculine journalistic culture is not exclusive to the music press. As Aldridge (1998) observes, a growing number of women have found careers in broadcasting and magazine writing but female journalists remain underrepresented within the staff of national papers. She comments that the professional organisation Women In Journalism (WIJ) was established only as late as 1993 'so powerful was the hegemony of lad culture' (Aldridge, 1998: 123). Other critics acknowledge that an increasing number of women are undertaking journalism courses and have attained journalistic positions in recent years but that there is often a lack of appropriate representation of women in the senior positions of management and editing (Lavie and Lehman-Wilzig, 2003; Rush et al., 2005). Such observations regarding career progression within journalism certainly have pertinence to the field of rock criticism. As McLeod argues, senior staff within rock publications are 'overwhelmingly male' and business practice within the rock critic establishment often 'resembles the classic "old boy network"' (McLeod, 2001: 56–7). The following case studies, however, are not principally concerned with how a culture of masculinity is evident in the working environment of journalism. Rather, the concern here is to examine how particular (and highly gendered) discursive themes are prevalent within journalistic accounts. As McLeod (2002: 95) has recently argued, rock discourse has an important role to play in helping to 'sustain gender inequality' as 'the specifics of what is said influence the way taste communities and other networks are formed, which in turn connect with the larger social and economic institutions of the music industry'.

Case studies: representations of 'madness'

In order to examine gendered tropes within music journalism this chapter focuses on one common motif within rock writing: that of 'madness' and mental anguish. Using this theme the chapter examines different ways in which journalists construct narratives and ascribe meaning to rock musicians. Drawing on five case studies of indie rock performers the discussion examines how images of madness and mental suffering are commonly drawn upon by journalists to comment on the processes of artistic expression and to enunciate the figure of the creative artist. The motif has been selected because of the diverse ways in which critics have employed it within reviews: sometimes to reinforce the image of the creative individual as a sensitive and pained soul, and, in other instances, as a device to place the subject at a remove or mark out them out as deviant. The following discussion will argue that the ways in which notions of madness and mental anguish are put to work within music reviews are often informed by a discourse of gender. Examining different media profiles it considers how these representations are bound up with particular constructions of masculinity and femininity. The chapter will examine instances where the notion of mental torment is used in reviews of male musicians to construct a profile of the tortured romantic artist and how, in other examples, associations with mental ill health are called upon by journalists to dismiss or 'other' female performers.

Foucault's study of the birth of the asylum explores the label of madness by considering how this institution operated by reinforcing the values of the larger community: 'The asylum reduces differences, represses vice, eliminates irregularities. It denounces everything that opposes the essential virtues of society: … debauchery, misconduct … laziness.' (Foucault, in Rabinow, 1991: 149). Here behaviour at odds with the dominant culture could be disavowed by association with insanity and sanity accorded to those who operated within society's moral frame:

> The operation as practised by Pinel was relatively complex: to effect moral synthesis, assuring an ethical continuity between the world of madness and the world of reason, but by practising a social segregation that would guarantee bourgeois morality a universality of fact and permit it to be imposed as a law upon all forms of insanity. (Foucault, in Rabinow, 1991: 150)

Foucault's analysis of the asylum revealed how 'troublesome' elements within society could be controlled through the operation of a discourse that diagnosed unruly social behaviour as indicative of insanity. Foucault's discussion of the links between ascription and power is pertinent to an examination of how public figures are mediated in ways that replicate existing power relationships. The following discussion will explore how the diagnostic discourse described by Foucault can be applied to musicians to frame them in particular ways. It will argue that, when applied to rock artists, discourses surrounding madness and mental ill health are often nuanced in order to frame performers in particular gendered ways. On the one hand, the label of madness can be used as a trope that helps explain an artist's creativity; on the other hand, it can be used to reduce their credibility or throw their artistic agency into question.

The label of madness defines the individual as behaving beyond accepted social norms and as such acts as a powerful tool of exclusion. It is a means of defining the irregular as unacceptable and divorcing it from any position of power or legitimacy. However, not all of the cultural associations of madness are negative as it has also been linked to notions of genius and creativity. Historically in art, music and the media, links have been drawn between creativity and madness.[6] In these instances 'madness' has been understood as an aspect of an artistic persona. As the case studies below demonstrate, this link has been a recurring trope within rock journalism, with certain constructions of madness or interpretations of ill health being used to communicate particular understandings of musicians and their work.

The following discussion focuses on press responses to five songwriters and vocalists. The first three case studies examine how the written media have responded to musicians who have reportedly experienced episodes of mental ill health. Three artists have been selected for consideration in this regard, all of whom are, or were, songwriters, vocalists and guitarists in 'indie' rock bands: Richey Edwards of the British band Manic Street Preachers; Kurt Cobain, front person in US band Nirvana; and Polly Jean Harvey, front person in the British band PJ Harvey. A selection of press reports is used to highlight divergent responses to mental ill health and consider the implications of these within the discourses of gender. Analysis of press reports on Edwards and Cobain will be confined to those published after Edwards' disappearance and Cobain's death.[7] The media profiles of the solo artist Björk, and Courtney Love, solo artist and former lead vocalist and songwriter with US band Hole, are also considered, as both of these performers have been presented in the press as 'mad'. The examination of Courtney Love's press coverage over a number of years will be presented in a detailed case study, while Björk's press coverage is dealt with in less detail and thus will serve as a comparative example. The analysis uses these examples to explore the ways in which a range of writers use the motif of madness as a metaphor to describe sounds and behaviours, and as a device to frame musicians.

Kurt Cobain and Richey Edwards

Both Kurt Cobain and Richey Edwards were documented in media reports as suffering from depression and mental ill health. Cobain was the singer and guitarist in the three-piece US band Nirvana, who released their debut album *Bleach* in 1989 on Sub Pop Records. The album was a critical success and Nirvana were hailed as a significant force within the so-called 'Seattle scene'. The band later signed with Geffen and released what was to be the platinum-selling album *Nevermind* in 1991. The success of Nirvana's music brought Cobain a huge amount of media attention. Nirvana went on to release a compilation of outtakes and old singles under the title of *Incesticide* (1992) and a further studio album entitled *In Utero* (1993). In March 1994, while touring in Rome, Cobain overdosed on a mixture of champagne and tranquillisers. He returned home to Seattle to recuperate, amid rumours that the incident in Rome had been a suicide attempt rather than an accidental overdose. On 8 April Cobain's body was found at his home by an electrician who was fitting an alarm to the property. He had killed himself with a shotgun.

As Jones (1995) notes, the circumstances of Cobain's death did not integrate with other more 'typical' rock star deaths from drug overdoses or traffic accidents. In light of this Jones argues that press coverage attempted to 'make sense' of Cobain's suicide and to draw on a broader social commentary often tied in to themes of authenticity and mass culture. The tendency to not only relay the fact of Cobain's death but to explain the causes of his unhappiness was certainly in evidence within journalistic responses. Cobain's suicide was described in daily newspapers, style magazines and the music press as understandable and even noble. He was presented as an authentic, gifted, honest musician who extricated himself from the corruption of the music industry rather than face contamination by it: 'Cobain got caught in a vice between the glory and the lie ... he was compelled to pay up with his own life' (Fricke, 1994: 29). This explanation placed death not as an easy 'get out' but as a way of staying true to oneself. *LA Times* critic Robert Hillburn stated that Cobain 'hated the corruption he saw in mainstream rock and worried that he might be adding to that corruption by assuming the role of a spokesman' (Hillburn, 1994: F1). According to this logic, Cobain's suicide was as an escape from the corruption 'inherent' to being a major rock star. Furthermore, there was often the implication that Cobain's death was somehow symbolic. By placing his suicide into the context of an insidiously corrupting 'mainstream' Cobain became the personification of the struggles over incorporation, appropriation and 'selling out' that were ideological mainstays of indie rock culture in the 1980s and 1990s. Thus, while Cobain's mental health problems were widely reported they were often posited as a 'rational' response to his particular material conditions.

The media portrait of Richey Edwards has parallels with that of Cobain. From the early days of the Manic Street Preachers Edwards' mental health problems were significantly foregrounded in media representations of the band. Press reports documented that Edwards suffered bouts of depression and engaged in self-harm. At the beginning of the band's career Edwards caught press attention by carving '4 REAL' into his left arm with a razor blade in front of Steve Lamacq, live music editor of the weekly UK music paper the *NME*. Despite the fact that Lamacq later claimed that there was serious debate about whether to print the '4 REAL' pictures in the *NME* (Lamacq, 2000: 65), the images were given prominent coverage in the news section of the paper. The image was subsequently reproduced many times in the music press and was even used in a campaign aimed at 'breaking' the Manic Street Preachers in the US. In addition to mutilation, the press reported that Edwards' self-harming included alcohol abuse and, allegedly, 'some kind of anorexia' (Harris, 1995: 5). In 1994 he spent eight days in a Cardiff hospital before being checked into a London clinic suffering from mental exhaustion and depression. On 1 February 1995 Edwards walked out of the Embassy Hotel in West London and was not seen again. He left behind a packed suitcase, credit cards and medication. His car was found abandoned at Aust Service Station near the Severn Bridge in Wales on 17 February. Detective Superintendent Stephen Morey, who led the case, concluded that Edwards had probably killed himself.

As has already been noted, labelling someone as mentally ill often has a disempowering effect on them as their actions are understood to be aberrant, illogical or unreasoned. However, journalists tended to offer a particular portrait of Edwards as a reflective individual. He was presented as cognisant of his own condition: 'the most striking thing was his ability to analyse his sickness in a detached way, act as doctor and patient' (Price, 1996: 25). This cerebral understanding of his own condition restored intellectual credibility to Edwards. Moreover, Edwards' condition was presented as an understandable, even rational, reaction to the spiralling insanity of social order in contemporary society: 'if anything, Richey is too sensitive and intelligent for a brutal and crass world' (1996: 25). Thus readers were encouraged to understand his illness not as a personal failing but as testimony to his sensitivity. His apparent suicide was presented as a Christ-like self giving in response to the shallow stupidity of the outside world, 'to some, he's become a stigmata martyr – "He bleeds For Our Sin"' (1996: 25). This presentation is crucial to figuring Edwards as an important rock icon. All the negative associations of mental instability were removed from his public persona. He was presented as a figure to be understood and admired rather than pitied.

Journalists were keen to maintain the credibility of Cobain and Edwards by offering selective understandings of the origin and nature of their mental ill health. These musicians were salvaged from the negative associations of 'insanity' and presented as figures worthy of regard. One of the methods adopted by writers was to closely associate their mental ill health with the nature of artistic genius. John Mulvey, in an article for the *NME,* drew clear links between mental anguish and creativity: 'Often, perversely, it is the low points and black moods and only-just bearable disasters that inspire artists to their greatest triumphs' (Mulvey, 1994: 15). Mulvey argued that it was testimony to the artistic integrity of Cobain and Edwards that their spirit had become shattered while attempting to grapple with the darker side of nature: 'the stars… were now paying the psychological price for their honesty' (1994: 14). Other writers endorsed this interpretation, referring to Cobain as a 'tortured hero' (Wallace, 1994: 8) and, in an article on Edwards' disappearance, lamenting the star process 'that turns sensitive human beings into garish cut-outs' (Harris, 1995: 5). Another critic argued that blame should be placed on the myopia of present society for its inability to offer adequate regard to Edwards' heroic nature: 'Had he been born in another age, he would have sipped coffee laced with absinthe in gilt-edged drawing rooms, hurled grenades over buckling barricades. But Richey found himself here, and now' (Parkes, 1994: 12). It is thus suggested that Cobain and Edwards should not be viewed as irrational figures but as sensitive intellectuals who found little comfort in the mechanics of everyday life. Cobain and Edwards were both framed as authentic artists whose personal anxieties were reflective of their artistic sensibilities.

Both Cobain's and Edwards' mental anguish was understood by most critics as having a significant cultural echo. In both cases they were presented as indicators of the disillusionment and unhappiness of contemporary youth. Cobain was repeatedly referred to as the voice of a generation (Ali, 1994: 96; Gaines, 1994: 128–32; Mcdonald, 1994: 20; Sullivan, 1994b: 19; Tredre and Vulliamy, 1994: 3) and linked to other deceased male icons. One UK report commented 'Kurt's death is every bit the defining moment for this generation that Lennon's was for another' (Greene *et al.,* 1994: 81), while US journalist Lorraine Ali reflected: 'Now, like my mom with President Kennedy or my father with Anwar Sadat, I, too, have a moment etched in my mind' (Ali, 1994: 98). It was stressed, however, that Cobain had not aspired to be a spokesperson. His fame had been born from talent not arrogant ambition. The British tabloid paper the *Daily Mirror* described Cobain as 'the reluctant voice of a generation' (Wallace, 1994: 9) and the British broadsheet *The Sunday Times* argued that, while he resisted this position, 'Kurt Cobain came closer to fulfilling that role than any other popular musician of the 1990s' (Sandall, 1994: 19). Such an accolade elevated the position of these performers, interpreting their personal difficulties as an articulation of a wider social concern. Their problems with living were to be understood as emblematic of difficulties experienced by the twentysomething 'generation X'.[8] As Mazzarella (1995) discusses, in a comprehensive review of press reports immediately following Cobain's death, the tendency of journalists to link Cobain's suicide to the problems faced by contemporary youth was part of a myth-making process that presumed the homogeneity of a whole generation and worked to commodify Kurt Cobain.

Representations of these artists within the press have remained relatively consistent in the years since Edwards' disappearance and the death of Cobain. Both remain acclaimed artists whose work appears regularly within critics' polls and reviews of 'classic' works. To illustrate, attention can be given to articles published in the UK press to commemorate the tenth anniversary of Cobain's death. Many of these accounts, in common with press immediately following his death, reflect on the impact of Cobain's suicide by drawing comparison with the deaths of other music icons including Lennon, Presley, Gaye, Vicious, Morrison, Joplin, Lynott and Hendrix (Bicknell, 2004: 4–5; Leith, 2004: 7; Mohan, 2004; O'Hagan, 2004: 39). John Robinson (2004: 23) of *The Guardian* suggests an even wider social impact by commenting that the event was 'analogous in significance to the Kennedy assassination'. All these accounts confirm Cobain's status as a highly important figure within the rock canon, often reinforcing the notion that he was a spokesperson for a musical movement and attendant youth culture. For some commentators the passage of time has allowed them to present his death as the close of a particular chapter within music history. Critics refer to him as 'the last great rock star' (Mohan, 2004), 'the nihilistic voice of grunge' (Harris, 2004: 18), and 'the voice of his generation' (*Bath Chronicle*, 2004: 10), whose 'suicide marked the end of the punk era' (Arnold, 2004: 22–3). Cobain's mental anxieties are again framed as indicative of his artistic sensibility within these accounts, where he is understood as 'a unique and troubled musician who made art of his neuroses' (Chick, 2004: 16) and offered 'an anguished howl that seemed dredged up from the pit of his tormented stomach' (O'Hagan, 2004: 39). Despite the fact that some critics (Harris, 2004: 18; O'Hagan, 2004: 39) include acknowledgement of the way in which Cobain's life has been mythologised they tend to construct a familiar narrative of a doomed figure burdened by the cares of disaffected youth, who cared too much about his integrity to 'sell out'. The mediation of Cobain and Edwards and the media treatment of their respective mental conditions can be directly linked to recurring romantic tropes of masculinity within rock culture. The following discussion considers how conceptions of mental crisis are woven into the media narratives relating to three female artists, examining how these portrayals are also structured along particularly gendered lines.

Polly Jean Harvey

Polly Harvey formed the eponymously titled three-piece band PJ Harvey in 1991. Their debut album *Dry*, released in 1992 on the indie label Too Pure, was critically acclaimed by the UK and US press. In 1993 PJ Harvey signed to Island Records and released their second album, *Rid Of Me*, in the same year. Since then Polly Harvey has recorded with a number of musicians, including John Parish and Nick Cave, and has also worked on various music projects including writing and producing material for Marianne Faithfull. In 2001 PJ Harvey's fifth album, *Stories from the City, Stories from the Sea*, featuring the original band line-up, was awarded the Mercury Music Prize. During the early 1990s media accounts alleged that Harvey had experienced a number of nervous breakdowns and some journalists suggested that she had battled with an eating disorder. Analysis will concentrate here on these early media reports in order to discuss how Harvey's music and persona have been discussed in relation to her health.

Polly Harvey's media profile contrasts markedly with the heroic representations of mental crisis found in news reports on Cobain and Edwards. As Davies has commented in a review of the British music press, 'An angry image, with the hint of self-destructive tendencies that this implies, is viewed as heroic and exciting in a man, but women with such an image are pathologised' (Davies, 2001: 307). While Cobain's and Edwards' illnesses were projected onto a broad cultural canvas, Harvey's first reported nervous breakdown was represented in primarily personal terms. Instead of ascribing her problems as indicative of the fragility of the human spirit in an abrasive environment, journalists focused on Harvey as an individual suffering a personal sickness.[9] Most reports, while being sympathetic, rested upon particularly gendered tropes. One key motif in media representations of Harvey at this time was that of domesticity. Here, her separation from a close-knit family and rural domestic life was represented as contributing to her problems. Furthermore, her family life was consistently referenced as her 'escape' from an alienating metropolitan environment. *The Independent* newspaper related that her condition was such that, 'clinically unstable, she was pulled out by her family and taken home' (Cavanagh, 1995: 30) while a feature within *The Guardian* explained that 'she was fetched by her mother and brought back to Dorset to recover' (Sullivan, 1993a: 8).

Second, Harvey's 'breakdown' was further framed within the realms of the personal in that it was described as partly resulting from a failed relationship. Employing a particularly condescending tone Ted Kessler of the *NME* described how: 'little Polly was in a bad way during this time. Lost in a flat in Tottenham, buried in a failing romance, she broke down. She couldn't hack the business ... Her mum came and took her home' (Kessler, 1995: 33). In this account the music business is represented as a tough environment within which a musician must show strength of character in order to survive. Harvey is presented as vulnerable, unable to cope, in need of parenting and traumatised by her separation from a slow-paced, domestic environment. A similar portrait was painted in other accounts. The London listings magazine *Time Out* reported 'She looked tired – not at all the fresh faced, positive art college undergrad I'd met in the pub just eight months before. ... an unhappy spell holed up in a Tottenham flat was the last straw for Polly, who had never lived away from her parents' rural farm. ... she cracked' (Davies, 1993: 20). Even more problematically, in a lengthy interview report for *The Observer*, Andrew Billen paints a portrait of Harvey as 'barely out of her teens, the virgin from the sticks had become a London pop singer with a recording contract and a boyfriend problem' (Billen, 1995: 8). While adapting to her metropolitan environment and coming to terms with her success may have placed Harvey under stress, the ways in which these events were mediated is significant. They are indicative of the way in which the pressures of the domestic/personal are often highlighted within representations of women rock artists. For instance, in the media accounts of Janis Joplin discussed in Chapter 1 and in the following discussion of the press treatment of Courtney Love, the domestic is highlighted in ways that would be unthinkable for a male artist.

In other ways, however, representations of Harvey's mental state seem congruent with wider journalistic conventions relating to 'madness', creativity and the transmission of emotion. Media accounts of Harvey have not only documented her moments of mental crisis, they have incorporated these crises into interpretations of her music. In some instances it is described as a vehicle through which Harvey exposes her psychological turmoil: '*Rid Of Me* serves up a brilliant boot-to-the-gut testament to Harvey's ongoing psychic purge' (Manaugh, 1993: 39). Similarly, Sullivan comments: 'In an era of unglued women using pop as therapy, this much is unequivocal: no one is doing it like Harvey. ... *Rid Of Me* is the sound of psyche being scraped with sandpaper' (Sullivan, 1993b: 14). These reviews follow the common practice within music journalism of equating lyrical and musical expression with the personality of a performer. Themes of mental anguish and breakdown have frequently featured within rock writing as journalists have often implied a link between mental suffering and creativity. For instance, in a celebrated 1970s review of Van Morrison's album *Astral Weeks* the US journalist Lester Bangs explicitly equates the emotional intensity of the record with Morrison reaching a low point in his life. Here, mental ill health is positioned as symptomatic of the intensity of the artist's emotions. Bangs describes Morrison's songs as testament to the songwriter's depth of feeling, intensity and poetic skill. He presents Morrison as a visionary who is able to express the often brutal 'truths' about the troubles of the human psyche, giving an aside to readers that if they don't like the album it reflects their inability to cope with its strength of emotion: 'A lot of people couldn't take it; the editor of this book has said that it's garbage, but I think it made him squeamish' (Bangs, 1991: 24). The links between emotional intensity, creativity and mental suffering are perhaps unsurprising given the way in which emotions have been understood and represented within music criticism. As Jon Stratton has argued, it is frequently 'taken for granted' that 'the one crucial thing that defines rock music is that it aims for emotional involvement' (Stratton, 1982: 280). The emotional states of depression and breakdown are therefore easily incorporated into this core discursive construct of rock journalism. Indeed, many of the major male romantic figures of rock music (from Jim Morrison and Ian Curtis through to Cobain) have been presented in such a way.

Many press accounts of Harvey draw upon this journalistic tradition, explicitly referencing the concept of madness and employing metaphors relating to illness and emotional turmoil. In a review of the album *Rid Of Me* for the British music magazine *Select*, David Cavanagh wrote that the album was 'so vicious and committed it defies adequate diagnoses. It's ... a true hospital record. ... Scratched, banged, stroked and wrung, Harvey's guitar is the sound of bandages being gnawed at. Frightening stuff' (Cavanagh, 1993: 85). The use of metaphor is a common device in journalism to describe an emotional state or a sense of sound. Cavanagh's words make it explicit that *Rid Of Me* is an emotionally charged record that, the journalist feels, conveys a sense of mania. A similar technique is used by Gina Morris in a review of the single '50 Ft Queenie': 'another startling, emphatic slab of potent punk rock, delivered in a flurry of intensity, which again highlights Polly's ability to manoeuvre her voice to sound spent, torn and bleeding in emotive tension' (Morris, 1993b: 18). In these instances the motif of madness is not related to 'feminine rage' but is used to describe the emotional intensity of Harvey's performance. These examples illustrate how within the context of a music review a journalist must explain how a record had a personal and emotional impact, and then move from this to offer a judgement on the recording. As Frith has pointed out, this shift from a personal opinion to an authoritative judgement is problematic, as 'the language of music criticism still depends on the confusion of the subjective and objective, on the championing not so much of music as a way of listening to music' (Frith, 1998: 67).

The media framing of Harvey in relation to the themes of creativity, emotion and madness is not gender neutral. It is evident from the metaphors selected by reviewers of Harvey's work that gender often informs the ways readers are invited to listen to her music. The images employed are frequently related to femininity, 'otherness' or conceptions of female 'nature'. An album review in the *NME* used two constructions of womanhood in order to explain how *Rid Of Me* expressed emotional contrasts and vocal aggression: 'She is the sweet, crooning girl, then she is the mad, avenging woman wild with hurt. She understands the dark side, the great, raging feminine archetypes' (Page, 1993: 29). David Cavanagh's review in *Select* also focused on how Harvey's music conveys a sense of dynamic contrast. Cavanagh described Harvey as a witch whose songs act like evil spells: 'Some lyrics sound hopelessly gauche, and are probably meant to. The bulk of them sound like a gigantic Polly hex levelled at anyone mad enough to drive her mad' (Cavanagh, 1993: 85). This portrait of Harvey as a bewitching figure features in a number of other articles. For example, in a lengthy article for the *NME* Ted Kessler used the image of a witch to describe Harvey's stature and presence: 'She's small, almost frail and dressed entirely in black. She wears her hair in a kind of floppy bob. She looks like a good, homely, kindly witch. She extends a bony hand' (Kessler, 1995: 32).

The tendency to frame Harvey as a witch or mad woman has become so marked that some journalists have acknowledged the overuse of such archetypes. Steve Sutherland's review of the album *Is This Desire?* compares Harvey's music to a new album release by Hole:

> Courtney Love has taken the challenge of being branded a witch and crafted a glorious big rock out of it that, in its very radio-friendliness, will achieve revenge over all of those who wish her to fail. Polly, on the other hand, has retreated into a small, dark, private place and is basically taking her troubles, dressing them up as dolls and then dismembering them. (Sutherland, 1998: 94)

While Sutherland refers to the fact that both musicians have been publicly constructed as witches, he nevertheless works with this image in order to convey the dark quality of Harvey's music. Similarly, the media appetite for narratives of the 'tortured artist' is discussed explicitly in an article on Harvey by Caitlin Moran.

Moran remarks that readers are much more interested in the cult of personality around this musician than in her music making:

[Harvey is] far happier talking about her music: her face lights up like a birthday cake when she talks about a little mini-studio that Björk recommended to her. But I try to explain that this is of absolutely no interest to anyone, including myself. I want to know what it is that feeds the sense of extreme, and hunger, in your music. What do you do with your life? (Moran, 1999: 13)

This insightful remark reflects Moran's awareness that she, like others, trades in the well-established mythologies surrounding 'creative artists'. These articles demonstrate how dependent journalists are upon easily identifiable images in order to communicate difficult concepts to readers, and how the images selected within rock journalism are often informed by gender stereotypes.

Courtney Love

The discussion so far has illustrated how representations of the mental suffering of rock performers within the rock press have been demarcated along gendered lines. The application of terms such as 'witch' and 'mad, avenging woman' (Page, 1993: 29) in reviews of Harvey's work clearly offer a different set of connotations to the profiles of Cobain and Edwards as 'troubled' or tortured souls. The gendering of rock discourse is even more apparent within the media representations of the performer Courtney Love. Courtney Love founded the US female-centred band Hole in 1989. Their debut album, *Pretty On The Inside*, was released to critical acclaim on the independent record label City Slang in 1991. In 1992 Hole signed a record deal with the major label Geffen and in the same year Love married Kurt Cobain. Hole's second album, *Live Through This*, was released in 1994, the same year that Love suffered the suicide of her husband and the death of Hole's bass player, Kristen Pfaff, from a heroin overdose. The band released a third album, *Celebrity Skin*, in 1998 before officially disbanding in 2002. In 2004 Love released a solo album, *America's Sweetheart*, on Virgin. A vast amount of media attention has been devoted to Love, generating a considerable mythology around her persona. She has been at the centre of a number of controversies relating to her public behaviour, criticism of the record industry and control of the release of Nirvana material. Due to the number of articles about her, in magazines and newspapers in the UK and the US, the study offered here is both selective and limited. This section is based upon a study of 86 articles published between 1991 and 1995. These articles were taken from music papers and magazines such as *Select* (UK), *Spin* (US) and *Rolling Stone* (US), newspapers such as the *Sunday Mirror* (UK) and *The Guardian* (UK), as well as style and women's magazines such as *Vanity Fair* (US) and *Vogue* (UK). The following discussion examines how Love's music and public behaviour has often been linked to particular representations of madness that are very distinct from the 'rational' interpretations of the mental processes of Cobain and Edwards.

Several journalists draw on stock images of 'the insane' in order to paint their particular portrait of Love. Caitlin Moran, for instance, opens an article on Hole by situating the band in a landscape of madness and unrest: 'This is America – a land that buckles and heaves with schizophrenia and madness and beauty and incomparable ugliness' (Moran, 1994: 13). John Peel's review of Hole in the British newspaper *The Guardian* draws on the concept of the madhouse in order to convey an image of Love as an out-of-control, frightening spectacle: 'Swaying wildly and with lipstick smeared on her face, hands and, I think, her back, as well as on the collar of her dress, the singer would have drawn whistles of astonishment in bedlam' (Peel: 1994). An earlier review similarly places Love outside the realm of the rational by presenting her as a rather menacing figure: 'In her loose-fitting frock she begins to resemble a dangerous mental patient' (Grad, 1992: 6). In each of these instances, the profile offered is one laden with threat or danger rather than a picture of a figure burdened by mental anguish.

A number of journalists have pathologised Love's behaviour, with descriptions that again suggest a dangerous quality to her personality. Amy Raphael described her as having a 'strangely addictive personality' (Raphael, 1993: 36), while Moran commented on meeting her, 'that phrase "car crash personalities" makes sense' (Moran, 1994: 13). The image of a road accident is evoked in a number of articles. Jon Hotten refers to the Hole album *Live Through This* (released in the same month as Cobain's suicide) as having 'car crash timing' (Hotten, 1995: 44), while Liz Evans describes Hole's appearance at the UK's annual Reading Festival as being 'like watching someone climb from the wreckage of a car crash' (Evans, 1995: 38). Both of these accounts, published in 1995, acknowledge that Love has been victim to bad luck. Certainly a display of anguish may be understandable from a person who has suffered the suicide of a spouse and the accidental death of a fellow band member. However, the choice of phrase is significant for it suggests that Love offers the spectacle of unpredictable danger. Earlier accounts also place Love in the role of victim, suffering from mental torment. However, rather than soliciting an empathetic response, critics often warn against Love's frightening unpredictability. An article written in the US music magazine *Puncture* refers to her 'vulnerable psyche' yet notes that this is often hidden by a 'pissed off explosion' (Mills, 1992: 43), whereas Liz Evans, writing for the women's magazine *Elle*, offered a more pronounced warning, stating: 'Her tattered dresses, black roots and scarlet pout give her the air of a victim who is horribly in control' (Evans, 1993a: 12).

The profile drawn of Love is a specific one: she is presented as offering a public display of madness. The portrayal of Edwards as an individual burdened by mental illness evokes a sympathetic response but Love's persona, by contrast, is presented in theatrical terms. She is presented as a freak show to be gawped at rather than understood or engaged with. *NME*'s Taylor Parks commented on the tendency of journalists to present Love in the, supposedly, strong role of survivor. However, he qualified this by reducing her attraction to the lure of the spectacle: 'Never mind that this "strength" fascinates you simply because it might just snap any second and vindicate your muffled life, or that you turned up tonight hoping to see a woman die, preferably photogenically, preferably spectacularly and preferably on stage' (Parkes quoted in Wise, 1995: 39).

It is important to recognise the media practices that encourage mythologies surrounding an artist to be maintained and reproduced. Analysis of media reports on Courtney Love and Hole reveals how dependent journalists are on existing media accounts for their background research. As Aldridge (1998: 118) has pointed out, investigative journalistic reporting in the current economic climate is now the exception rather than the rule due to costs in staff time and the potential for costly libel claims. Consequently there is a trend within journalistic practice towards '"passive" news gathering', which may be noted in 'the use of promotional materials of all kinds – rewritten news releases, attendance at staged events, briefings and news conferences; material borrowed from other media more or less shamelessly' (Aldridge, 1998: 118). Journalists are particularly likely to echo media reports of celebrity scandal in order to capture the attention of readers. A very clear example of this is the first major article on Love in the US fashion magazine *Vanity Fair*. This article itself has taken on mythic proportions because of the way it framed Love as an irresponsible parent. The article alleged that Love used heroin while pregnant, and was accompanied by a photograph of her, heavily pregnant, in a flimsy negligee holding her hand aloft. The magazine had reportedly used an airbrush technique to remove a cigarette from the picture. The removal of the cigarette from the picture suggested that this image was too shocking for magazine readers to see. This apparently doctored photograph of Love's 'scandalous' behaviour was subsequently reprinted in other magazines and music papers. The allegations made in the article caused such concern that Love and Cobain were subject to welfare investigations concerning their parenting ability.

Whether or not these allegations had any basis in truth was of little account in subsequent reports. The *Vanity Fair* article provided reporters with a reference point. Thus they were able to echo the substance of the allegations while deferring to journalist Lynn Hershburgh as the source of the rumour. Bonnie Vaughan, in *The Guardian* supplement, *The Guide*, delighted in reminding readers of 'the infamous *Vanity Fair* article which revealed that, throughout her pregnancy, Courtney and Kurt sat at home all day, in the dark, drinking and smoking and shooting up' (Vaughan, 1994: 14). Reporters could escape personal culpability for their reports and engage in scandal-mongering under the guise of giving their readers background information on this artist. A further illustration can be taken of an article published in *Elle* magazine entitled 'Here Comes Trouble' (Evans, 1993a: 12–15). The editors of the magazine, recognising the marketability of scandal, advertised the article on the cover as 'Heroin, Babies and Me by Courtney Love'. The title suggested an inside exclusive, though the report relied solely upon quoted claims made by British tabloid papers the *Daily Star* and the *News of the World,* that Courtney went 'on a drugs binge during her pregnancy' (Evans, 1993a: 12). These statements were refuted by the musician in the body of the text.

The tendency of writers to use past reports as source material has resulted in mythic profiles being reinforced rather than deconstructed. Moreover, the regurgitation of previous news stories resulted in the information on Hole in the articles under consideration remaining within a narrow framework. An article by Avril Mair published in the British style magazine *ID* in April 1994 provides evidence of this practice. In January 1993 Liz Evans reported, 'Courtney embodies the ancient anti-feminist mythology in 20th Century form. She is MedUS, Pandora, Lilith, reincarnated as the bad girl of rock' (Evans, 1993a: 12). Mair's piece reproduces this observation, informing readers 'She looks like an embodiment of anti-feminist mythology reincarnated as the bad girl of rock' (Mair, 1994: 39). It is tempting to dismiss this example as lazy journalism. However, such appropriation illustrates the heavy reliance by journalists on past media accounts. This repetition of negative associations served to fix the public image of Love. Mair's account thus re-presents a select view of Courtney Love, endorsing previous summaries of this musician. Indeed it reiterates, word for word, a comment made in the *NME* (Sutherland, 1993: 26) a year earlier that 'Courtney Love is not so much a character to be interviewed as a cause to be championed – or a witch to be burned' (Mair, 1994: 39).

Several critics reinforced the perception of Love as a frightening figure by introducing the concept of witchcraft. Articles in the women's magazine *Elle* and the British style magazine *The Face* mentioned her reputation as the 'Wicked Witch of the West' (Evans, 1993a: 12–15; Raphael, 1993: 36) and Caren Myers, in an article for the *Melody Maker*, described her live performance as being 'like a witch at the teddy bears picnic' (Myers, 1993: 16). Of course these are not threatening allegations but rather examples of glib prose. However, the choice of the term 'witch' is significant as it has historically been used to present the 'fragile sex' as dangerous.[10] In an inquiry into institutional psychiatry Tomas Szasz argues that the concepts of witchcraft and madness share important similarities:

> ... witchcraft and mental illness are imprecise and all-encompassing concepts, freely adaptable to whatever uses the priest or physician (or lay 'disgnostician') wishes to put them. ... the belief in mental illness and the social actions to which it leads have the same moral implications and political consequences as had the belief in witchcraft. (Szasz, 1971: xix)

Ways in which the notion of woman as 'other' is reinforced and magnified when the female subject is identified as 'mad' have already been considered. The label of witch, as Ussher comments, adds a further dimension: 'witches are doubly guilty, for being both woman, and wicked' (Ussher, 1991: 43). The conception of Love as a force of evil was presented in a number of articles, although journalists usually stated within their work that this depiction was not their personal opinion but an image in common use within the media: 'many reporters had Courtney nailed as a smackhead witch who was draining the lifeblood from her new husband' (Evans, 1995: 36). The relationship between Love and her partner was highly significant, for a witch is supposed to have the ability to 'alter men's minds to inordinate love or hate'.[11] Thus witchcraft could be used as a metaphorical key, allowing journalists to suggest that Cobain's wife had unnatural power over him: 'we dined out on the speculation that she'd ball busted Kurt into romantic submission; that she'd put a spell on him, had laced his food, or worse' (Vaughan, 1994: 14). Love's reported manipulative spirit was used to explain Cobain's personal problems, thus absolving him from any blame. A news item in the *NME* picked out the claims made in *Vanity Fair* that 'Love resorted to religious chanting to "capture" Cobain', 'was having a divisive influence on the band' and was allegedly responsible for 'introducing Cobain to heroin' (Morton, 1992: 5).

Other reports discussed how Love had been positioned within the media in a range of other meddlesome roles. In 1992 Everett True conducted an interview with Love and Cobain, which was supposedly aimed at silencing critics who 'have cast Courtney as a scheming parasitic bitch who's ruthlessly exploited her feeble, unwitting husband' (True, 1992: 12). Yet while True positioned himself above such misguided journalism, his questions demonstrated an obsession with myth making. Instead of steering away from such accounts, True guided the interview into the issue of Love's power over her husband, asking 'Do you feel poisoned by Courtney, Kurt?' (1992: 13). Other critics invited condemnation of Love through association, likening her partnership with Cobain to that of Sid Vicious and Nancy Spungen or John Lennon and Yoko Ono. Writing in the *NME*, Steve Sutherland used a visit by Cobain to the barber's as an opportunity to draw yet another comparison, this time from the Bible: 'He'd cut his hair by now and was wearing glasses. People said he was like Samson and she was his Delilah. Or worse' (Sutherland, 1993: 27). One end-of-year account in 1992 described Love as presenting a combination of personality types, stating that during the year 'Courtney went from being Nancy Spungen to rock 'n' roll's Lady Macbeth' (*Melody Maker*, 1992b: 46). The charge of overweening ambition and female ruination features in each of these comparisons.

In addition to these historical or mythic figures, Love has often been framed by journalists within other female archetypes. An article published in the US music magazine *Spin* in 1995 began by offering a list of roles that, it suggested, she slips between: 'Heroine, villain, feminist, slut, poet, punk, fashion plate, gossip, punching bag, bitch, survivor, wife, mom' (Marks, 1995: 45). Admittedly these personas are divergent. However, this attempt to define and label Love may be noted in almost all of her press coverage. Ignoring her achievements as a professional musician, press accounts have tended to position Love in relation to her partner, Cobain. Over time she has been presented in the role of girlfriend, wife, mother and widow. These may be understood as limiting roles as they suggest certain behavioural patterns. Naming Love as a wife extends beyond informing readers she is married. It presents an ideal model of faithfulness and care against which she may be judged. Her resistance to the standards demanded by these feminine roles was such a point of interest to journalists that frequently comment on Hole's musical performance was greatly restricted.

The practice of positioning Love within specific feminine roles was particularly apparent after Cobain's death. As a journalist for the British weekly music paper *Melody Maker* commented, 'the thick, dark ghost of Kurt follows Courtney everywhere, even overshadowing Hole … From now on, she is The Widow' (LeClaire, 1995: 17). In grieving for her husband Love did not adopt the passive stoicism associated with widowhood and so was targeted for criticism. The *Daily Mirror* ran an article entitled 'A Hole Lot of Love: Hell-Raising Widow's World of Shocking Sexploits' (Pringle, 1994: 19), which presented a portrait of her as a manipulative, promiscuous, drug-addicted careerist. The article began with the denouncement: 'even when her husband Nirvana grunge rocker Kurt Cobain killed himself earlier this month in the most horrible way, Courtney Love still managed to plug her group Hole in his wake' (1994: 19). Likewise, a documentary entitled *Kurt and Courtney*, produced by Nick Broomfield in 1998, relied upon well-worn clichés associated with the couple. Broomfield's documentary traded on gossip and rumour, and even included an allegation that Love had tried to hire a hitman to kill Cobain.

This review of articles published between 1991 and 1995 has demonstrated how these press accounts constructed and sustained an image of Love as dangerous and unstable. Press accounts written to commemorate the anniversary of Cobain's death reveal how the conception of Love as a negative force on her husband has been sustained. One such account, written on the tenth anniversary of Cobain's suicide, reinforces earlier press depictions of Love by describing her as 'modern day Yoko Ono and former groupie' (Mohan, 2004) thereby evoking characters that have become emblematic within the media of female interference and fame-hungry sexual availability. In a number of these retrospective articles journalists have sought to reinforce the image of Cobain as an authentic voice within rock music by constructing Love as his opposite: a figure of brash insincerity. For instance, a feature published in *The Guardian* (1999: 11) on the fifth anniversary of Cobain's death listed Love as one of five 'facile "alternative" icons who have benefited from Kurt Cobain's suicide', while in 2004 Robert Thicknesse commented in *The Times* (2004: 8) that 'Kurt might have done the decent thing and taken Courtney with him.' Love's musical output, as front person in Hole and in her subsequent solo career, is dismissed within many of these articles, which demonise her as a bothersome, unstable, manipulative opportunist. This characterisation of Love is offered in particularly exaggerated terms in a feature in the UK press by Gina Arnold. Arnold (2004: 22–3) dismisses Love's embrace of feminism and casts her as 'a manic, mouthy mess' who 'got rich and powerful by getting pregnant'. Arnold's denouncement of Love as 'desperately trying to garner some cheap facsimile of Cobain's phenomenal fame' (Arnold, 2004: 23) positions her as emblematic of the vacuity of commodity culture and thus creates a foil against which to construct Cobain as an anti-corporate, sensitive hero.

Björk

The final case study of this chapter considers how press reports have constructed singer-songwriter Björk as mentally unstable. The Icelandic singer and musician first gained attention in the British music press as lead singer in the indie band The Sugarcubes. In 1993 she received critical acclaim in the British press with the release of her first solo album, *Debut*, which reached number three in the British album charts. Björk co-wrote the title track to Madonna's *Bedtime Stories* album in 1994 and released her second album, *Post*, in 1995. Following the success of *Post* she was awarded International Newcomer and International Female Solo Artist at the Brit Awards. Björk has won considerable critical praise and commercial success with her subsequent musically experimental releases *Homogenic* (1997), *Vespertine* (2001), the vocal-based album *Medúlla* (2004) and *Volta* (2007). She has also written two soundtrack albums and taken on film roles including acting in Lars von Trier's *Dancer in the Dark* for which she was named Best Actress by jurors at the Cannes Film Festival in 2000.

As with the previous discussion of Love's media profile, the way in which the press has framed Björk has constrained and limited her image as a musician. However, Björk's media persona is sharply distinct from that of Love as it is generally devoid of associations with danger. She is instead othered as an exotic eccentric whose quirkiness is positioned as symptomatic of impenetrable cultural difference. In Anglo journalistic representations Björk's supposed madness is presented as an amusing quirk of her personality and culture. The terminology used to describe her is colloquial and condescending. Johnny Dee's review of Björk's *Debut* album employed the words 'weird' and 'bonkers', informing readers 'This woman is quite patently barmy' (Dee, 1993). This media representation has persisted, with other critics using the terms 'loopy' (Mcbeth, 2000: 6; Morris, 1993a: 12), 'quirky' (O'Brien, 1994: 127), 'daffy' (Fricke, 1995: 25; Barber, 1998: 4), 'nutty' (Callan *et al.*, 2002), 'Bjonkers' (Blackstock, 1994: 35; Carey, 1996: 25), 'wacky' (Dingwall, 1996a: 26; Mcbeth, 2000: 6; Taylor, 2001) and 'Bjorking mad' (Dingwall and Oxley, 1996: 12) in their reviews and news articles. With an acknowledgement of the frequency with which these descriptive terms are applied to the performer, Kitty Empire (2003: 11) remarked in one review that 'If Bjork ever actually loses her mind, we will never notice.' All of these terms temper Björk's artistic image, often overshadowing any meaningful investigation into or discussion of her music.

Furthermore, journalists constantly place Björk within a fairy-tale landscape where she features as a 'happy little pixie' or 'the Icelandic princess' (Morris, 1993a: 12). The images chosen tend to refer directly to her physical appearance, emphasising her small stature by selecting words such as 'doll-sized' (Sullivan, 1994a: 7), 'pixie' (Fulton, 1997: 56; Porter, 1998; Cairns, 2000; Powlson, 2000: 4; Callan *et al.*, 2002; Verrico, 2004: 18) and 'elfin' (Cornwell, 1995; Dingwall, 1996b; Murray, 1997: 15; Sandall, 1999; Billen, 2001). Moreover, Björk is constantly described in childish terms. Placed at a remove from sexual and intellectual maturity, she is likened to 'a mischievous child' (Morris, 1993a: 12), 'a kittenish child-woman' (Gray, 1994), who charms her audience by 'emitting little gurgles' (Sullivan, 1996: 41), speaks in a 'little girl lost voice' (Taylor, 2001) and makes her viewers 'come over all gooey and protective' (Lester, 1994: 24). People who have worked with Björk testify to the laughable fiction of this media image. Jon Fugler, who remixed two of her singles, commented early in her career that 'She's more concerned about her son's school than all the crap of being in a band' (*Select*, 1994: 13). Pat Savage, her accountant, concurred with this, stating: 'She has a good head for figures and is in control of her own destiny, not just in terms of money and property, but her career and life' (*Select*, 1994: 16). Björk's impressive career as a recording artist, songwriter and actor seems to confirm this endorsement. Nevertheless, journalistic representations of Björk continue to be fairly restrictive.

The hackneyed use of these stereotypes within reviews of Björk's work has not gone unacknowledged by critics. For example, within the UK broadsheet papers, a number of journalists have noted how Björk has been 'pigeonholed as pop's mad Artic cutestress' (Sullivan, 1998: 12) and labelled by the media as 'barking mad' (Connolly, 2001) when they have found her to be 'quite normal' (Gordon, 2002: 13). Yet this image of Björk has become so much part of her media characterisation that, even when choosing to present an alternative portrait, critics still feel it necessary to reiterate the notion of Björk as a mad elfin creature. Indeed, within the aforementioned articles the writers used this image as a framing device for their work, introducing each piece with a suitably teasing headline: 'Don't call me pixie' (Sullivan, 1998: 12), 'Off the wall?' (Connolly, 2001) and 'I'm glad you think of me as a nutter' (Gordon, 2002: 13).

Ways in which the label of insanity places the individual in the position of 'other' have already been discussed. This parallels the way that de Beauvoir (1952: 249) argued gender relations work by normalising the (sane) masculine subject and distinguishing it from the (aberrant) feminine 'other'. This model also has application here in reference to nationality, as presentations of Björk's 'strangeness' have often been married to her Icelandic origin. In an industry where Anglo-American performers are normative, Björk's nationality translates as otherness. Stereotypical representations associated with Iceland inform descriptions of Björk within the press. In 1994 the British monthly music magazine *Select* opened a lengthy article on Björk with an introductory headline billing her as a 'berserk little Eskimo' (*Select*, 1994: 13). An earlier review in the *NME* described her voice as 'an alien screech that coughed up puffin feathers' (Dee, 1993: 35). Just as her individuality is understood as quirkily amusing, her 'foreignness' is presented as an entertaining facet of her persona. Linguistic errors made during interviews or performances are often quoted verbatim (see, for example, Thorncroft, 1994: xxiv), and her difficulty with the English language is emphasised and parodied in reports.[12] In one instance Björk's supposed mental imbalance is explained as a direct product of her country of origin: 'That she has been born and raised in an unusual country which boasts a population of a mere 250,000 and the highest suicide rate in the world ... *verifies* her *natural* madness' (Morris, 1993a: 12, my emphasis).

The repeated references to Iceland by reviewers should be considered within the context of everyday journalistic practice. Journalists are expected not only to present facts about an artist but also to offer an insight into their personality. They are thus under pressure to offer readers a framework for understanding musicians and their work. Björk's Icelandic origin provides journalists with a convenient way to construct their presentation. A glance at the titles of a range of articles published about Björk in British broadsheet newspapers illustrates journalists' reliance upon her national identity as a framing device: 'Nordic But Nice' (Spencer, 1996: 13), 'The Ice Melts' (Brown, 1997: 4) and 'Norse Code' (Baker, 1997: 12). Images of the landscape of Iceland inform not only descriptions of Björk but also her music. A review in the *Independent* describes 'arctic waves of violin and cello' (Brown, 1997: 4), while a review by Neil Spencer in the *Observer* (1996: 13) begins with an allusion to the weather and landscape of Iceland by describing a 'blast of Icelandic pop ... her current live show emphasised the darker, Nordic undertow of her music. For all its eruptions of passion, there remains an odd sense of detachment to her work.'

Examination of articles within the UK press that discuss other musicians from Iceland reveals that there is an identifiable tendency within British music journalism to peculiarise Icelandic artists, and to suggest links between their personalities, creative output and country of origin. Journalistic responses to Björk in this regard can thus be viewed as indicative of a tendency within the press to exoticise Icelandic artists and to present them as different and separate from the norm of Anglo-American musicians.[13] Reviewers often liken the work of these artists to aspects of Iceland's austere landscape, describing the music in terms of physical terrain, weather phenomena and the patterns of the seasons. For example, in a review in *The Sunday Times*, Flynn (2005: 6) presented Mugison as an 'alien apparition from the edges of the pop world' who produced 'what sounded like a North Atlantic storm through a laptop' while another reviewer described how the artist possessed 'a voice like the aurora borealis', commenting 'ice melted when he sang' (RT, 2005). Similar references can be found in reviews of other Icelandic artists: one reviewer describes the 'glacial beats' of Gus Gus (Clarke, 2003: 22), while another discusses the impact of 'Iceland's unique, magma-hewn landscape' on Mum's 'spartan soundscapes' (McNair, 2001: 13). Moreover, Icelandic artists are frequently presented as 'eccentric' or 'idiosyncratic'. Again this characterisation of 'strangeness' is often explained with reference to Iceland's 'spectacularly alien geography' (Lynskey, 2005: 6) or 'isolated position' (Gill, 2003: 18–19). Furthermore, this alleged tendency towards eccentricity is often 'evidenced' with recourse to the public image of Björk (see, for instance, Culshaw, 2005: 25; Lynskey, 2005: 6). In a round-up review of a number of Icelandic acts, McNair (2001: 13) acknowledges the triteness of this depiction while simultaneously reinforcing the stereotype 'ever since Bjork brayed, donkey-like, on the Sugarcubes' 1987 single "Birthday", the British media have tended to portray Icelandic musicians as nutters. It's a patronising generalisation, but it holds true with regard to Kanada.'

While Björk's Icelandic nationality has provided a convenient point of reference for journalists, the way that this has been discussed in the written media has changed over time. This reflects the need for journalists to periodically reposition the image of a musician in order to sustain reader interest.[14] These media repositionings, usually coinciding with the release of new material, help to sustain the longevity of a music career as performers are presented as having produced a fresh sound that reflects their 'development' as artists. The release of Björk's third album, *Homogenic*, in 1997 was an opportunity for journalists to recreate her public profile. Press accounts discussed the new 'maturity' in her work (Baker, 1997: TT12; Sullivan, 1997a: T20; Porter, 1998), linking artistic development to various biographical details:

> Naturally, she long ago outgrew the Nordic-pixie persona of her first album, *Debut*, … this unapproachability is a new thing. You don't need to be a shrink to link it to the tumultuous period of her private life that began with a letter bomb from a deranged fan and ended with the highly public break-up of her relationship with junglemeister Goldie. (Sullivan, 1997b: 7)

A live review in the British broadsheet paper the *Independent* reflected, 'the new Björk is less a hyperactive child, more a genuine nervous wreck' (Brown, 1997: 4). However, while accounts offered a different public image of Björk, often these new descriptions continued to draw upon images of Iceland: 'It's the most famous thing about her, that balmy, shrieking eccentricity. … But then Björk does hail from Viking territory. Iceland is an extreme place if ever there was one' (Baker, 1997: 12). Björk's image as a quirky pixie was downplayed by many journalists who re-presented her as an icy personality who harboured brooding mysteries. These articles offered Björk's nationality as explanation for her creative input, likening the sounds on the album to aspects of Iceland's landscape. The processes of creative production were somewhat naturalised within these accounts as Björk was presented as a conduit through which the language of Iceland's geography could find a voice. Journalists reflected that 'The album is apparently a kind of audio-synaesthetic impression of Björk's return to her native Iceland' (Gill, 1997: 19), the vocals 'feel cool and Nordically restrained' (Sullivan, 1997a: T20), and 'while you can take Björk out of Iceland, it seems you cannot take Iceland out of Björk's music' (Sinclair, 1997).

Consideration of the press response to the work of Björk and other Icelandic musicians has revealed the clear tendency within UK journalism to present Iceland as an alien landscape that necessarily produces unusual or 'strange' artists. Björk has thus been placed in the position of 'other' through her nationality. However, this brief examination of the language used within press reviews exposes that Björk is subject to a doubled process of othering. Her public image is further constrained by the tendency of journalists to diminish her credibility by adopting a particularly gendered language of criticism that styles her, patronisingly, as a 'little pixie'. The associations of madness have further been used by journalists to undermine the seriousness of Björk's image or to reinforce their construction of her as an outsider.

Conclusion

This chapter has drawn out different significations accorded to mental ill health and explored how these are used by journalists to frame performers. It has shown that the written media do not adopt a singular or common approach to this subject. Rather, the meanings ascribed are selected and applied in order to enhance or reduce a performer's artistic status. Although the chapter restricted the number of performers under consideration, it has shown how the discourses of gender inform public profiles. It has also demonstrated how images related to mental ill health are frequently drawn upon within the rock press in ways acutely differentiated along gender lines. Female musicians are seldom offered the title of tortured genius. More often the concept of mental ill health is presented as a personal shortcoming to be understood either with patronising concern or guarded against as a dangerous female loss of control.

Clearly no article offers a neutral presentation for each seeks to define and transmit a readily understandable 'type' to its readership. The weight of Courtney Love's media coverage has resulted in reports offering conflicting profiles from grieving widow to whore-queen of rock. The contradictions in the images used to describe Love are highlighted when reporters attempt to offer a composite media profile. Mair's article in the British style magazine *ID* may be used as illustration. Unable to meld the apparent lack of continuity in Love's public persona, Mair decides to pronounce that 'there are two Courtney Love's' (Mair, 1994: 41). The first, she declares 'is considered, intelligent, loving and loved in return. The other is tortured, a bitter realist, a woman who wages war within herself' (1994: 41). It is significant that Mair chose to separate the role of wife and mother from that of tortured individual and placid intelligence from bodily anguish. Such a representation is indicative of the way in which journalism trades in labels as an effective way to contain the individual.

The case studies in this chapter have traced how music criticism employs the concept of madness to understand music and music makers. Of course, music journalists use a wide range of descriptive terms and metaphors in order to characterise performers and to offer a sense of sound through the written word. However, these descriptions are not presented in the press as simply personal opinions but as authoritative interpretations, and as such they have the potential to shape the way in which we understand performers and the music they produce. The word 'potential' is crucial here for, as Simon Frith points out, 'the adjectives [of music journalism] turn description into interpretation and are effective only to the extent that we are prepared to agree that, yes, this is how musical sounds mean' (Frith, 1996: 67). As Marcus Breen (1987) and Jason Toynbee (1993) have argued, readers are encouraged through various journalistic strategies to take the interpretations offered by the press as valid, even authoritative, interpretations. Readers who invest emotionally and financially in music outside of the canon of prescribed taste are scolded in sarcastic editorials, knowing asides and polemic prose. However, as this chapter has argued, not only should these interpretations be questioned on aesthetic grounds, they must also be examined in order to reveal an underlying discourse of gender.

Notes

1   For an account of the range and variety of music magazines and papers worldwide see Leonard *et al.* (2003).

2   While the structure of the music press has changed considerably since Frith made this observation, it retains its significant cultural relevance, albeit in a rather more diffuse sense. Frith was writing in the period when the UK music press was at the height of its cultural power. Four consumer weeklies were published in Britain in 1981 (*Melody Maker*, *NME*, *Sounds* and *Record Mirror*) with 'a combined circulation of 600,000 to 800,000' (Frith, 1981: 166). However, circulation figures for British weekly music papers have dropped considerably from the late 1980s, with both *Record Mirror* and *Sounds* closing in 1991, a trend that continued unabated right up until the closure of *Melody Maker* in 2000. During the same period the music press responded to changes in the market with differing formats aimed at different consumer demographics and specialised taste cultures. In the 1980s and 1990s a number of glossy, monthly colour magazines dedicated to music were launched. While some of these were short-lived (such as *X-Ray*, *Select*, *Vox*, all broadly dealing with 'indie' and 'alternative') others (such as *Q*, *Mojo*, *Uncut*) have gone on to establish healthy circulations and a distinct place within the market. The music press in Britain now comprises a diverse range of publications dedicated to particular niche markets that encompass a range of music genres. These publications include *Mixmag*, *DJ International* (dance), *Straight No Chaser* (jazz and hip hop) and *Word* ('classic' rock).

3   With regard to many UK broadsheets this distinction has become less acute in the 2000s, where strategies to capture the lucrative 16–35 market have included extended popular music coverage in the *Independent*, *Times* and *Guardian*, and the launch of a specialist monthly music magazine in the *Observer*.

4   For a critique of the male dominance of rock journalism and a celebration of the contribution made to the form by female writers see McDonnell (1995).

5   Examples of such work are collected in Kent (1994), Bangs (1991), and Kureishi and Savage (1995).

6   See, for example, the chapter 'Art by the Insane' in Rhodes (2000: 48–103), Gisbourne (1996) and Kavaler-Adler (1993).

7   See the special issue of *Popular Music and Society* edited by Mazzarella, S.R. and Muto, J. (1995) for further analysis of press coverage following Cobain's suicide.

8   Taken from the title of a novel by Douglas Coupland published in 1991, 'generation X' became a catchphrase within the media referring to people typically aged in their twenties who felt alienated by contemporary mainstream society and used irony to negotiate poor employment opportunities.

9   As I have dealt only with press reports published after Cobain's death and Edwards' disappearance, it might be expected that press representations of these musicians are informed not only by constructions of gender but also by the tendency of journalists to heroicise performers who have died. However, posthumous celebrations of stars are also often informed by constructions of gender. As discussed in Chapter 1, the late Janis Joplin has been presented in journalistic accounts not as a heroic 'hellraiser' but as an insecure and tragic figure.

10   For discussions of gender and witchcraft see Ussher (1991), Blécourt (2000), and Hallissy (1987).

11   Scot, R. (1584) *The Discoverie Of Witchcraft*, New York: Centaur Press, p. 31, quoted in Ussher (1991).

12   The same media treatment was afforded to the all-female Japanese trio Shonen Knife in the 1990s. Their misapprehension of reporters' questions allowed journalists to present their answers as surreal soundbites from a kookie collective.

13   Stephen Amico offered an interesting discussion of this tendency in his conference paper 'Desired Exotics: American and Icelandic Popular Musics in Contact', presented at the 12th Biennial Conference of the International Association for the Study of Popular Music (IASPM), McGill University, Montreal, July 2003.

14   See Toynbee's (1993) discussion of the practice of 'periodisation' in the British weekly music press.

Chapter 4

Strategies of performance

This chapter considers how the image of a band (not only their visual look but also the ways in which they construct themselves discursively) is created and promoted through the adoption of various performance strategies. It will concentrate attention on the contexts in which bands perform, examining how musicians work with different performance traditions. It argues that performances are not simply an outlet for creativity but an attempt to communicate to and engage with an audience. As Jason Toynbee comments, performance does not simply consist of the production of sound as it also has another intent, for when 'musicians perform … they not only show off but also try to reach the audience' (Toynbee, 2000: 67). The opening section of this chapter will discuss the effect of performance on listeners, looking at how particular performance strategies by female musicians have been understood by journalists and critics. In presenting a performance musicians intend to provoke a response from their listeners or spectators, whether they are loyal fans or record company representatives.

It is conventional to consider performance as taking place within the live setting of a gig or concert. This chapter focuses attention on the performance of female-centred indie bands within and across four 'sites', including not only the stage but also promotional videos, press interviews and photo shoots. This approach to understanding performance can be linked to the discussion in Chapter 2, which explored how particular contexts of music practice and production allowed for different modes of gendered behaviour. This chapter is not concerned with individual performances but with the relationship between performance and the concerns of marketing, artist development and the aesthetics of particular music genres. It argues that performance can and should be conceptualised broadly because, by focusing on live music events as *the* site of performance, critics have ignored the variety of ways in which musicians construct their public images. While a photographic print of a performer or band is a frozen image, it has been realised through a process of enactment. The gaze of the performer, their attire and pose may all be understood as performances for an imagined viewer. In a similar sense the press interview should not be thought of as an event in which a musician reveals their 'true self' but as a site in which the musician performs their public identity. The press interview may be understood as an instance in which the musician acts out a constructed 'true' self. Thus in each of these performance sites the image of a band or performer is constructed in a way that contributes to an apparently 'authentic' and coherent public identity. As Auslander (1999) argues, it is important to recognise the ways in which mediatised images and live performances inform and lend credibility to one another. He comments that, rather than regarding the live performance as authentic and in conflict with 'manufactured' mediated forms, one should consider how live performance 'has become the means by which mediatized representations are naturalised ... if the mediatized image can be recreated in a live setting, it must have been "real" to begin with' (Auslander, 1999: 38–9). This chapter looks at how different forms of production – the live gig, the music video, press interview and the photo shoot – actually inform and reinforce one another in producing a consistent and, generally genre-specific, image of the subject or band.

This broader application of the term 'performance' to include staged photographs and press interviews draws attention to the constructedness of the public identities of musicians, and to the strategies of production through which these public performances are achieved. In selecting four sites of performance I discuss how each performance relates to conventions and aesthetics within rock music and to notions of the creative artist. This analysis is also concerned with how musicians construct themselves as gendered beings through their performances: whether using dress codes, bodily postures or witty asides to journalists. Judith Butler's theorisation of gender as performance is particularly useful here. Butler argues that gender does not exist as an 'ideal' or 'essence' but instead is constituted from a series of performed acts that actually create the notion of gender. She argues that while gender appears to be an identifiable fact it is instead a construction that is *treated* culturally as if it were a fact:

> Gender is, thus, a construction that regularly conceals its genesis; the tacit collective agreement to perform, produce, and sustain discrete and polar genders as cultural fictions is obscured by the credibility of those productions – and the punishments that attend not agreeing or believing in them; the construction 'compels' our belief in its necessity and naturalness. (Butler, 1990: 140)

In accordance with this, consideration will be given not only to how gender is negotiated by female rock performers but also to how particular aspects of rock practice, such as the press interview, may be understood as performances rather than moments where the 'real' or 'true' person behind the star persona is revealed.

Subversion and performance

Interpretations of live music performance are influenced by a number of factors including the setting, the sound and volume of the band, the choice of instrumentation, the stage clothes worn, the interaction with the audience and the standard of the musicians' performance. The physical gestures of the musicians, their interaction with one another and their style of playing generally fit into modes of performance established within particular music genres and subgenres. For instance, as Walser comments, 'Visually, metal musicians typically appear as swaggering males, leaping and strutting about the stage, clad in spandex, scarves, leather, and other visually noisy clothing, punctuating their performances with phallic thrusts of guitars and microphone stands' (Walser, 1993: 109). Walser's comments indicate how established such performance conventions have become and illustrate how a viewer may decode certain performance styles as a display of masculinity. However, heavy metal performance has little in common with contemporary indie rock, although certain elements of heavy metal performance are sometimes employed. These genre-specific conventions of performance contribute to a continuing and diverse history of rock practice and become part of a store of possibilities for the contemporary musician to copy, reference, ignore or parody.

Just as the performance of heavy metal has become associated with male musicians, other roles, such as the solo pop vocalist or the singer-songwriter, have come to be culturally understood as legitimate or even prescribed roles for female performers.[1] While not exclusive to female performers, the role of the pop singer or folk vocalist accompanied by an acoustic guitar can be viewed as tapping in to and reinforcing conventional notions of femininity. In turn, this 'cashing in' of traditional gender stereotypes has a self-perpetuating effect upon both the logics of the music industry and the performative roles that are adopted by female performers. In other words, the amount of record company investment in female singer-songwriters and pop vocalists has encouraged women to view these roles as legitimate ways to break into the record industry. Female musicians who have departed from conventional feminine gender identities on stage (whether performing pop, rock or country) have often been understood by journalists and critics as subversive. Even commercially successful artists such as Siouxsie Sioux, Madonna, Annie Lennox and k.d. lang have been described in this way.[2]

Punk performer Siouxsie Sioux of the well-known British band Siouxsie And The Banshees offered a visual challenge to conventions of female stage performance during the late 1970s by adopting a confrontational, overtly sexual stage persona. In the Banshees' live performances, Siouxsie dressed in militaristic style, thigh-high boots, black satin shorts and a T-shirt printed with an image of a pair of breasts. Her face make-up was heavily applied, creating a mask rather than acting as conventional cosmetic enhancement. The image she presented, along with other female punk performers of the time, was intended to challenge conventional female 'prettiness'. As Reynolds and Press comment, she 'invited the voyeuristic gaze only to punish it' (1995: 302). Other female artists have sought different effects, whether through the asexual suits worn by vocalist Annie Lennox when performing in the British pop duo The Eurythmics,[3] or in the heterosexual drag of the highly successful solo artist k.d. lang, who collected her first Canadian Music Industry Award wearing bridal wear and trainers.[4] Even when a female performer such as the internationally acclaimed US artist Madonna has worn conventional feminine attire, this has been understood critically as an ironic mimicry, a subversive enactment. It may be queried whether one such definitive reading can ever be authoritative, and indeed whether all these instances are truly subversive rather than just enticing spectacles or smart image making. However, the concept of 'subversion' has been a dominant mode of understanding female musicians who offer different interpretations of gender identities.

The change in the style choices of Courtney Love, front person in US band Hole, in the mid-1990s, from battered antique dresses and heavily applied smudged make-up towards a highly groomed, glamorous, feminine public image, provides another example of how even shifts towards more 'mainstream' visual styles of female performance may be read as subversive. Some fans accused Love of 'selling out' as she divested herself of the clothing styles that were consistent with her image as an indie rock musician and as Hole releases and tours were temporarily suspended while Love developed an acting career. However, other fans and critics delighted in Love's new 'disguise' as a 'conventional' female and took pleasure in the absurdity of her appearance at film awards[5] and as a fashion model for a new line of clothing from well-known Italian designer Versace. Gayle Wald has commented on the appearance of this 'new' Courtney on a US television programme hosted by the well-known chat show host Barbara Walters. Wald explained that Love appeared on the show, entitled *Most Fascinating People of 1995*, wearing a beige suit. She commented:

> … just as Love uses her trademark smudged red lipstick to parody conventional femininity and bourgeois tastefulness, so there was something oddly askew about her rehearsal of female virtue: a curiously compelling disjunction between composure and distraction, propriety and vulgarity, that suggested nothing less than the spectacle of bourgeois white femininity in drag. (Wald, 1997: 151–2)

Courtney Love's public persona and her history and cultural status as a rock star prevented her new public image from truly being understood as a belated capitulation to feminine norms. Love's new image in the mid-1990s, when read against existent information and mythologies linked to the performer, could be understood as a *performance* of normality, or as Love gatecrashing conventional society.

Undoubtedly, certain performances by female-centred bands can be read as consciously subversive. A number of queercore[6] bands in the late 1990s presented stage shows intended to mock and challenge conventional heterosexual identities. Performances by the lesbian five-piece band Tribe 8 from San Francisco provide a good illustration of this. During some of Tribe 8's shows, singer Lynn Breedlove took off her shirt and produced a dildo from the fly of her jeans. During the course of these shows, in a song about gang rape entitled 'Frat Pig', Breedlove cut the object away using a hunting knife (occasionally using a chainsaw) and threw it into the audience.[7] Breedlove's corporeal enactment of a sexually aggressive (and self-mutilating) androgyne challenged heterosexual morality and operated as a performance of a queer identity. This presentation by Tribe 8 featured regularly in a number of their live shows. However, the band also presented this performance during the recording of a US cable television programme named *Luke's Peep Show* presented by Luke Skywalker, a front person for the gangsta rap act 2 Live Crew. The producer of *Luke's Peep Show* decided to book Tribe 8 to play on one of the shows in the series as, reportedly, she was annoyed by the overt sexism within the show's content. The band's subsequent appearance presented Tribe 8 playfully satirising the programme's content, slipping between performances of themselves as coquettish guests and sexualised lesbians, and ending their programme debut with the aforementioned simulated physical violation.[8] The subversive and confrontational nature of Tribe 8's performance was heightened within the context of television programming where it is general practice to tone down any risqué elements that may appear in live performances. Perhaps not surprisingly the recorded show was never broadcast. An alternative example may be taken of the live shows of the female-centred band Bikini Kill,[9] based in Washington DC. At several gigs, while singing a song about incest, lead singer Kathleen Hanna exposed her left breast and repeated the song line 'Suck my left one'. Situating herself within the performance traditions of punk rock, Hanna used her body to shock and confront the audience.

Bands such as Tribe 8 and Bikini Kill present unique and clear challenges to sexual and cultural mores within their live performances. Their shows directly engage with issues of sexuality and gender though physical gesture, lyrical content and in their relationship with audience members.[10] Of course, not all female-centred indie bands offer such clear examples of subversive performance. In a study of women in Japanese popular music, Jennifer Milioto compares the public images and performance traditions of mainstream Japanese pop (j-pop) performers and female punk, hardcore and indie musicians in Tokyo. Focusing her analysis on a live event showcasing a number of contemporary all-female indie bands, including Super Junkey Monkey, Buffalo Daughter and Cibo Matto, Milioto comments that while each band presented a different musical experience, each positioned itself against the dominant j-pop music. Milioto states that: 'There is a rejection of dominant female style as visual object and more focus on musical ability. Even a resistance of expected female behaviour, as one dives into the audience, or performs in an encoded masculine vocal style' (Milioto, 1998: 487). Milioto argues that through their live performances and photo shoots these bands offer alternative and oppositional images of female musicians to the dominant pop culture. However, while a comparison of indie and pop performers can offer an explanation of the conventions of each respective music genre, such an analysis cannot offer a sophisticated account of the subtle variations and signifying systems within each genre.

Genre and performance

Some staged performances such as those already discussed are clearly intended to be provocative and subversive. However, often female rock performers appear to be labelled as subversive simply because they do not display or conform to particular modes of feminine behaviour. To peculiarise such artists as 'subversive' naturalises the relationship between biological sex and feminine gender patterns. This point is remarked upon by Reynolds in respect to the all-female post-punk band The Raincoats. He comments: 'The Raincoats ... looked slightly scruffy in a way that would have been unremarked-upon in an all-male band during this era. Coming from women, though, it took on the quality of radical gesture, a strident abstention from glamour and showbiz' (Reynolds, 2005: 214). Furthermore, critical readings of the performance strategies of female artists as subversive frequently fail to take account of the nuanced relationship between popular music performance and genre. The screaming vocals of US artists Courtney Love and Kat Bjelland and the vintage baby-doll dresses they wore in their early careers may be read as subversive of traditional representations of mainstream adult femininity, yet they can also be read as consistent with particular conventions of music practice and female display within indie rock music. Thus while many of the performative practices of female indie rock musicians are intended to be challenging and engaging, they may not necessarily be understood as subversive if related to the signifying systems of indie rock music culture.

**Figure 4.1   Amelia Fletcher, lead vocalist with Oxford-based indie band
Marine Research, performing at the Reading Festival, 1999**

Indie musicians and fans cannot merely be understood as reacting against
a particular set of conventions but also as working within certain conventions of
performance and display, which in turn may be read as oppositional. Milioto's
description of a 'resistant' female musician diving into the audience may equally be
read just as the description of a participant within a particular music (sub)culture.
It is problematic to generalise about indie or subcultural conventions because the
category of indie rock encompasses a variety of subgenres and a diversity of musical
and stylistic practice from lo-fi punk to electronic rock experimentalism. However,
the composite of stylistic choices made by indie bands generally work with reference
to established genre-specific customs. For example, the wearing of vintage clothing
has become an established tradition within indie culture,[11] and 'baby doll' clothing
styles can be set within a tradition of the fetishisation of childish things within a
certain strand of indie music.[12] Examples of such styles include: the faux naive
performance style of Oxford-based indie band Marine Research, whose lead singer
Amelia charmingly swings her arms, taps a tambourine and grins at the audience
(Figure 4.1); the children's hairslides worn by many riot grrrls; the cartoon characters

used to represent the members of the Glasgow-based band bis in their publicity and merchandise; or the stickers, crayons, coloured felt-tip pens and cartoon 'Hello Kitty' ink stamps used by many British fanzine writers to adorn letters and envelopes when mailing out issues. As US indie singer-songwriter Lois Maffeo comments:

> I think a lot of this imagery of girls and baby doll dresses and stuff like that is because so much of punk rock culture came from being the misfit, the one who was beaten up, the weaker, the smaller. In the world of rock 'n' roll, there's also the icon of the eternal teenager, wanting to stay at that arrested state of, 'I'm 16' and, 'rock 'n' roll forever.' For women, you can't just wear black jeans and black Converse sneakers and still maintain that mystique of being 16 forever, so they go back to a slightly more adolescent model, the baby-doll look. (quoted in Juno, 1996: 131).

Implicit within the concept of subversion are the issues of intent and effect. The subversive act is intended to mock, undermine or overturn well-established or dominant modes of thought, power or behaviour. Wilson (1993) questions the power of 'transgression' because it implies a binary relationship as an act that opposes dominant norms. Set against these norms, the transgressor may certainly challenge the status quo but the power balance is such that it is doubtful that they can overturn them. Wilson comments that the words 'transgression', 'dissidence', 'subversion' and 'resistance' are thus words of weakness since they do not in themselves create change (Wilson, 1993: 113). She concludes that transgression 'can only be a tactic, never a total politics' (1993: 116) as the intention must be for transformation rather than for a mere strategy of resistance: 'we have to have an idea of how things could be different, otherwise transgression ends in mere posturing' (1993: 116).

This notion of 'mere posturing' is particularly salient with regard to the marketing of popular music performers because notions of subversion and rebellion have often been employed throughout the history of rock music in order to market or 'hype' an act. In fact, subversion has been a significant trope in rock culture since the 1960s. Harron (1990), for instance, describes the way in which The Rolling Stones were consciously marketed as rebellious while Harker (1980) notes that, in the late 1960s, the major recording companies were very quick to incorporate the radicalism of the US counterculture into their promotional strategies. Bands or artists who are understood to have crossed or blurred the line demarcating acceptable conduct are regularly granted cultural cachet and media attention. This is not to disregard the power of such performance strategies but to recognise that subversion or radicalism has become a central framing narrative within the music industry. With regard to issues of gender and sexuality, the concept of posturing becomes rather problematic. While some stage shows and performer images may be read as an ironic comment on established gender roles, they may also be interpreted in other ways. The sexualised performances within Madonna's live shows, for example, may not be read as 'resistant' or 'ironic' by every member of her audience.[13] As Radio 1 broadcaster John Peel reflected:

> If ever there is any area of human activity which is liable to be misunderstood, it is by someone trying to deflate, or remove, the menace from sexism by being grotesquely sexy.

You are really playing with fire there and there are not many people, including Madonna, who manage to pull it off. (personal communication, 17 February 1994)

Appraising an act of 'transgressive' gender performance is problematic not only in terms of how the success of that performance is open to interpretation but also because a concentration on gender alone might leave out other important dimensions for analysis. Gayle Wald (2002) has highlighted this concern in her consideration of the seemingly transgressive manipulation of girlhood by the US singer Gwen Stefani, solo artist and lead vocalist of ska rock band No Doubt. Wald argues that, by considering only gender representation in an analysis of Stefani's performance style, one misses out other crucial dimensions of representation concerned with race and national identity. She comments: 'seemingly transgressive gender play within contemporary rock music cultures often "fronts" for far less transgressive codings and recodings of racialized and nationalized identities. At its worst, such recuperation of girlhood has been staged in terms that equate girlness with whiteness' (Wald, 2002: 194).

Sound, genre and gender

Across a range of popular music genres particular musical instruments, music technologies[14] and sounds have become associated with masculinity and femininity. For example, the jazz trumpet has been associated with performative masculinity (see Darrington, 2000), whereas in the nineteenth century the performance in the home of songs on instruments such as the piano or harp was considered a genteel and feminine pursuit for women (Miller, 1994). Within rock certain sounds, such as an amplified overdriven guitar riff, have also become associated and codified as emblematic of performative masculinity. It is of course fallacious to define sonic events as naturally male or female. However, it is valid to discuss how particular musical sounds have come to be understood in gendered terms and how these gendered significations have become associated with particular music cultures. Research on how people associate certain sounds with masculinity and femininity has been undertaken by a number of scholars. Tagg (1989), for instance, has conducted research that explores how gender stereotypes and associated imagery are conveyed in western instrumental music. With reference to rock music, Robert Walser has described the standard tropes of metal music as 'impressive feats on the electric guitar, counterposed with the experience of power and control that is built up through vocal extremes, guitar power chords, distortion, and sheer volume of bass and drums' (Walser, 1993: 108–9). Walser has related these musical elements to a performance of 'fantasies of masculine virtuosity and control' (1993: 108–9). Yet it is not only these rock sounds that have become codified as masculine, the very performance of these sounds has come to be understood as a male occupation.

Just as with the performance of certain rock instruments,[15] the vocal style of rock singing, characterised by harsh, abrasive timbres, contributes to the cultural association between rock and masculinity. Indeed Frith and McRobbie have discussed how the music, lyrics and vocalisation of 'cock rock'[16] performance communicate messages of masculinity: 'the music is loud, rhythmically insistent, built around techniques of aroUSl and climax; the lyrics are assertive and arrogant, though the exact words are less significant than the vocal styles involved, the shouting and screaming' (Frith and McRobbie, 1990: 374). John Shepherd (1991) has examined the 'macho' vocal sound of 'cock rock' in more depth, comparing its harsh vocal timbres with those of 'soft' rock or top 40/AM ballads. Robert Walser has also reflected on how harsh vocal sounds are a powerful generic signifier of rock music: 'before any lyrics can be comprehended, before harmonic or rhythmic patterns are established, timbre instantly signals genre and affect' (Walser, 1993: 41). The screamed vocals of indie rock performers such as Jon Spencer of the Jon Spencer Blues Explosion or Jack White of the White Stripes, are effective in communicating not only a rock sound but also emotional intensity and an articulation of force and power.

Since the rock vocal style has frequently been characterised as masculine, it is interesting to consider how it has been understood when adopted by female singers. Shepherd suggests that the cultural understanding of rock is such that the female rock vocalist who adopts the 'rasping timbres of "cock" rock' is positioned as 'actively becoming "one of the boys"' (Shepherd, 1991: 171). Such an understanding defines rock as masculine and presents the female musician as effectively offering masculinity in drag. However, this depiction of the female rock vocalist engaged in becoming one of the boys has not been the only interpretation. Numerous press reports present rasping female rock vocals as an articulation of (specifically) female anger.[17] For example, Polly Harvey has been described as 'the screeching visceral indie harpy … She makes records that wring every last bloody drop of mental anguish from her tortured life' (Fowler, 1995: 80), while Kim Gordon has been described as singing 'in a voice like teething razors about a wide variety of boy-baiting subjects' (Morton, 1996: 5). Such descriptions of vocalised female anger have not been restricted to journalism but are also repeated within scholarly criticism. For example, Holly Kruse describes 'powerful, unconventional female voices' as signifying 'both to the singers and to the audience: the visceral expression of female pain, rage, and frustration. This scream of female anger poses a direct threat to patriarchy, which attempts to cover both the existence of such anger and the structures which engender it' (Kruse, 1999: 90–91).

The equation of screamed rock vocals by female rock artists with 'female rage' is a problematic interpretation as it veers into essentialism. Such an interpretation ignores the performance conventions that female vocalists tap into and presents their delivery as something essentially female and personal. The performers are not understood within the rock tradition where harsh screamed vocals by male performers are normative. Rather, the vocal delivery of women rock performers is understood in these instances as something separate from this tradition and as essentially female. The understanding that these performers are expressing the anguished, and previously constrained, rage of womanhood removes them to some extent from the realm of the professional performer or the creative artist. Their delivery is understood as a channelling of internal rage rather than as the adoption of a rock convention. Moreover, song lyrics that express anger or defiance are frequently understood as the personal testimonies of the female vocalist rather than as an invented lyrical narrative. Thus the boundaries between performance and performer are collapsed as the listener is encouraged to understand the female vocalist as a conduit through which 'female anger' is expressed.

Such interpretations illustrate how gendered readings of sound operate within rock discourse. These interpretations of female rock vocalists close off alternative explanations and peculiarise female rock performance. By prioritising the masculinist representations of rock they ignore the way in which female performers are engaging primarily with a musical form and with established conventions of performance. For example, when describing the album *Spanking Machine* by Babes In Toyland, Simon Reynolds commented that lead vocalist Kat Bjelland 'snarls bitter recriminations, releases volcanic eruptions of fury or lets loose a sustained banshee howl' (Reynolds, 1992: 27). Lori Bambero, drummer in Babes In Toyland, offered a more mundane explanation of Bjelland's vocal technique: 'Kat screams when she sings and one of the reasons is because our PA was so bad in my basement. It was just like a little speaker and that is how we practised. So that is the way she has learned. But now that is how she sings' (personal communication, 10 July 1994). What these examples highlight is that the understanding of rock as a masculine practice colours the interpretation of particular rock sounds and affects the way in which that music is generally understood when performed by a woman. Auslander (2004) notes this process in his analysis of the repertoire and performance strategies of Suzi Quatro. He comments that Quatro's showy performance style, reminiscent of earlier male rock performers, has led to criticisms that she is trying to be 'one of the boys'. However, Auslander argues that such an interpretation is too uncomplicated as Quatro 'no more becomes a man (or some very near equivalent to a man) by wearing leather and rocking out than David Bowie became a woman by wearing a dress and mincing around the stage' (Auslander, 2004: 9). Instead, he argues, Quatro presents an intriguing blend within her performances as her body and voice are encoded as feminine while her songs and gestures are encoded as masculine. Rather than viewing Quatro as offering a 'masculine' performance Auslander highlights how she 'enacts the polymorphousness, undecideability and performativity of identity' (Auslander, 2004: 13). In a similar challenge to media interpretations of female rock performers Kennedy argues that the US rock performer Joan Jett cannot simply be dismissed as 'an inferior copy of male rock musicians' (Kennedy, 2002: 89). Drawing on Halberstam's discussion of female masculinity Kennedy argues that Jett offers a performance of female masculinity that 'is not an imitation of male masculinity but rather, a distinct gender identity that exists in between middle-class definitions of appropriate masculinity and femininity' (Kennedy, 2002: 91).

This analysis will now move from a general discussion of performance to an examination of how indie rock is understood and enacted in different performance 'sites': those of the stage, the promotional video, the photo shoot and the press interview. Discussion of specific sites allows attention to be paid to the ways in which musicians manipulate their public performances in order to communicate notions such as sincerity, credibility and creativity to different audiences, whether they are physically present (at a gig or concert), a magazine readership, a loyal fanbase or a potential market.

The stage: live performance and audience response

All performances, whether given in a rehearsal room, recording studio or on the stage of a concert hall, are produced for a present or imagined listener. However, the success of a live music event crucially depends upon the positive reception of the performance by the assembled audience. In selecting and ordering the songs they play live, musicians are aware of the need to entertain and communicate effectively. As Toynbee argues:

> There is a self-conscious awareness on the part of musicians and audience of the gap between them, a gap which even the most naturalistic of performers in the most intimate of environments (a pub back room, say) have to confront. From this perspective creation includes the struggle by musicians to *get across* to an audience. So, performance mediates creativity and pushes authors into taking account of it. (Toynbee, 2000: 53–4)

The stage is thus a crucially important performance site as it is from here that musicians are challenged to entertain or overpower an audience, build a fanbase, impress an A&R scout[18] or inspire a journalist to write a favourable review. The live music event, where music enthusiasts share a physical proximity with an artist, has been privileged as a more authentic musical experience than listening to recorded sound.[19] Ironically, as Thornton has commented, 'the demand for live gigs was arguably roused by the proliferation of recordings, which had the effect of intensifying the desire for the "original" performer' (Thornton, 1995: 27). In addition, Auslander argues that it is important to acknowledge that, within rock culture, live performance and the recording share a relationship of mutual endorsement: 'the rock recording calls up the desire for a live performance that will serve to authenticate the sounds on the recording' (Auslander, 1999: 82–3). Today cultural cachet is still accorded to those who attend live gigs and watch the development of an artist over time by following successive tours.

The artist's interaction with a live audience and the response of that audience is thus crucial to the way in which the performance is received and evaluated. However, the reaction of an audience to a live performance cannot be read as spontaneous. The audience act according to certain established conventions, which may also be understood as performance, and which include styles of dancing or body movement and the expression of appreciation or frustration (whether clapping, foot stomping, whistling, heckling or singing). In her study of British indie gigs Wendy Fonarow reflects on the way in which sections of the audience occupy different areas of non-seated venues. She comments on how 'participants place *themselves*; they choose where to stand and what to do with their bodies within the parameters of expected behaviours. This different participatory structure significantly impacts on how the event is experienced' (Fonarow, 1997: 361). While the individual response and behaviour of an audience member cannot be predicted, the 'language' of an audience, in this instance the way in which an indie rock crowd operates, can largely be anticipated.

The notion and importance of 'authentic' performance has implications for the way in which live events are staged, discussed and evaluated. Musicians may, for example, attempt to play down the theatricality of performance in order for their stage shows to be understood as moments of direct communication. When questioned about live performance Helen, vocalist in the band Bêtty Noire, commented:

> My feelings on image is to get up there and don't practice an image. ... To just get up there and feel it. Because until you have got the audience out there I don't think you know how you are going to react and feel. It just gives you a buzz. Sometimes I think if you try and say 'Well, let's do this and do that', it can come across ... as really false. It is as though you are watching yourself almost. (personal communication, 4 March 1999)

Similarly, Barry Shank observes in his study of the rock scene in Austin, Texas, that:

> sincerity is the quality most highly valued in Austin's rock 'n' roll aesthetic, from punk to mainstream folk-rock. Its presence guarantees the validity of a musical style and, by extension, of a way of life. Its importance is enhanced by, and in turn enhances, the intimate emotional connections between musicians and their fans. (Shank, 1994: 153)

The sincerity and credibility of a performer or band is frequently assessed according to criteria that reflect the different aesthetics and nuances of indie scenes and subgenres. Review pages in the British weekly music press illustrate how the legitimacy of a performer is assessed according to varying standards dictated by musical genre. For example, a positive review of the UK female band Twist focuses on their imperfection and lack of experience: 'Twist are – yikes! – *girls*. Young girls at that. ... singer Emma Fox. All eyeliner and hair, she's the spellbinding rough diamond you hope refuses to be polished' (Grogan, 1999: 34). Twist's youthfulness and brash noise are understood in this context as hallmarks of an exciting, immediate and unpretentious rock performance. By contrast, in a live review of the UK band Marine Research, song structure and composition was commended for fitting into pop aesthetics: 'With their deft skill for classic songwriting touches, their ease with timeless girl-group choruses, they are perfect, and they are pop' (Chick, 1999: 29). By describing their crafted song structures and delivery as 'free of kid gloves preciousness', the reviewer presents Marine Research as sincere and credible performers who fit with the aesthetic criteria of pop as stylised and upbeat. The selection of evaluative criteria is crucial. For example, if Marine Research had been judged in a different way, perhaps against the value-laden aesthetics of rock, they may have received a damning review for lack of intensity or seriousness.

Yet the sincerity of a rock performer is established not only in journalistic discourse but in the context of the live music event. The physical performance of the musicians (their style of playing, gestures and expression) contributes to how sincerity is communicated to their audience. Moreover, when considering the communication between band and audience, it is worth noting not only musical performance but also inter-song banter and other forms of interaction between audience members and the on-stage musicians. The next chapter discusses the riot grrrl 'network' and considers how female-centred bands such as Huggy Bear and Bikini Kill challenged established conventions at live gigs by halting their music 'set' to pass the microphone to female audience members in order to involve them in the performance. In these instances audience response and interaction were prioritised over the planned performance of selected songs.

While these Huggy Bear and Bikini Kill gigs are noteworthy in their efforts to involve the live audience, other artists often use inter-song chat to create a bond with their audience. As Berger states: 'most bands try to involve the audience with devices such as between-song patter, sing-along sections, eye contact, and a vocabulary of flashy stage antics' (Berger, 1999: 43). For example, a Hole gig in April 1995 in Wolverhampton, which was staged to promote the band and their records, was also an opportunity for front person Courtney Love to engage with media stories surrounding her celebrity. During the band's set, Love made references to her wealth and visual image, and challenged media reports predicting her demise and the cessation of her band's activities. Making several references to her late husband, Kurt Cobain (vocalist and guitarist of Nirvana), Love shouted at crowd members wearing Pearl Jam[20] T-shirts to take them off, promising 'I'll give you twice what you paid.' Love suggested that by supporting the band Pearl Jam, Hole fans were committing a betrayal to the memory of Cobain. Pointing skywards she remarked solemnly that 'He's watching!' Love requested the audience to 'get your Pearl Jam records and your Nirvana records and separate them. Forever!' The live event was an opportunity for Love to quash industry rumours and to distance herself from the commercial slur of the US 'grunge movement' as characterised by Pearl Jam. The live setting worked as an opportunity for Hole to articulate their sincerity, enhance their credibility and demonstrate their connection with 'underground' music.

A number of musicians interviewed for this book discussed how they strove to control how they were represented and interpreted when playing live by commenting that they carefully selected the clothes that they wore on stage in order to project a distinctive image during performance. Lisa Eriksson and Anna Schulte from the band Schulte/Eriksson, for example, discussed the difficulty of deciding upon a stage persona and communicating a set of intended affects to their audience. Lisa reflected:

> I have read so much about it that in the end I just feel that whatever you do it is very difficult. It is going to work against you. I have worn a skirt. Sometimes it is because I am ironic. I have things in my hair that are ironic but also [the problem with] irony [is people] usually don't understand it really. You don't know. It can give the wrong signals. ... So I try to just do my thing as good as I can and not judge myself too much ... Maybe it is bad but at least I try to get up on stage. (personal communication, 20 March 1999)

Anna and Lisa felt that paying attention to their music was more important than concentrating on their stage performance. Consequently, they had tried to deflect attention away from the band members on stage by screening video projections during their live shows. Other musicians pointed to the familiar dilemma that, while they wished to present an interesting stage show, they were wary of wearing revealing clothes that might encourage male audience members and venue workers to judge them solely on their looks. Jae, the keyboard and saxophone player in the all-female band Bêtty Noire, described how one man who was working with the band had attempted to influence their image:

He always made comments about 'Why don't you wear more colourful clothes? Why don't you do this?' And I think it was all his idea of what we should look like and we have had a lot of blokes make those kind of comments. Like: 'Oh, if you wore short skirts you could go down really well' and I think you tend to resist even more. (personal communication, 4 March 1999)

Many female musicians discussed their awareness of the need to create an image and to offer an immediate visual impact when performing live. Bass player Emmy-Kate Montrose and vocalist Lauren Laverne from the band Kenickie considered the visual presentation of Kenickie on stage to be part of the marketing of the band:

Emmy-Kate: If people are paying, they are not just coming to hear you because they hear you when they play your records. They are coming for a visual package.

Lauren: A sensual package extravaganza.

Emmy-Kate: Even if you are not particularly pretty then you are stupid if you are going to go on looking like shit.
(personal communication, 9 May 1997)

Claire Lemmon, vocalist and guitarist with the all-female band Sidi Bou Said, referred to the connection between the band's visual presentation on stage and their record company's desire to promote a particular image of them for commercial gain. She commented that at the outset of their career the band members 'were very much new to this marketing game' (personal communication, 13 May 1995) and tended to wear somewhat plain clothes that they felt comfortable in and they believed would allow them to be taken seriously. She reflected that their record company subsequently 'had trouble marketing us ... because we weren't really one thing or another'. With an increased awareness of marketing concerns and sales figures, the band developed a more striking image: 'this album round, we tried to do something about it really ... we got co-ordinated'.

Sharon, vocalist and songwriter in the band Pooka, addressed the issue of on-stage image differently, by relating it to the musical output of the band. Pooka's first album was folk influenced and during the accompanying tour Sharon and Natasha wore jeans and checked shirts. It can be argued that there was a cultural fit between the music performed and the image selected. However, Sharon described how, when touring their second album, she had consciously selected clothes that were less 'everyday' in order to create a distinction between the clothes she wore in leisure time and those she performed in. She commented that she enjoyed 'the idea of going on stage and being a different person' (personal communication, 9 October 1997) and that this sense of transformation could be achieved by costume changes. The link between stage dress and particular musical genres was something to which members of Bêtty Noire also alluded. Alice (drums) and Helen (vocals) discussed the way in which their stage appearance helped to position them as indie performers:

Alice: I think we are quite happy with the way we look. We look sort of quite indie. We sort of go with the music. I think anything else would be too contrived.

Helen: We could look almost like a show band and it would make it ten times worse for us being female. If we even got into that territory, to try and keep indie would be really hard. We would almost be like a Robbie Williams band.
(personal communication, 4 March 1999)

The promotional video

A music video is a performance site where an artist or band's image is enacted, reinforced, developed or reinvented. The opportunity to promote a song is combined with a presentation of visual signifiers that communicate particular narratives about an artist. In purely economic terms, videos are largely used as a promotional tool for a new music release. Indeed, the number of agencies that deal with both video and advertising production confirms the strong association between video production and marketing.[21] The usefulness of music videos in marketing an artist is reflected in the amount of money invested by the industry in video production.[22] Record companies allocate considerable budgets to music videos in the hope of ensuring an innovative and engaging work that will receive widespread television coverage. Indeed, record companies sometimes finance the production of two totally different videos to promote just one song, so that they can target them at the different markets of Europe and the US, adapting the content to suit different geographical regions and different marketing strategies. Even editorial decisions on music videos are geared towards meeting the demands of the marketplace. The fast cutting between scenes is not only an aesthetic choice but also a financial imperative, ensuring that the videos are suitable for editing into short snippets for television broadcast.

The degree of financial commitment made by a record company to a promotional video influences the direction, style and content of the final product. Justine Frischmann of Elastica, for example, discussed how the band's editorial control over their videos was tied to their economic input:

> We've had complete control of our videos because we've had to pay for them 'cause our record company's quite small and everything and couldn't afford it and that's been really good. ... we've been allowed to do exactly what we want and we've storyboarded them ourselves and sat there in the editing room and said 'we want that and that. (personal communication, 13 February 1994)

This reveals the sliding scale of control a band or artist has over aspects of their professional life at any point in time. The amount of control that a performer can exercise in any given situation, whether on a video or photo shoot or during a press interview, must be understood as peculiar to that particular context. It relates to a host of variables including star status, contractual obligation and economics. It is useful to describe this as a sliding scale of control because it is not fixed throughout an artist's professional life nor is it consistent in all situations at any point in their career.

Leaving the issue of control and economics to one side for now, the discussion will turn to how video performances situate particular musicians within generic musical categories and work to shape the public associations of a performer or band.

While a set of images used in a video may be unique to a band, their presentation is generally consistent with particular stylistic and generic conventions. Thus while an almost infinite range of objects and settings may be featured in a music video, their style of presentation enables viewers to readily understand them within the signifying system of a particular music genre. Indeed, these conventions are so established that even when one is shown a reel of videos with the sound turned down, one is usually able easily to identify the musical style and genre from the mode of presentation. However, as John Mundy comments, despite this visual and musical 'fit', academic work has often 'ignored the ideological loadings associated with specific music genres' (Mundy, 1999: 241).[23] Indeed, as Goodwin has earlier discussed, academic studies of music video have all too often downplayed the importance of the music within music video and ignored the 'visual discourses in pop' (Goodwin, 1992: 2–3). The appearance of a performer in a video, their mode of dress and any knowledge one may already hold about them also assist the viewer in decoding the communication of the video. However, readings are also dependent on other elements, such as the selection and use of imagery, the lighting of the video, the speed of cutting the images, the framing of the singer, and the setting for the shoot.

Hole's video for the song 'Violet' may be taken as an example.[24] The video includes a succession of apparently unrelated images including twirling ballerinas, the crowning of a child beauty queen, a man's hand plunging into a jar of pickled eggs, and a number of rats scuttling along the floor. This montage of images is intercut with shots of band members posing on a couch, performing in a basement, playing before a crowd and stage-diving. The intense performance style of the band indicates that this presentation should be read as a rock video: Patty bashes the drums with great force; Eric, the guitarist, is bent over his instrument in a fury of playing; Melissa, the bass player, rocks back and forth; and Courtney Love offers a very agitated and physical vocal delivery, and in some sections of the video also plays guitar. The 'live' performance element serves a double function as it not only locates the montage of disparate images within a rock context but also connotes a sense of immediate and direct communication between the band and their audience. As Gracyk comments, 'live performance is so prominent in rock videos and the images of rock promotion and packaging ... for its totemic function. Images of live performance encourage fans to imagine that they can be in an immediate and thus genuine relationship with the musicians' (Gracyk, 1996: 78).

The entire video is shot in dim light, using a sepia filter for some sections, and the visual appearance is that of grainy, scratchy video footage rather than even-toned film stock. There are no clear establishing shots showing the performance space or slow panning shots of individual members of the band. Instead, the video has quite a jagged feel, with fast edited cuts between images. Rather than using carefully composed shots of the band performing, the camera pans shakily across the individual members of the band; images are sometimes half out of frame and the camera frequently drops in and out of focus. There are moments when the footage of Love singing does not synchronise with the recorded track being played. The fast cutting of the video and the unsteady camera angles convey a sense of energy and urgency. The dark feel of the video is a further indicator that this cannot be read as a pop performance. The grainy reproduction, dark lighting and shaky recording are all conventions that encourage the viewer to understand the presentation as an 'authentic' indie rock performance. The adoption of low production values and avoidance of slick camera techniques offers a sense of raw, direct communication reminiscent of documentary footage.

John Mundy has compared music videos to numbers in a Hollywood musical, reflecting that: 'these performers exist both within and outside the text, so that the performance in a specific text draws upon, amplifies and resonates with all those performances by that artist which exist in one form or another elsewhere' (1999: 243). Building from this, it can be argued that the viewer brings to the video not only any recollections they might have of other performances by that artist, but also any media mythologies, subcultural connections or artistic associations that may be connected with that artist. The example of the Hole video for the single 'Violet' may be taken once more. In this video Love wears an antique Victorian-style lace dress and, at another point, a ballerina costume with a multilayered lace tutu. This selection of battered antique lace dresses became almost a trademark of the singer during this period of her career and was christened the 'kinder whore' look in the print media.[25] The mode of dress reinforces Love's established public image and connects her with a particular underground indie fashion. The depiction of Hole performing in a basement and Love stage-diving into a densely packed crowd is a sequence of the video that offers a visual reference to US alternative rock and associated subcultural practices. Love is also presented on stage in a pole-dancing club, an image that has resonances for viewers aware of her previous, much publicised employment as a club stripper. The video operates not only as a publicity device for a new release but also as a way of reinforcing Hole's image as a credible indie rock band.

The press interview

The press interview can also be read as a performance site as it is a staged event where musicians are given the opportunity to project an image of themselves, to cite their influences, and to describe or situate their work within a particular personal, cultural or political context. Of course, the way in which a journalist uses this material may alter or shift the emphasis given by the performer in interview. As Negus comments, a journalist can 'assert their autonomy by reporting things which have been said off-the-record or by relaying events which contradict the image of the act. In addition a journalist may misrepresent the artist by being selective with quotes, can be bluntly sarcastic or simply resort to personal abuse' (Negus, 1992: 124). As discussed earlier in this book, female performers are frequently presented in the print media in ways that are distinct from the treatments afforded male performers. However, it is important not to view the rock interview as a space where a musician reveals their true self, but as an opportunity for the musician to present or reinforce their public image. The comments of the female-centred band Kenickie illustrated the difficulties faced by musicians when undertaking a press interview. Members of the band described how the angle a journalist wished to take was obvious from their line of questioning. Bass player Emmy-Kate Montrose and guitarist Marie du Santiago commented:

> Emmy-Kate: You can usually tell by their line of questioning. You go 'the album, the album, the album', [and they ask] 'So then, are you the thin fat slags?'[26]

> Marie: They will go: 'I like your songs. Do you like sex?', and you'll go: 'Is this relevant?', and they'll go: 'I mean sheds ...'
> (personal communication, 9 May 1997)

The band explained that generally journalists approached the interview with certain preconceptions about the band, which were often replicated in their written articles through the careful selection of quotes that fitted with that image. A press interview can thus be understood as a meeting where both the artist or band and the interviewer attempt to direct the topics under discussion and to control the information revealed. Active within this process is the artists' press officer, whose role is both to attract media attention to their clients and to attempt to ensure that the attention is favourable. As a number of critics have pointed out, the nature of the music industry is such that publicists and record companies attempt to court a favourable reaction from the media through a system of gifts or a guarantee of interviews with sought-after artists, while 'punishing' disobedient journalists and music papers by withdrawing access to their artists or advertising revenue.[27] Naturally, Kenickie had such a media guardian in their out-of-house press agent.

Little academic attention has, however, been given to the 'management' of interviews by musicians themselves.[28] Keith Negus has undertaken qualitative research with industry insiders such as record company representatives, public relations officers, managers and music publishers. In a discussion of music journalism, Negus offers a detailed account of the role of the record company publicity officer in courting journalists and arranging interviews. However, he does not draw on any interviews with musicians or consider how they are active within the publicity process. Kenickie discussed the different ways in which they directed interviewers away from certain topics and on to other discussion points. Marie du Santiago stated that she would actually reprimand writers who asked her 'stupid questions'. Remarking that many writers wished to compare them only with other female artists, lead vocalist Lauren Laverne commented that she would tell journalists she did not like any other female bands, in order to guide the interviewer towards a different emphasis. While the topic of 'women in rock' is an obvious tack for journalists interviewing female-centred bands to take, Kenickie noticed that journalists sometimes switched their angle when an alternative interesting topic arose during the interview upon which the final written piece could pivot. The band reflected on an interview they had undertaken with a journalist from a music paper who was trying to goad them into talking about gender issues or drug taking:

> Lauren: As soon as our Socialist tendencies came to the fore, his sheets blew across the room and he knew where his questions were going.

Marie: You say 'Yes, I do think I'm a feminist' or 'Yes, I do think I'm a socialist' and he goes 'Brilliant! They are communists!'
(personal communication, 9 May 1997)

A number of interviewees mentioned that journalists frequently attempted to steer the conversation towards sensationalist topics. Conscious of what sells copy, writers predictably ask questions about sex and drug use. Kathleen Hanna, of US band Le Tigre and founder member of Bikini Kill, commented that during the time she performed with Bikini Kill journalists repeatedly asked her questions about the men that she associated with, her sexual past and work she had undertaken in a strip club (personal communication, 29 November 2000). She reflected that questions about her music were left out in a pursuit of more salacious copy. This tendency was also noted by Miki Berenyi, who was vocalist and guitarist in the female-centred UK indie band Lush. She discussed one press interview where the writer said: '"So, you have got a bit of a reputation as smackheads". We were like, "Fuck off! We have never really had a reputation as a drug band". He was obviously waiting for us to say "Yeah, we've dabbled". Talking bollocks just to get a quote out of you' (personal communication, 20 January 1996).

The interview is a site where a musician makes public supposedly private thoughts or reflections on their personal life and music. However, the frequency with which particular phrases appear in interviews indicates that musicians employ certain standard answering techniques to commonly asked questions. These stock phrases are relied upon by performers regardless of their gender. These replies may be understood as strategies for managing the interview situation and attempts to deflect any unwanted associations from their public image. For instance, music papers and style magazines frequently group a selection of contemporary artists together and present them to their readers as a particular trend, such as 'female-fronted bands', or as a new and emerging music movement, such as 'the new wave of the new wave' heralded in the music papers in the mid-1990s, or the rather short-lived 'movement' of 'yob rock'[29] in 1996.[30] There is a danger in being grouped as part of a transient fad as this could potentially limit future media attention and result in a drop-off of the public profile of a band. In order to be viewed as individual and distinct, band members often refuse to ally themselves with any of their contemporaries or to describe themselves as part of a current scene.

Moreover, musicians often try to promote the worth of their music by emphasising the challenging and contemporary nature of their work. This self-promotion is a common response to requests by the interviewer to name comparable artists. For example, Luke Haines of UK band Black Box Recorder stated of a new record release, 'although it's an obvious thing to say, this is a more realistic record of the time. It reflects England now; I'm not a fan of nostalgia' (O'Connell, 1998: 10), while in another interview Australian singer-songwriter Ben Lee commented, 'I want to speak the language of the time I'm in' (Martin, 1999: 10). Such responses are most often given by new and emerging bands, or established artists who wish to reposition their public image as, in these instances, it is crucial that the musicians are perceived as offering music listeners something new and worthwhile. While responses such as 'we aren't following, we're creating something *completely* new'[31] may seem rather trite and unhelpful to the music buyer, they do help to prevent an artist being lumped together with other artists and viewed as just offering another version of the 'same old thing'.

However, this is not to say that musicians seldom compare themselves to other performers. As press interviews are opportunities to play the role of the 'rock star', performers may wish to situate themselves within a lineage of rock celebrities. To avoid the problem of being classified with other similar performers competing for the same market, artists are highly selective in their cited reference points. Musicians most frequently compare themselves to older classic or critically acclaimed artists or to contemporary, credible, but little known bands. The comments of Daniel Boone, guitarist with London-based band The Crocketts, are a case in point: 'We just listen to crooners like Jim Reeves, Max Boyce and Elvis. They're the only people we agree on' (Myers, 1998: 10). In early interviews, female-centred band Elastica cited the Buzzcocks, Wire and The Stranglers as their influences. Lead singer Justine Frischmann remarked:

> I think it does help people to get a very simple message across because you really can only get a very simple message across when you are presenting yourself in the music papers or whatever and sort of giving people a clue about how to listen to you or how to view you can help. (personal communication, 13 February 1994)

These conventions within press interviews indicate high media literacy among musicians and demonstrate their agency in shaping their own public images. Unfortunately, there is not room to discuss a large number of common interview statements and replies in detail. Nevertheless, by considering the interview as a site of performance, one may understand common and repeated phrases not simply as rock clichés but also as tactics in developing a successful public persona.

Photo shoots

By examining the photo shoot as a performance site this section focuses on the *process* involved in producing a photographic image of a band or artist. While a photograph of a band is a frozen moment, very rarely is it an innocent capturing or recording of the daily life of a group of musicians. Photographs used to promote a band may be taken from carefully staged photo sessions or selected from a commissioned set of prints taken during a live performance. As Gracyk points out, 'What we seldom see, in photographs or videos, is the reality of the creative process. The images in which rock is packaged and promoted tend to deny the recording process' (Gracyk, 1996: 76). Indeed, as Gracyk (1996: 75) argues, photographs of rock musicians 'are highly selective and distorting'. Analysis of the production of band photographs can consider how the composure and staging of such photography taps into particular rock aesthetics, mythologies and marketing aims.

The commissioning of photography to market artists shares a number of similarities with video in its intention to communicate certain visual significations to a music-buying public for promotional purposes. As Goodwin has pointed out, the visual has always been important in the promotion of popular music, as demonstrated in early rock 'n' roll films, record covers, advertising and photographs in newspapers and magazines (Goodwin, 1992: 8). Each element within the composure of the photograph (from the way that the musicians are standing, their facial expressions, the clothes that they are wearing, to the location and whether they are featured with or without their musical instruments) contributes to the way that the visual semiotics are decoded and the artist's musical reference points are understood. As Negus comments, the images produced in photographic shoots 'are often highly imitative of existing styles, and initially articulate an artist's identity in terms of a series of visual clichés which translate the classification of performers into long term career acts and short term fashion dependent acts into a series of natural/artificial codes' (Negus, 1992: 67).

A number of musicians communicated their acute awareness of the aesthetics involved in promotional photography and the difficulty they had in deciding upon a workable image. I noticed differences in attitude and agency between bands that were in possession of a recording contract and those that were unsigned. Helen, lead singer with Bêtty Noire, commented on how conventions of indie band photo shoots influenced the way in which the band decided to stage their promotional pictures and selected the clothes that they wore:

> We have always tried to have a sort of indie image on the photos rather than a type of 'aren't we cute?' type of image. So we have had ones where we are all wearing dark clothing and looking quite solemn and things like outdoors casual clothing type of setting. (personal communication, 4 March 1999)

In this instance, as the band had not signed a record deal, the band's image evolved through a discussion between band members and a local photographer. At this stage of Bêtty Noire's development the framing of the image was crucial as it was important that the photograph could communicate ideas about the band's sound and attitude to people unfamiliar with their work, such as venue and event promoters, A&R scouts and record company executives.

By contrast, at the time of interview, Pooka held a major label record deal. The band had recently released their second album, *Spinning*, which featured a photograph of the duo on the front cover. Photographs of the band were commissioned for both albums and appeared on each release. A shift can be noted in the stylistics of the photographs. The first album presents a very 'natural' image of the band members, free of any cosmetics, while the image on the front cover of the second album, and those printed on the CD inlay, offer a very styled image of the band that is much more akin to fashion photography. The front cover of *Spinning* pictures Natasha wearing a black, low-cut sleeveless top and lace-edged skirt and Sharon wearing a sleeveless top and black trousers. Both women are sitting on the floor by what appears to be a hotel bar. The photographs included within the CD inlay present Sharon and Natasha in various outfits with the backdrop offering glimpses of a hotel interior. The change in the visual presentation of the band forms part of an artist development strategy wherein the performers' musical progression and innovation is signalled through their remodelled image. The band linked the music that they produced on the two albums to the choice of different imagery. As vocalist and co-songwriter Natasha commented:

> our image suited that [first] album. It was very stripped down, very naked music. Also the pictures in the album cover are quite straight. There is no make-up on. They are quite close up. It shows that vulnerability. It is quite naked. With this album, it is dressed up a bit. It is a bit more flamboyant, a bit less emotional. So that suits the image. We have discussed what we want the album to look like and stuff. (personal communication, 9 October 1997)

However, the band did not suggest that the development in their music style had a natural echo in their image and style choices. Instead, Natasha and Sharon discussed how their photographs had been staged with the aim of best promoting their new release and under the guidance of a stylist commissioned by their record company. As Sharon remarked:

> We made the album a long time ago … and they [the record company] wanted a new marketing angle on us. We felt like this is a new beginning. … So when they came up with this fresh approach to marketing it, they wanted to have us on the cover as well. I don't have a problem with that because I think that will help with the marketing to have us on the cover. (personal communication, 9 October 1997)

Such comments give the impression of a healthy degree of consultation between musicians, photographers and record companies, and a considerable amount of control and input by the artist. Yet, while it would be erroneous to draw a general principle from these individual cases, these examples serve to show the motivations and intentions that contribute to the selection and composure of band photographs. However, the dynamics between photographer and musician change dramatically when the agent commissioning the images is altered. One may take the example of photographs taken for a magazine or music paper. The brief behind the commissioning of these shots is obviously to produce interesting and striking images of musicians that will help to engage the interest of the reader. It is not in a picture editor's brief to prioritise the marketing strategies of the featured artists but to consider the marketing aims and demographics of the publication. This is not to ignore the close relationship between record company press officers and publications, but to highlight that while both depend on the figure of the artist, their relationship is distinct. Thus, as a number of musicians commented in interview, the control artists have over these images is more restricted. As Justine Frischmann reflected: 'with photo sessions usually a magazine will pay for a photographer. They kind of are a bit arsey with you if you don't do what they ask you to' (personal communication, 13 February 1994).

Julie Cafritz, former member of US band Pussy Galore and member of the female-centred four-piece band Free Kitten, explained how the demands of press photography were such that the performer is often in a position of reduced control. Cafritz described one press shoot she had been involved in, which was organised to accompany an article in a music publication. The photographer requested a particular staging of the shoot and asked her to hold a gun. While she expressed unhappiness at the type of images being used, she was encouraged to comply with the photographer's request on the understanding that a picture of the band would be used on the front cover of the publication. She commented:

> The whole thing was: 'This is going to be the cover. Possibly a cover shoot!' ... I was saying to the photographer, 'I don't want to do this. ... Do I look like a James Bond girl?' ... The label guy goes 'I will make sure he doesn't use these shots but this is a cover we are shooting.' And of course it wasn't on the cover and they used the fucking picture where I am kissing the thing, with my butt out with the gun. (personal communication, 9 January 1995)

This anecdote gives an indication of the pressure felt by artists to conform with photographers' requests in the hope of advantageous publicity. Cafritz's comments also highlight the tendency within the music press to sexualise female performers through the commissioning and selection of photographic images, a trend noted by Davies (2001: 304) in her study of the British rock press. Kim Gordon, bass player in the US band Sonic Youth and fellow band member in Free Kitten, suggested that the reluctance of artists to compromise themselves in magazine photo shoots has led to the development of a notable aesthetic: 'That's why there are so many pictures of bands standing around looking bored. ... It is hard to photograph four or five people and get a good photograph but nobody wants to do that thing with props' (personal communication, 9 January 1995). Some artists have attempted to avoid the 'problem' of press shoots altogether. UK band Belle And Sebastian, for example, have submitted photographs of friends instead of picturing themselves; London-based Linus sent a drawing of themselves in response to a request for a photograph by a magazine; and the US band Le Tigre have insisted in some instances on selecting the photographer for press shoots. The images used in publications, while dependent upon individual photographers, also reflect the agency of the musicians involved and their ability to 'manage' the press.

Conclusion

This exploration of some of the performance sites of female-centred bands indicates that performances are not produced from an endless chain of creative possibilities but are selected and produced within financial and stylistic constraints. This statement is not intended to give the impression of formulaic productions or highly redundant images and sounds. Indeed it is desirable that the images and sonic dimensions of a band performing live or on video are fresh and engaging in order to excite the interest of the viewer or fan. However, it is important that these dimensions are understood within the signifying systems of particular musical genres to aid classification of the music, identification with an audience and marketing of an act. The interview material reviewed here illustrates how sensitive musicians are to these concerns. This discussion of photography and image making has not mentioned issues of sleeve design for music releases, band logos or the use and design of associated imagery. Admittedly these elements are not sites of performance for individual band members. However, they do represent related areas of complementary image making that tap in to and exploit established conventions within music genres.

Moreover, although this chapter has focused on female-centred bands, the principal concerns of representation and control are applicable to all bands. Within each area of performance it is clear that the final production is dependent upon a number of factors, including the creation and maintenance of artist image, the relationship with an audience (whether physically present or conceived) and the resources available. Further to this, the performance is reliant upon the interaction and input of a number of interested parties, from band members to producers, advisers, stylists and publicists. By choosing to explore a range of performance sites this chapter has considered how artists adapt and refine their public selves in sympathy with different mediums, whether through the 'direct communication' of the live event or the mediation of a press interview.

Notes

1   See Strachan and Leonard (2003) for a discussion of the singer-songwriter.

2   See, for example, the discussion of the girls of 'punk subversion' by Press (1997: 293–301), comment on Lennox in O'Brien (1995: 252f), discussion of Madonna by Kellner (1995: 263–96) and comment on Madonna by Paglia (1992: 6–13).

3   Annie Lennox's comments on this are printed in O'Brien (1995: 252).

4   k.d. lang's public identity as a lesbian worked to satirise her performance of conventional heterosexual matrimony. For a discussion of this and of lang's changing public image see Bruzzi (1997).

5   Courtney Love was nominated for 'Best Actress' at the US Golden Globe Awards in 1997 for her role in Milo Forman's film *The People Versus Larry Flynt*.

6   Queercore refers to a number of punk rock bands with gay and lesbian members whose lyrics are concerned with sex and sexuality. Among the bands who have been labelled as part of this 'movement' are the all-female band Tribe 8 (San Francisco), the female-centred group Sister George (London), the band God Is My Co-Pilot (New York) and the male band Pansy Division (San Francisco). For a further discussion of the subject see Daly and Wice (1995: 196–7), Gill (1995: 168–70) and Kearney (1997: 207–29).

7   A number of critics have offered comment on this performance. See, for example, Fuchs (1998: 101–18), Kearney (1997: 207–29), McDonnell (1997: 453–63) and Padel (2000: 320–21).

8   For an account of this television appearance see Hopper (1997: 66).

9   Bikini Kill were prominent promoters of riot grrrl from the early 1990s. A detailed discussion of riot grrrl is given in Chapters 5 and 6. However, it is worth noting that there is a certain amount of crossover between the categories riot grrrl and queercore. Indeed Bikini Kill appear on the EP 'There's A Dyke In The Pit' (Outpunk) with the all-female US bands Tribe 8, Lucy Stoners and 7 Year Bitch.

10   A discussion of live performances by Bikini Kill may be found later in the book.

11   With reference to this see, for example, McRobbie (1989: 23–49), Reynolds (1989: 250–51) and Davies (1995: 124).

12   For a discussion of this in relation to British indie music of the 1980s see Reynolds (1989: 250–51).

13   For critical accounts of Madonna see Franks (1995) and hooks (1995).

14   See Théberge (1991) for a discussion of the targeting of music technologies to male readers of music magazines in the 1980s, and Keightley (1996) for a consideration of gender in relation to hi-fi technology in the late 1940s and 1950s.

15   See, for instance, discussions by Steward and Garratt (1984: 112–26) and Bayton (1997).

16   Frith and McRobbie (1990: 374) define 'cock rock' as 'music making in which performance is an explicit, crude, and often aggressive expression of male sexuality – it's the style of rock presentation that links a rock and roller like Elvis Presley to rock stars like Mick Jagger, Roger Daltrey, and Robert Plant'.

17   Feigenbaum's (2005) study of the press reception of folk-rock artist Ani DiFranco reveals that the dominant reading of this artist's performance is the label 'angry female singer'.

18   A&R (artist and repertoire) personnel of record companies are responsible for 'talent spotting' musicians and groups. Duties of A&R personnel include the evaluation of unsigned artists, negotiation of record company contracts, and liaison between artists and other music industry personnel. For a discussion of the activities and beliefs of A&R departments see Negus (1992: 38–61).

19   See Shuker (1998: 218) and Thornton (1995).

20   The US all-male band Pearl Jam were labelled as part of the 'grunge' rock movement of the early 1990s. They released their debut album *Ten* in the same year as Nirvana released the platinum-selling album *Nevermind*. Despite their commercial success Nirvana continued to enjoy a popularity and credibility within 'underground' indie rock scenes. During the 1990s Pearl Jam, while eventually outselling Nirvana, were not critically acclaimed by indie rock critics or within underground scenes as they were viewed as corporate (or major label) representatives of the grunge movement. Indeed, in reference to Pearl Jam, Kurt Cobain remarked to a journalist, 'I would love to be erased from my association with that band and other corporate bands like the Nymphs and a few other felons. I do feel a duty to warn the kids of false music that's claiming to be underground. They're jumping on the alternative bandwagon' (Azerrad, 1994: 35).

21   As Keith Negus rightly points out, there are clear differences between the production of an advertisement and a music video in terms of budgets, time frames and the restrictions imposed by the need to promote an artist. However, a person who gains the experience of directing a music video (using on-screen promotional devices) can later develop their career producing advertisements (Negus, 1992: 99).

22   For example Jack Banks (1998: 295), drawing on trade magazine reports, notes 'the average budget for videos rose from $15,000 in 1981, to $40,000–50,000 in 1984, and $50,000–60,000 in 1988, remaining at $60,000–80,000 in the 1990s.'

23   An exception being Mark Fenster's (1993: 109–28) article on country music video. Here Fenster argues that country performance videos 'differentiate themselves from those of pop or rock not only through the song, but also through set design, costume and the singer's style of performance' (1993: 120). See also Strachan (2006) for a discussion of indie rock video.

24   I shall leave aside a discussion of the motifs and narrative elements of the video. These appear to be concerned with images of femininity and the male gaze.

25   Many references were made to this particular fashion by writers in the style and news media. The look was discussed in detail by Joan Smith (1994: 52–4) and Sarra Manning (1998: 72–6).

26   'The Fat Slags' are cartoon characters featured in the satirical Newcastle-upon-Tyne publication *Viz*. As Kenickie were based in Sunderland, this was an obvious (albeit tiresome and insulting) frame of reference for journalistic copy.

27   See Negus (1992: 124), Stratton (1982: 168–9), Hesmondhalgh (1996: 129) and Wade (1972: 263).

28   An exception being a paper by Spencer Leigh (1999) based upon Leigh's experience of interviewing musicians for the UK regional radio station BBC Radio Merseyside and various music magazines.

29   'Yob rock', used as a category to describe bands such as Oasis, Northern Uproar and 60ft Dolls, was debated in *Melody Maker*, 29 June 1996: 30–33.

30   For a further discussion of this practice see Toynbee (1993).

31   Julie Sims of the UK band Tiger, quoted in Upton (1996: 55).

Chapter 5

The riot grrrl network: grrrl power in indie rock

So far this book has considered the importance of gender within indie rock culture and within the media coverage and performance strategies of indie rock musicians. It now proceeds to relate this analysis to the emergence of 'riot grrrl', a feminist network initiated by female-centred indie rock bands. Riot grrrl developed in 1991, out of the 'underground' indie music communities of Olympia, Washington and Washington, DC. It was first promoted by members of the female-centred bands Bratmobile and Bikini Kill, who voiced the idea of girls and women asserting themselves through underground music. This chapter does not aim to present a synopsis or definitive version of riot grrrl but rather to give a series of impressions of it by detailing the words and activities of some of those involved from its outset. Riot grrrl is particularly relevant to the present discussion as members of this network critiqued the masculine culture of indie rock music and the wider music industry.[1] Moreover, riot grrrls disrupted conventions within the live performance of indie rock and presented new ways of relating to music journalists.

Riot grrrl's development parallels the way in which a number of youth subcultures have established themselves. It emerged from within 'underground' music circles; was promoted through gigs, events and zine networks; and was greeted with considerable levels of fascination by the mass media. This chapter will investigate to what extent subcultural theories and approaches offer useful frameworks for understanding riot grrrl. It will consider how from the beginning riot grrrls demonstrated a clear awareness of themselves as cultural curiosities, often attempting to thwart the efforts of journalists and critics to neatly summarise their activities and significance. Focusing on the beginnings and development of riot grrrl the discussion will highlight the challenges of theorising and representing such an evolving and self-reflexive music culture.

Context

Both the time at which riot grrrl emerged and its promotion by indie musicians are significant. The increasing visibility of female performers in this music genre by the early 1990s was evident from the high media profile enjoyed by female-centred bands such as Babes In Toyland and L7, and female musicians such as Kim Gordon of Sonic Youth and Free Kitten, and Kim Deal of The Pixies and The Breeders. The signing of Hole by Geffen records, reportedly for the largest amount ever paid for a female-centred band, demonstrated the growing economic investment in 'women in rock'. In the same period, a number of feminist organisations were founded by female rock musicians. Exene Cervenka of the band X, along with the rock promoter Nicole Panter, founded the Bohemian Women's Political Alliance, aimed at promoting sexual awareness and feminism, organising voter registration, recommending candidates and organising benefits. In defence of women's reproductive rights the all-female alternative rock band L7 and the associate editor of *LA Weekly,* Sue Cummings, helped to implement 'Rock For Choice' benefits. Supported by the Feminist Majority Foundation and Fund, concerts were organised across the US 'to encourage audience members to educate themselves, speak out, register to vote and learn what they can do to protect their right to abortion and birth control'.[2] In 1993 a small group of New York women formed Strong Women In Music (SWIM), 'to discuss their roles as women in the music community, and work out possible group solutions/supports/actions to problems that women have previously had to deal with on an individual basis'.[3]

The activities of riot grrrls should be situated within this context, but they also have connections with other groups. An obvious link may be made with the queercore movement within 'underground' rock music. As du Plessis and Chapman discuss in their consideration of queercore, by creating a compound of 'queer' and 'hardcore' participants in this movement 'signalled their allegiances to post-punk subculture, but also positioned themselves as equally distinct from lesbian and gay culture and the masculinist tendencies of hardcore punk' (du Plessis and Chapman, 1997: 48). Female-centred bands connected with riot grrrl, such as Huggy Bear and Bikini Kill, specifically link themselves to this, stating: 'punckrock [*sic*] is a queer scene / punkrock is queercore a call to the multi trajectorised sex'.[4] This identification with queercore was also made by many riot grrrl zine writers,[5] who discussed issues such as lesbian visibility, promoted queercore bands and included personal accounts by girls about their sexuality. As Cateforis and Humphreys (1997) reflect, in their study of a riot grrrl group in New York City, the New York hardcore scene of the 1980s had alienated many gay and lesbian members due to a number of homophobic incidents. In contrast, Riot Grrrl NYC attracted many lesbian and bisexual women 'because for the first time they had an opportunity within their own musical scene to express their desires and explore their identities' (Cateforis and Humphreys, 1997: 328). With respect to this issue of identity construction Halberstam has argued that the association of certain rock genres with particular productions of masculinity, far from being off-putting to queer women, might actually be a point of appeal. She points out that in existing and

> recent work on girls and subcultures, there tends to be little recognition that some girls, usually queer girls, may in fact involve themselves in subcultures precisely because of the 'strong masculine overtones' associated with the activity. Thus, a young queer girl interested in punk will not be put off by the masculinity of the subculture; she may as easily be seduced by it. (Halberstam, 2003: 322)

Certainly this dimension should be acknowledged in building a picture of riot grrrl for, as Kearney (1997) has pointed out, it is important not to ignore the connections between lesbianism, queercore and riot grrrl in developing an understanding of this initiative.

Terminology

Journalists employed a range of different terms to describe riot grrrl. Some writers chose to describe riot grrrl in terms of an identifiable collective: the *New York Times* referred to riot grrrl as a 'scene' (Japenga, 1992: 30) while *US Today* detailed 'an underground group of punkettes'[6] (Snead, 1992: 5D). More common were the descriptions of a new 'movement' (found in US publications such as *Fiz* and *LA Weekly*, and UK music magazines such as *Select* and *The Zine*) and the term 'network', which appeared in numerous articles including the coverage by *Crack DC* (US), *Lime Lizard* (UK) and *Elle* (UK). Publications produced by those involved in riot grrrl reveal a similar range of collective terms. A zine produced by a New York group of riot grrrls highlights how differing descriptions were encouraged and valued. It includes a selection of comments by different female writers that offer a variety of definitions of riot grrrl as 'a support network', 'a state of mind', 'a group of women (grrrls) who work together' and 'a community of co-operative young women' (*Riot Grrrl #5*, NYC: 1–2, 21). This chapter employs the term 'network' to refer to riot grrrls collectively, for while it identifies lines of interconnection, it does not suggest a singular voice or aim. The term is also particularly apt because of its reference to the process of making contacts through informal society meetings. Riot grrrl developed and spread through social communication at gigs and through zines. Moreover, as Pinterics has commented, third-wave feminism places considerable emphasis on 'synthesis, coalition building, and networking' (2001: 16). The employment of the term 'network' here also aids a conceptualisation of riot grrrl as sympathetic with, or indeed an example of, third-wave feminist initiatives.

The utilisation of the neologism 'grrrl' sets the agenda for this network. The traditional feminist insistence on the use of the term 'woman' has, it can be argued, to some extent reduced the value of the term 'girl'. Where 'woman' has been equated with an empowered feminist adult, 'girls', defined by their immaturity, have been depoliticised. Riot grrrl was then a reclamation of the word 'girl' and a representation of it as a wholly positive term: 'she [a grrrl] can do anything she wants ... she (you) are [*sic*] a powerful person to the degree that you can hold the powers that enable you to be free of a lot of things – sexism, phat-ism, racism, homophobia' (*Notta Babe!* #1: 46). The term 'grrrl' was invested with a new set of connotations. It signified a feisty, assertive girl or woman, who relished a political engagement with feminist issues. Kay, co-author of *Intimate Wipe*, commented on the strength she found in bridging definitions: 'Not a girl because of the easy cook rice & the late bedtimes. Not a woman because of the pre-pubescent dresses, the messy bedroom & the toys' (*Intimate Wipe*: 2). Those involved in the network celebrated the use of the term riot grrrl as an empowering label.

The term 'riot' is also very significant. Magazine reports, in attempting to understand the origins of the 'phenomenon', stated that a friend of Allison Wolfe, of the band Bratmobile, coined the term 'riot grrrl'. Inspired by the Mount Pleasant riots in Washington, DC, in 1991, she reportedly wrote to Allison proclaiming a desire for a girl riot in the DC underground music scene. Some of those involved with riot grrrl were less keen to historicise the network, concerned that this may have the effect of curtailing its dynamic energy. Whatever the origin of the phrase, it is effective both as a call to action and as a description of a state of rebellion. The use of the phrase has a further dimension for it draws on the exaggeration of media language. Terry Ann Knopf's comments on the use of the term riot are relevant. She notes, 'the continued media use of the term contributes to an emotionally charged climate in which the public tends to view every event as an "incident", every incident as a "disturbance" and every disturbance as a "riot"' (Knopf, quoted in Cohen, 1980: 32). The network of grrrls who used this term revelled in the media use of this terminology to create public trepidation. Riot grrrl so named itself in incubus, inviting alarm and drawing on the concept of disobedience, when no action had yet been publicly taken.

Totally grrrl powered: beginnings and development.

The International Pop Underground Convention of August 1991, organised by Calvin Johnson and Candice Pederson of the independent label K Records in Olympia, Washington, was a demonstration of what Bikini Kill named 'revolution grrrl-style now!'[7] The first night of this five-day event was 'Girl Night', when female musicians performed, grrrl zines were distributed, and female audience members collectively countered instances of sexism. As information about riot grrrl spread, networks of girls and women in the US and Britain became involved, communicating by post, at meetings and through zines. Riot grrrl offered a vehicle for empowerment for many of those involved. As Angel states, 'it's about love and communication and networking and productivity and learning. ... we can get a lot done and have a lot of power if we just pool our ideas and resources' (*Persephone's Network*: 12).

Visible instances of the spread of this network in the US and the UK were the emergence of new zines (Figure 5.1) and female bands identifying themselves as riot grrrls. It is very difficult to ascertain how many zines connected with riot grrrl have been produced since 1991, as they were often produced in very small numbers with restricted distribution. During the research for this book 162 publications were collected (the majority of which were concerned with riot grrrl), but this is of course a mere fraction of the number of zines produced in the name of riot grrrl. A list of the zines collected, along with dates and place of publication, is presented in Appendix 1. The distribution of zines was aided by the foundation of the Riot Grrrl Press in Olympia, Washington, which endeavoured to copy and distribute any grrrl zine that was forwarded to it. The number of bands inspired by riot grrrl is also difficult to establish. In December 1993 Karren, a British zine writer, identified 47 new grrrl bands that had formed that year.[8] Of course, a very considerable number of bands has since formed in Europe, Australia, the US and beyond inspired by the activities and legacy of riot grrrl. For instance, ten years after Karren's initial statement Clair, a member of Riot Grrrl London, described how she had formed a female-centred band where 'all three of us were inspired by Riot Grrrl and had the positive "we can do it" vibe, which I think came from this inspiration' (personal communication, 28 July 2003).

Figure 5.1   Selection of zines published in the UK

Performance

The musicians involved in riot grrrl challenged the notion that indie music was free from the discourse of patriarchy. On their joint tour in 1993 Bikini Kill and the British band Huggy Bear problematised the gendered way in which an audience views a live performance. I attended two of these gigs: one that took place in Derby in the English Midlands and another in Newport, Wales. Before the bands performed they issued handouts that requested girls and women to stand near the front of the stage rather than towards the back. The handout commented that the front-of-stage area usually excluded women due to the violence of slamdancing or the potential for harassment.[9] Moreover, the text stressed the importance of female address and identification, stating: 'I really wanna look at female faces while I perform. I want HER to know that she is included in this show, that what we are doing is for her to CRITICIZE / LAUGH AT / BE INSPIRED BY / HATE / WHATEVER' (Bikini Kill/ Huggy Bear handout, 1993). The bands thus forced a renegotiation of the spaces that girls and women traditionally inhabit at gigs. Moreover, live performances would regularly be stopped and house lights brought up when male audience members refused to move to the back or vocalised their irritation at the bands' policy of prioritising female audience members. The banter between the band and audience, with the temporary halting of a performance, actually became a regular part of these live gigs. The two shows I attended were especially notable in this respect. During the gig in Derby a member of Huggy Bear was physically assaulted by an audience member causing disruption of the show. Disruption of the performance was also an element of the gig in Newport when Bikini Kill objected to the presence of male security workers guarding the front-of-stage area. Whether or not this conflict was encouraged by the performers or an inevitable outcome of challenging convention, the gigs forced the issue of how people negotiate performances in a gendered way. Reflecting on this strategy Kathleen Hanna of Bikini Kill has commented that she felt that her request had an important impact: 'I think it worked really well. I think that even saying girls to the front even once just echoed through the woods and through the trees and everywhere' (personal communication, 29 November 2000).

Similarly Pete Dale, co-founder of the UK-based independent record label and distribution network Slampt, reflected that these gigs had a considerable impact:

> I went to about half the shows on the Huggy Bear/Bikini Kill tour of the UK in early '93, in fact our band Pussycat Trash were the extra support at a few of the gigs, and as far as I could tell the 'Girls to the front' policy worked a treat – the band would request it, the girls would do it, the boys would get pissed off – perfect! I think the Riot Grrrl-era helped to improve the self-policing behaviour of people at punk shows, and it remains improved to this day. (personal communication, 5 November 1999)

These gigs also undermined other music performance conventions. Riot grrrl opened up the gig environment as a place for debate, not just an area of passive viewing. By requesting that people change their viewing habits Huggy Bear and Bikini Kill stimulated a response. They ignored the customs usually employed in maintaining distance between performer and audience, thus breaking down their ideological separation. Kay, co-producer of the zines *Intimate Wipe* and *Go Go Girl*, recalled the impact that these gigs had on her as an audience member:

> The extent to which power structures are enforced through the spatial politics of fun didn't really sink in until then and I wasn't even at the more infamously violent gigs on that tour. The other thing I enjoyed about those shows was the greater level of interactivity. Backstage was pretty much open access, the bands were much more talkative (in fact people were in general), and the microphone was handed round in between the songs and left on in-between sets. (personal communication, 23 August 2000).

Hecklers were engaged with rather than ignored, and girls at the front of the stage were passed the microphone to voice their anger at harassment at gigs. Margaret, author of the US zine *Quit Whining*, commented that this new approach to performances was demonstrated on 'Girl's Night', the evening of female performance that formed part of the International Pop Underground Convention: 'Girl's Night seemed to be more than just a show; there was a sense of sharing between the performers and the audience. A forum. The arrangement of acts was informal and somewhat of a open mike, no order of importance' (*Quit Whining* #1: 5).

In addition to dismantling the power relationship between performer and audience, these shows allowed other voices to be heard. The New York-based spoken-word performer Juliana Luecking commented on the encouragement she received from Kathleen Hanna of Bikini Kill, who reduced the length of her own spoken-word set in order to grant Luecking time to recite a monologue. Luecking described how the audience was very receptive of her monologue, in which she talked about the events and lifestyles of the people that surrounded her, and about issues of sexuality. Luecking commented that she enjoyed performing at music gigs as the other venues in which she regularly performed, such as galleries and community centres, did not have the same potential for communication with the audience. She explained that when she performed between music sets, she would receive a direct reaction to her material both in the response of the crowd as a whole and through the individuals who came to talk to her after her performance: 'This audience of homo friendly punks is my absolute favourite. I learn more from these individuals … than I do from someone telling me about how my art fits into other artistic periods or groups' (personal communication, 20 August 1994).

The riot grrrl gigs also allowed for previously silenced voices to be heard. An incident that occurred at the International Pop Festival in 1991, recounted to me by Juliana Luecking (personal communication, 20 August 1994), provides a striking example.[10] A group of women became aware of a man who had allegedly harassed and date raped a number of women in the area. In response they composed a short written account of this behaviour to which they added an explanation of date rape and advice on what to do if readers had experienced this act of violence. The text was produced as a 'flyer' and approximately 100 of them were distributed to the crowd. One woman, on receiving this flyer, informed the group that she had been raped by the man they mentioned. These activities were followed by a live music performance by the US band Fugazi. In response to these events the lead singer, Ian MacKaye, took a break from one of the band's songs about street harassment (entitled 'Suggestion') to talk of the problems faced by victims of sexual aggression. At the band's invitation, the woman who had earlier identified herself, climbed on stage and sang the close of the song. This highly emotive incident, while distressing in its acknowledgement of the prevalence of violent crime, demonstrates the opportunities for empowerment that were opened up by riot grrrl. The incident allowed for a rape survivor to vocalise her distress and speak out against her attacker.

Display and spectacle

Many of those involved in riot grrrl challenged traditional images of female display. Members of Bikini Kill would write such words as 'SLUT' across their midriff and arms in marker pen. This personal labelling pre-empted any derogatory term that might be directed at them. These women thus confronted spectators with the very terms designed to prohibit female display. Numerous other riot grrrl bands also wrote slogans on their bodies, which allowed them to offer spontaneous responses to hecklers and to play with codes of display. Moreover, many grrrls chose to adopt particularly feminine dress codes, wearing bunched hair and hairslides with patterned dresses. These women offered a critique of feminine etiquette by juxtaposing their attire with bold words such as 'whore' written on their bodies. While riot grrrl was not merely a spectacle, a point that will be discussed later, there was a clear intention behind such modes of presentation to shock and confront gender conformity.

Riot grrrl zines also critiqued conventional forms of female display. US and UK zines commonly included detourned images from fashion magazines, comic strips and advertising posters. In this respect the zine writers employed the Situationist techniques that the visual artist Jamie Reid[11] utilised as part of the punk movement, by taking texts from mass culture and endowing them with new and subversive meanings. Zine writers also borrowed the Dadaist project of communication through a collage of cut-up words and images. The collage of photographs of smiling women, lingerie advertisements and soft pornography featured in *Girls Annual* provides a good example. Words and phrases such as 'bitch', 'anorexic/absolute beauty' and 'the psychology of rape' are scattered across the images, thereby inviting debate about societal constructions of beauty (*Girls Annual*: 5–6).

This method of communication linked riot grrrl directly into a punk tradition, though the context and audience for these messages offered a new frame of reference. The author of *Discharge,* for example, reprinted an advertisement for a slimming product previously published by the US magazine *Sassy*. The advertisement featured a photograph of a smiling girl in a bikini alongside a page of text encouraging readers to buy the product. The advertisement heading ran: 'Get the look that boys notice. How to lose weight fast and look great. You can have the cute, thin body you've always wanted – the kind of body that really gets boys attention ...' (*Discharge* #3: 13–14). The zine writer placed the original advertising copy 'under erasure' by writing on top of the text in marker pen her own summation of how the advertisement might be paraphrased: '... How to lose weight fast and look like an anorexic with the body of a fucking twelve year old! Then you'll be the kind of girl every boy wants to fuck real hard. Order now.' Clearly it was intended that readers should read both the original text under erasure and the handwritten text. Rather than a random attack on the advertising industry, the writer had launched a feminist attack on a magazine aimed specifically at teenage girls. The criticism was specific as *Sassy* had championed the riot grrrl 'cause' by featuring zine reviews and riot grrrl information. The editors of the magazine had even released a single, 'Hey Baby', highlighting the problem of street harassment, under the name Chia Pet. The writer of *Discharge* was not alone in pointing to the disparity between the politics of the writers of *Sassy* and its advertisers. For instance, the zine *Kingfish* included criticism of a similar *Sassy* advertisement (*Kingfish* #2: 12). These zine writers critiqued the ways in which the construction of femininity is conveyed to women through the mass media and offered their readers alternative ways of constructing personal identity.

Riot grrrls did not limit their activities to the rhetoric of the zine, but rather aimed at mobilising grrrls to meet together and engage in activities such as music production. In the early 1990s the Leeds and Bradford 'chapters' of the riot grrrl network organised a workshop event, entitled 'Bitch Schirmish', where they amassed musical equipment in a club and invited girls to experiment. Karren, author of the Leeds-based zine *Ablaze!* and an organiser of the event, explained that the idea was to 'give girls a chance to try stuff out, to get comfortable with the idea of playing guitar without any expectations'.[12] Other events organised by this group included girls learning how to DJ and organise gigs. This illustrates how, as information about riot grrrl spread, local groups of grrrls began to meet together and offer collective responses to the initiative. A zine produced in Arlington, Virginia, informed readers of weekly meetings and encouraged involvement: 'the zine you hold in your hands is just one aspect of what riot grrrl is about. Riot grrrls meet and talk, and are also planning a workshop to learn how to run [a] sound board and equipment, and other cool stuff as well. ... come on by!' (*Riot Grrrl* #6, Virginia: 1).

Punk rock dream come true

The DIY ethic, zine culture and music of riot grrrl situates it within a punk tradition. Rather than claiming to reinvent the punk movement, participants placed themselves within its ongoing tradition. This point is clearly expressed by Tobi Vail of Bikini Kill in her sleeve notes to the album *Stars Kill Rock*, a compilation featuring several riot grrrl and queercore bands. Vail comments: 'despite the much publicised notion of the non-existence of such a thing, underground music is very much alive'. She warns against the 'dissemination of an ideology indicating otherwise' promoted by those 'busy trying to convince themselves that simply because they are no longer punk rockers, punk rock must no longer exist'.[13] New riot grrrl bands adhered to the punk ethos of creating music regardless of previous training: 'who cares if the boring musos whinge that we "haven't learnt to play our instruments properly" ... anyone can write and play for as long as there's ATTITUDE/ANGER there' (*Kookie Monster's Free Peach Thingy*: 1). Members of the band Tsunami, who ran the Simple Machines independent record label, showed a dedication to the DIY spirit of punk by producing an information booklet on how to produce your own records.[14] Maintaining the energy of the original punk (and so-called post-punk) periods, riot grrrls built on the contributions made by female-centred bands formed in the late 1970s such as The Raincoats[15] and The Slits, and presented a new 'punk rock feminism' (*Kookie Monster's Free Peach Thingy*: 6). A contributor to the zine *Quit Whining* comments on the inspiration that this has given her: 'until Girl's Night, I never knew that punk rock was anything but a phallic extension of the white middle class males frustrations' (*Quit Whining* #1: 5).

While the activities of riot grrrls may clearly be understood as feminist, those involved identified with and celebrated a broad range of feminist viewpoints. The authors of several zines demonstrated their familiarity with feminist and women's literature through the inclusion of book lists and recommended texts. Several zines recommend the work of Toni Morrison, Alice Walker and Luce Irigaray, authors often featured in university programmes which may be linked to the fact that many zine writers were students. However, there is by no means a canon of riot grrrl literature. Several grrrls eschewed 'traditional' feminist texts, identifying instead with more 'radical' writers. Kathleen Hanna provides an illustration of this, citing author Kathy Acker and performance artist Karen Finley as her main influences (Arnold, 1992: 45). Responses to feminist texts by zine writers were varied and conflicting. While some chose to valorise Valerie Solanas, founder of the Society for Cutting Up Men (SCUM) and author of the *SCUM Manifesto* (1983), others distanced themselves from such texts: 'although I am politically active... I don't share a lot of Grrrl's views of "radical feminism"' (*Persephone's Network*: 12).

Riot grrrl as youth subculture?

So far this chapter has explored how riot grrrls challenged conventions of performance and female display, including ways in which they created spaces of communication at gigs and through zines by encouraging involvement and motivating girls and women to assert themselves. This section will examine whether the emergence and growth of the riot grrrl network has commonality with the development of earlier youth subcultures and will investigate to what extent it is useful to conceptualise riot grrrl using subculture theory. There are inherent problems in doing so, not least of which are the very terms 'youth' and 'subculture'. The term 'youth' does seem to be something of a misnomer as the ages of riot grrrls ranged from around 14 upwards. While most riot grrrls were below the age of 30, older women also aligned themselves with the network. As Tye, publisher of *The Meat Hook* zine, commented: 'my mom and I are doing a zine together (she's 51) and I know she loves the idea of Riot Grrrl!' (Vale, 1996: 72). It is with such problematics that this discussion will grapple, re-examining the theoretical ways in which the relationship between 'subcultures' and the 'dominant' culture have been modelled.

There are clear reasons for examining riot grrrl against established subculture theory. While the statement 'every girl is a riot grrrl'[16] aimed to explode any notion of a definable 'subculture', one can decipher a certain knowledge shared by those involved. Details of live performances, record reviews and listings communicated a shared appreciation of indie music from the UK and the US, with bands such as Nation Of Ulysses, Bikini Kill, Tribe 8 and Voodoo Queens receiving frequent mention. Riot grrrls' identification with a continuing punk tradition further encourages a reading in subcultural terms, as does the frequent description of the network as a subterranean force: 'we're growing, we're underground, and we're denying their power by not talking to them' (*Ablaze!* #10: 15). Moreover, the response to riot grrrl in newspapers and magazines was consistent with the media attention given to new youth subcultures, as journalists attempted to explain this 'latest nastiest phenomenon' (Barrowclough, 1993: 27) to readers.

One of the flaws of subcultural theory has been its tenacious grasp of the concept of delinquency. Youth subcultures have often been positioned as oppositional to the 'parent culture' and thereby at odds with societal norms. For example, in *Working Class Youth Culture* Mungham and Pearson (1976) discuss the tendency of social scientists to present youth as a 'problem' category. However, despite this acknowledgement, they nevertheless romanticise deviancy and youth in this collection by selecting theorists dealing with this theme, albeit to look at the 'issue' of problem youth. Rather than redressing the balance, through this book Mungham and Pearson contribute to the notion of youth as problem, concluding that: 'youth is definitely troubled, and working class youth seems to be more of a trouble than most' (Mungham and Pearson, 1976: 9). However, by equating youth subcultures with delinquency one immediately marginalises their position and undermines their importance as legitimate modes of expression. This point has particular relevance with respect to riot grrrl. To place riot grrrl in a tradition of delinquent youth theory would be to ignore the nature of its protest and dismiss its feminist objectives as mere teen dissent.

The British tabloid media response to riot grrrl was indebted to this tradition of aligning youth culture with the character of the delinquent. The *Daily Star* published an 'exclusive' report on the 'new cult of outrageous, fast-living, dirty-talking, hard-drinking, all-girl bands ... set to shake the pop world'.[17] However, the picture painted of 'teen female rebellion' (Snead, 1992: 5D) and of riot grrrls as 'screaming brats' (Goad, 1994: 22) cannot be set in the same tradition as that of the media reaction to, for example, the mods and rockers (see Cohen, 1980). This response to riot grrrl was clearly informed by a gendered discourse. Riot grrrls were unacceptable or at least shocking, not because they rioted on Brighton's beaches, but because they subverted specific conventions of femininity.

Riot grrrl's status as a feminist initiative, and the decision by a number of its members to be straightedge,[18] gives good ground for questioning whether traditional ways of modelling youth subcultures are adequate with respect to this network. It seems that even in defining riot grrrls as 'adolescent rebels' (Brown, 1993: 27) one is forced immediately to qualify the statement. Riot grrrl certainly embraced the title of rebel, indeed Bikini Kill's 'Rebel Girl'[19] became something of an anthem and Huggy Bear's statement that 'this is the sound of revolution'[20] became a stock phrase. However, to simply describe riot grrrl as a rebellious youth subculture implies an opposition to a static (adult) dominant culture. As recent post-subcultural studies (Muggleton and Weinzierl, 2003; Bennett and Kahn-Harris, 2004) have argued, the models of subcultures put forward by cultural theorists in the 1970s and 1980s can be criticised for a number of reasons, including the fact that they tended to heroicise subcultures as authentic, coherent unities 'rebelliously' resisting incorporation by a monolithic mainstream. Such a conception is too static, binary and rigidly defined to be applied in an understanding of riot grrrl. However, as Bennett and Kahn-Harris suggest, the term subculture is still a useful concept not least because 'its identifiability and coherence provide an effective point of departure for contemporary research' (Bennett and Kahn-Harris, 2004: 15). Riot grrrl must be understood not as just acting out 'youth rebellion' but as having specific aims within a particular cultural context. Those involved with riot grrrl were rethinking their involvement with indie rock culture(s), setting up new networks of communication and offering new modes of female expression. As Emily White commented in *LA Weekly*, 'Bikini Kill's show is not just a vague, fuck-society gesture, but a focused critique of the punk scene itself' (White, 1992: 22). Riot grrrls may be understood, then, as contesting a particular male-dominated culture. Indeed, riot grrrl seems to offer a realisation of the 'all-girl subculture' that McRobbie looked towards, where members might have 'a collective confidence which could transcend the need for boys' and that could 'signal an important progression in the politics of youth culture' (McRobbie, 1990: 80).

British media networks

In the UK, riot grrrl was first given national publicity in the weekly music paper *Melody Maker*, which presented a highly favourable report on this new feminist network (Joy, 1992: 30–32). But while *Melody Maker* sought to publicise riot grrrl, it also attempted to define it, and thus exhibited a traditional media response. This initial publicity was then picked up on by other national and local papers.[21] This reflects the trend within journalism of 'passive newsgathering', which was discussed in Chapter 3. This is evident from numerous US reports which listed the other publications that had carried riot grrrl stories as evidence of the 'public interest' in this emerging underground culture.[22]

Although riot grrrl did not generate the media 'moral panic' often associated with youth cultures (Cohen, 1980), it did incite the moral indignation of a number of journalists. Anne Barrowclough's article in the *Mail on Saturday* fits neatly into the mould of journalistic moral panicking. Her emotive vocabulary constructs the image of invasive, irreverent, threatening youth: 'They screech, they spit, they snarl, they swear. Every word they scream is a prayer against men ... Meet the riot grrrls, the latest, nastiest phenomenon to enter the British music scene ... They call themselves feminists but theirs is a feminism of rage and, even, fear' (Barrowclough, 1993: 27). Yet, as Hebdige has remarked, while it is tempting to focus exclusively on such sensationalist accounts, it is often more typical for the press coverage of subcultures to display ambiguous reactions (Hebdige, 1979: 97). Daisy Waugh's article in the *Evening Standard*, adopting the stance of a fascinated outsider, illustrates this point. Having attended a Huggy Bear gig the journalist, 'retreated to where I knew I belonged, which was anywhere but there. To a quiet coffee bar nearby and with one of their damned elusive and utterly incomprehensible "fanzines" for company' (Waugh, 1993: 10).

It is worthwhile considering Hebdige's analysis of the punk movement when developing a model through which to understand riot grrrl. The extensive coverage that riot grrrl received in the weekly music press, national newspapers and monthly magazines[23] is consistent with the media fascination Hebdige highlights. Hebdige's theory that the media evolved subtle methods through which to contain punk also has some currency with regard to riot grrrl. Writers sought to limit the radical potential of the riot grrrl initiative by interpreting the age and gender of the participants as an in-built limitation. They sought to disarm the threat of this united 'other' by trivialising the network and couching praise in condescension: 'Their ideas may be babyish. But at least they have some' (Waugh, 1993: 10). As already discussed, riot grrrl traversed a broad range of feminist viewpoints and allegiances. However, several critics keen to locate this network within an academic feminist tradition, sought to undermine the validity of riot grrrl on the grounds that participants were not fully informed by feminist theory. In 1993 Anne Barrowclough remarked that riot grrrls had not read De Beauvoir or Germaine Greer (Barrowclough, 1993). Ten months later a *Melody Maker* journalist commented: 'The best thing that any riot grrrl could do is to go away and do some reading, and I don't mean a grubby little fanzine' (Manning, 1994: 35). While riot grrrls were collectively seeking to combat day-to-day sexism, dismissive journalists argued for a cessation of activity until participants were familiar with feminist theory. Again, this may be understood as a gendered response, as previous youth subcultures had not been directed to contextualise their dissatisfaction within an academic framework.

However, the temptation to slot riot grrrl into a simple model of media containment should be resisted. As McRobbie argues, analyses of news items covered in today's postmodern mass media require an appreciation of the complexity of communication systems and a revision of the old model of the moral panic (McRobbie, 1994: 198f.). To attempt to place riot grrrl in a model of media fascination and public appropriation seems a misguided pursuit. Coverage of the mods, rockers and punks can be explained by the theoretical frames, devised by Stan Cohen (1980) and Dick Hebdige (1979), of media moral alarm and exaggeration followed by resolution and/ or co-optation. However, riot grrrls demonstrated a sophisticated response to the media that demands a revision of these models.

Sarah Thornton, in her analysis of acid house and rave culture, has argued that there is a need to discard the notion of a binary opposition between the public mass media and the private sphere of the subculture (Thornton, 1994: 176–92). She demands that instead we should be aware of the networks of media communication in operation. Thornton takes issue with the notion of a romanticised 'authentic' culture, theoretically located outside of media and commercial structures. Instead she comments on how subcultures employ media networks. Thornton's description of the acid house 'craze' in Britain is one of a spread of information from micro-media such as rave flyers, niche media such as the weekly music press, through to the mass media of the tabloid papers. Thornton argues that the tabloids did not commandeer the rave scene but were fed information about it through the media systems of the subculture itself.

She further argues that, while the mass media are usually positioned as unwelcome intruders into the camp of youth, they simultaneously serve to emphasise the importance of that youth subculture. Noting how subcultures revel in the notion of rebellion, she comments that this is more a homage to the construct of the rebel than a threatening reality. She notes how the underground, 'Imagines itself as an outlaw culture, as forbidden just because it's unauthorised, and as illicit even though it's not illegal' (Thornton, 1994: 179). Moral outrage in the national press thus endorses the assumed rebel guise, authenticating its cultural status. Thornton's comments on media processes highlight the dynamic aspects of publicity and demonisation. Moreover, she demands that we should not view youth subcultures as 'innocents' unwillingly exposed to media forces.

The growth of riot grrrl and the expansion of knowledge about this network can be linked into the micro, niche and mass media communications that Thornton identifies. Information was spread and a community delineated through a network of zines. These activities were publicised in national music press coverage such as Sally Margaret Joy's article 'Revolution Grrrl Style Now' (Joy, 1992: 30–32). It is notable that this and future articles did attempt to 'construct as much as they document' (Thornton, 1994: 176). *Melody Maker* attempted to present definitive guides to the network in the form of top ten charts listing 'vital' releases, girl influences and 'cool' zines (Joy, 1992: 30–32). Subsequent articles collapsed the breadth of musical activity inspired by riot grrrl into the output of a small number of bands. By closely tracing the Huggy Bear and Bikini Kill joint tour, journalists claimed to be documenting the network. Tabloid and broadsheet attention further publicised as well as distorted the nature of riot grrrl.[24] The next section explores how riot grrrl compels a further refinement of Thornton's model in order to fully understand the relationship between a subculture and the mass media. Riot grrrls displayed a comprehension of the processes of containment and incorporation initiated by media interest and developed strategies of resistance.

Managing the media

Those involved in riot grrrl discussed the danger of being co-opted by the niche and mass media, translated into a new trend to be celebrated and then discarded. However, participants did not simply adopt an oppositional stance to all media attention, recognising the benefits to be derived from some publicity. In the UK, Sally Margaret Joy's initial coverage in *Melody Maker* was welcomed as a positive piece of publicity that encouraged girls and women to become involved. This coverage became a facet of the development of riot grrrl itself as it was instrumental in shaping its growth. A copy of a zine produced by riot grrrls in Leeds and Bradford states, 'we might be called RIOT GRRRL, but we're aware of the media deadtime deadlines that crush anything it discovers ... Seeing all that, we use their media while we sneakily construct girl lines of communication' (*Riot Grrrl!*, Leeds and Bradford: 6). As media interest grew, those involved with riot grrrl were responsive to the potential problems of usurpation. Jenn and Soph commented on this in their zine *Hair Pie*:

> I've noticed (as I'm sure you have) riot grrrl is getting more press (daily star) for fuck's sake, we've gotta stay underground and undermine the corporate rock press by doing it ourselves so we can talk about our beliefs to people without fear of being misunderstood or the truth being distorted. (*Hair Pie* #2: 1)

One repeated argument directed against press involvement in riot grrrl was that journalistic involvement might rigidify the network. Gwen, a zine writer from Northamptonshire, argued that press attention resulted in 'the music press defining the idea for us, claiming it to be something it necessarily isn't and putting their own expectations on it rather than giving girls/people the information and letting them interpret/use it as they wish' (personal communication, 24 December 1995). Riot grrrls continually adjusted their stance in response to differing media reports. As riot grrrls became characterised in the press as frequently writing words such as 'whore' on their bodies, one girl in the US responded by writing 'media scam property' on her torso and arms, a photograph of which was duly published in the US publication *Newsweek* (Chideya *et al.*, 1992: 84) and the British broadsheet newspaper *The Guardian* (Van Poznak, 1993: 8).

Musicians and zine writers also attempted to arrest journalistic misrepresentation through a refUSl to participate in the interview process. While they could not prevent inaccurate media reports, this strategy prevented journalists from selecting quotes to reinforce their opinion and was thus effective in exposing journalism's system of operation. Similarly, the band Linus initially refused permission for the publication of band photographs. As a journalist writing an article on Linus commented, 'there is no photo to accompany this article because Linus don't want there to be any; instead, they've drawn a picture of themselves. It's not wilful petulance, merely a desire to show up the interview process for what it can be' (Terry, 1993: 14). Journalists were placed in the perverse position of formulating articles on the subject of a media silence: 'This, in case you're wondering, is not an interview. It's an article written with the bands co-operation. My fee for the article will be donated to the King's Cross Women's Refuge' (Wells, 1993: 13). The media silence, with the accompanying media frenzy, returned authority to the riot grrrl participants.[25]

Another way in which riot grrrls evaded reappropriation was in their refUSl to invest in common semiotic signifiers. In order for the dominant culture to appropriate subcultural signs there has to be some consensus of opinion on what these signs actually are. The 'Destroy' T-shirt identified with the 1970s punk movement had first to be understood as a symbol of punk's nihilism before it could be capitalised on as a desirable, 'authentic', fashion garment. Riot grrrls did not offer such clearly identifiable symbols and this to some extent protected the network from reappropriation by the dominant culture. This is not to argue that riot grrrl has been devoid of any symbolic systems, but rather to comment that participants purposefully frustrated attempts to precipitate certain 'essences' from the fluidity of its underground network.

A number of publications in the US and the UK attempted to conceptualise riot grrrl in terms of fashion. The US magazine *Glamour* informed readers that riot grrrls 'mix baby-doll dresses and bright red lipstick with combat boots and tattoos' (*Glamour,* 1993: 134). The UK broadsheet *The Independent* published an article that stated: 'theoretically you could be a Riot Grrrl in Laura Ashley florals. However, it seems unlikely', commenting instead that, 'black and denim [were] de rigueur' (Matthewman, 1993). These descriptions did not, however, distinguish riot grrrl from the clothing styles worn by other girls and women who, while perhaps sharing an interest in indie music, would not describe themselves as riot grrrls. The attempt at such definitions was met with mockery by riot grrrls. Bidisha, author of the London zine *Girl Pride*, parodied the fashion magazine format to highlight the reductive tendencies of such reports and the inaccuracy of their copy:

> with this guide you can look and sound like – hey you can BE a riot
> grrrl without knowing anything about it – be trendy kids!
> THE CLOTHES
> D.M. boots (let's hear you squeak in those new boots)
> some kind of old dress
> cardigan or navy jumper… use Dad's sandpaper to make holes in the fabric.
> (*Girl Pride* #6: 10).

Of course, riot grrrl zines do not form a remarkable oasis of self-reflexivity within a greater field of popular culture. It may be argued that during the 1990s stylistic and musical movements became increasingly self-reflexive, as did publications such as *NME* and *Melody Maker,* which displayed many instances of self-parody. However, this self-awareness should be acknowledged when considering riot grrrl, especially if such instances of parody are to be understood as a form of resistance to 'outside' discourses. Riot grrrls further undermined attempts to limit the scope of the network by claiming that riot grrrl did not attempt to alienate any girls, stating 'every girl is a riot grrrl', and through their insistence 'this name [riot grrrl] is not copyright … so take the ball and run with it' (*Riot Grrrl*, Washington, DC: 2).

Subcultures have tended to be defined against the dominant culture. Their ideological location has been viewed in opposition to prevailing cultural practices or values. Media moral panicking has inflated the idea of these cultures as a threat to parental or 'straight' culture. However, within this frame, rather than affecting an erosion of the dominant culture through their existence, subcultures paradoxically depend on reinforcing its precedence and even exaggerating its cohesion and dominance. As Stewart Home comments, 'those whose identity is based on "their opposition" to the world as it is, have a vested interest in maintaining the status quo' (Home, quoted in Plant, 1991: 4). This highlights the irony of subcultural opposition. Many of those involved in riot grrrl have demonstrated an awareness of the way in which 'opposition' is framed by the dominant culture. As Karren states in her zine, 'We are aware of the dialectical nature of protest, which ensures that dissenters are relegated to the role of "other", thus playing a necessarily supportive role to the mainstream ideology. We refuse to give credibility to traditional modes of protest' (*Ablaze!* #10: 16). Instead, riot grrrls aimed to educate and empower other girls and women to achieve their potential, unfettered by an ideology of femininity. Rather than railing against a general conception of mainstream culture, riot grrrls tended to focus their activities, targeting the perceived sexism of the indie rock music scene and working towards specific feminist goals. Riot grrrl live music performances, for example, aimed to convey certain feminist messages within a gig environment to a particular music audience.

It can be argued that riot grrrl did not seek the legitimating force of the mass media to define itself as 'authentically' rebellious. The goal of many of those involved was not to gain mass attention but to encourage girls and women to communicate with each other. As Tobi Vail of Bikini Kill remarked, 'we're doing so much now that it [mainstream attention] seems kind of unimportant ... We've really aligned ourselves with the underground' (quoted in Arnold, 1992: 46). Rather than seeking to attain the status of rebel through inference, as might a youth culture associated with 'spectacular' modes of dress or subcultural display, the riot grrrl network purposefully defined itself as oppositional in its choice of a name and through its self-conscious critique of mainstream media and culture. By providing ways into a network of communication that was resolutely uncontrollable (and unable to be appropriated by the mainstream media), riot grrrl strove to protect and re-enforce its underground status. Moreover, riot grrrl continued to re-establish the suggestion of rebellion through song lyrics, such as Huggy Bear's 'this is the sound of revolution',[26] in slogans such as Bikini Kill's 'revolution girl style now'[27] and in zines such as *Girlfrenzy*, which discusses: 'Girlspeak. The organ of GIRL POWER INTERNATIONAL; a worldwide network of Girl Revolutionaries' (*Girlfrenzy* #3: 30).

Rather than attempting to offer a coherent conception of the 'riot grrrl revolution', many grrrls just offered their own definitions. Ella's comments in *Pariah* may be taken as an illustration: 'it's not my fault that words like "revolution" and "manifesto" have become so hackneyed and meaningless – because I MEAN THEM. It's not my problem, you know? I want to restore their power' (*Pariah* #1: 8). She follows her point by quoting Lewis Carroll: 'when I use a word, it means just what I choose it to mean ... The question is which is to be master – that's all' (*Pariah* #1: 8). Huggy Bear explain their use of the word revolution in their zine *Reggae Chicken* as a celebration of dynamic energy: 'REV-o-LUTION a going round thing ... cars racing, the hype-know-sis of motion itself ... revolution is toy. totally a phenomenon of temporaneity' (*Reggae Chicken*: 13). Yet while this explanation is put forward, Huggy Bear also recognise that the message of their text may get altered through individual interpretations by different readers. Rather than view this as a failure, this is noted as a positive quality, eluding stasis and stimulating new understandings: 'if it gets understood by some and misunderstood by others then hopefully you get all these interesting cross signals to stimulate thought rushes, confusion, random arguments bastard seed patch weeds could be revolution lets see ...' (*Reggae Chicken*: 13).

It might be suggested that the call to arms that riot grrrls issued and bands such as Huggy Bear articulated was a somewhat empty threat of revolution. Prophecy of a grrrl-powered end point, although commendably positive, may be criticised for its clear lack of a base in a concrete reality. A degree of female empowerment may result, but a desecration of all bastions of patriarchy was hardly achievable given the nature of the network. However, Huggy Bear acknowledged that utopianism is flawed by the very goal of its idealism. Thus, rather than postulate a purely teleological philosophy, they adopted a chimerical stance: presenting counterfeit manifestos and celebrating an indulgence in the fanciful. While issuing cries such as 'boredom – rage – fierce – intention ... the arrival of a new renegade ... her jazz signals our time now',[28] they acknowledged that goals are rarely achieved: 'revolution fails' (*Reggae Chicken*: 13). In a similar sense, while Huggy Bear were noted for their promulgation of manifestos, they also issued refUSls of adherence to rigid statements. On a cassette release of a live London performance they responded to their critics, stating: 'All you want is like simplistic responses and I'm not prepared to do it. You want manifesto, we don't give manifesto.'[29]

Whose herstory? Locating riot grrrl

So far this chapter has considered how newspapers and magazines attempt to define as well as document subcultures and how riot grrrls, aware of this tendency, employed techniques to return authority to those involved in the network. Yet it is important that, in writing this chapter, I should not extricate myself from this process. Academic analysis encourages scholars to also offer definitions and authoritative interpretations of their subject of study. This objective carries the potential for misrepresentation.

Any definition of a subculture demands common interests within a group, but it does not follow that one can extract a cohesive identity from all subcultures. This point has particular pertinence for this analysis, as it is tempting when analysing riot grrrl to extract identifiable strands of the network and to present them as constituting the 'essence' of the culture. Such a mode of investigation suggests a homogeneity that riot grrrls have resisted. Instead those active within the network allowed and encouraged individual responses to riot grrrl. In this sense riot grrrl echoes the shift within feminism to discuss feminisms rather than a canon of feminist theory, thus allowing for a variety of responses and ensuring that no viewpoint is excluded on the grounds that it does not fit with the dominant view. The sentiment voiced by

Liz Naylor, of the independent record label Catcall, in a *Melody Maker* debate surrounding the 'issue' of women in rock, provides an example of this perspective. The debate, published two weeks before *Melody Maker* 'discovered' riot grrrl, was an opportunity for female performers and women involved in the music industry to respond to inflammatory questions set by journalists. Liz Naylor expressed concern that some of the women felt they should present a united front: 'Why not criticise me? I hate that thing where women are supposed to be "politically correct" and, like, not slag a sister' (*Melody Maker*, 1992a: 27).

Riot grrrls demonstrated an awareness of, and posed a challenge to, the academic practice of locating and defining meaning in subcultures. Subcultural theorists have historically approached subcultures as interested outsiders whose role it is to decipher the systems of signification within the group and to explore the power relations it shares with the dominant culture. Theorists have distanced themselves from the culture under review while investing themselves with the authority to uncover its significant aspects and render their meanings. The self-reflexivity of riot grrrls arrested this method of investigation by challenging the authority of the cultural archivist. From the early 1990s riot grrrls displayed an awareness of themselves as academic curiosities. Karren commented in the zine *Ablaze!* that riot grrrl purposefully blocked any attempts at academic intrusion into the network: 'ACADEMIA IS A SHITTY PLACE for me ... So we thought we'd try something without them. Of course, they're [academics] very upset and rarely give up that fearful howling on our doorsteps, but you know that in a while they'll quieten down and leave us be' (*Ablaze!* #10: 15). This self-awareness demands a reassessment of the ways in which riot grrrl might be conceptualised. Moreover, the fluency with which several riot grrrls used theoretical language highlights the need to reconsider the relationship between researcher and subject. Riot grrrl may be understood as a network of activity that sought to elude the paralysis of reification. The previous quote from *Ablaze!* states the intent of preventing a flow of information about riot grrrl from entering the 'long tall twisting staircase' of academia (*Ablaze!* #10: 15). However, participants did more than block information: they actively sought to frustrate attempts to historicise the network and interpret its collective 'intent'. Since its beginnings there has been a continuing dialogue between those involved in riot grrrl and the academic community. For example, in October 2005 Ladyfest Brighton staged a discussion panel on the legacy of riot grrrl with original riot grrrl organisers Allison Wolfe (Bratmobile, Girl Germs) and Tobi Vail (Bikini Kill, Frumpies). The discussion included reflection on the merits and accuracy of academic accounts of riot grrrl, highlighting how those involved are active in researching and critiquing the ways in which the initiative has been historicised.

From its beginnings the awareness that several zine writers and bands demonstrated of the progress of the history of art was influential in directing their output and shaping their public statements. The content of many zines demonstrated an indebtedness to Dadaism and employed sloganeering and detournement practices used by Situationists. The London-based female-centred band Linus referenced avant-garde art in their zine by including quotes by artists and photographs of the work of Meret Oppenheim, Alberto Giacometti and Man Ray (*Plague Your Eyes*: 16–17). The name of their zine, *Plague Your Eyes*, also nodded in the direction of art activists such as Stewart Home, who have been involved in dismantling notions of individual artistic genius. A manifesto entitled *Towards Nothing*, issued by Home under the name of the Generation Positive, proclaimed: 'we affirm that plagiarism is the truly modern artistic method. Plagiarism is the artistic crime against property. It is theft and in Western Society theft is a political act' (Home, 1991a: 6). Just as with spectacular youth subcultures, the radicalism of art projects is subject to canonisation and conversion into commercial terms antithetical to its original purpose. One may consider the example of the art strike of 1990–93, when a group of 'militants' declared that they would 'cease to make, distribute, sell, exhibit or discuss their cultural work' (Home, 1991b: 1) for a three-year period. Those involved wished to draw attention to the hierarchy of the arts and extricate themselves from the capitalist consumption of art. However, the refUSl to create cultural objects was not a defence against historicisiation and cultural recuperation as the very notion of abstention became in itself an art statement, put forward by a notable few, located in time and subject to incorporation into the history of art. The knowledge that grrrl bands and writers demonstrated of the forces of recuperation informed the way in which they presented themselves.

One of the ways in which riot grrrls attempted to prevent the network from becoming static was through their use of contradiction as a tool. Many zines vocalised the problems that their writers faced in trying to develop a personal identity. They commented on how they felt that they were constantly having to negotiate different constructions of themselves as gendered beings: continually switching between the passivity of femininity and their need for 'girl action', and between their want to dismiss conventions and their desire to conform to standard images of beauty. Kathleen Hanna, then of Bikini Kill, expressed in the zine *Jigsaw* how this imbued her with a sense of displaced identity: 'Because I live in a world that hates women and I am one ... who is struggling desperately not to hate myself ... my whole life is felt as a contradiction' (*Jigsaw*, quoted by White, 1992: 23). Riot grrrls embraced this notion of a complex personal identity. Zines often contradicted one another and individual writers also presented conflicts in their texts. For example, Irene Chien, editor of the zine *Fake*, published in Potomac, Maryland, opened the publication with the statement: 'I don't claim to be revolutionary, consistent or even coherent in my feminist theory or anything ...' (*Fake* #0: 1). This acknowledgement of inconsistency and changing perspectives may be understood as a response to the complexity of female experience, and inhibited an easy reading of the author's stance. Emily White described this as having a definite subversive quality: 'creating a kind of paralysis, or night blindness, in the man/boy imagination' (White, 1992: 22).

While some women discussed the notion of contradiction in relation to their experience, others utilised the concept as a playful method of inviting debate, employing a scheme of anti-information to stimulate a response. This approach is articulated by Karren in *Ablaze!*: 'Our fight is adrenaline-fuelled and essentially fun, following no pre-set programme. ... We are prepared to (ab)use philosophy, to put forward statements we know to be untrue, in order to stir up stagnant ponds of thought into newly rushing fountains of debate' (*Ablaze* #10: 17). This mischievous refUSl to present a 'truthful' singular account is a way of allowing other discourses to come through the zine medium. Seeking to escape the construction of a definitive riot grrrl tract, those involved also dissuaded the reader from viewing the zine writer as author, encouraging the publication to be seen rather as a writerly text:

> Non passive reading – like a heckler with a brain as well as a tongue and a beer. A righteous interruption … so reader know that you aren't looking for a bottom but exploring the multi-trajectorised paths and cross roads of the text. There is no proper, no real, no single meaning. (*Reggae Chicken*: back page)

Conclusion

It is ironic that the attempt by riot grrrls, from their position as cultural curiosity, to adopt methods to control outside media and academic interest, further heightened the attention of such parties. In researching this subject I am acutely aware of my own involvement in this process. Other researchers writing about riot grrrl have also commented on the necessity of analysing their own position in relation to these girls and women. The experience of ethnographer Lori Taylor is most enlightening. The US publication *City Paper* rejected the article it had commissioned Taylor to write on riot grrrl as it considered it too sympathetic and was unhappy with her decision not to describe participants in terms of fashion. Taylor posted the article to her main riot grrrl contact, explaining what had happened. A defence of her standpoint was subsequently included in a Washington, DC, zine. Instead of being a detached ethnographer, Taylor had become a visible figure for riot grrrls. She has commented on the uncomfortable sense this gave her: 'I was pleased that I came out on the right side, but I was very embarrassed to have been noticed at all' (Taylor, 1993: 14). She stressed how respect for riot grrrls was her uppermost concern and how this experience caused her to reassess her role as researcher: 'Maybe girl culture should only be studied in the oral histories of women. Maybe any scholarly investigation of girl culture is an unjustifiable invasion of privacy. Maybe girl culture should remain an undeveloped wilderness preserve on our cultural landscape' (1993: 14). In another study, Gottlieb and Wald explain that their academic interpretation of riot grrrl met with resistance from participants because they had attempted to speak for this group (Gottlieb and Wald, 1994: 270).

This chapter has illustrated the complexity of riot grrrl through an exploration of some of its facets. The aim has not been to define the substance of a network that attempted to allude cohesion, but to highlight points of particular interest. Although bands and zines issued declarations of intent under the name of riot grrrl, they were quick to stress that these were not representative of all riot grrrls, but offered individual and sometimes conflicting responses. The chapter has considered how participants reworked conventions of female display and performance, allowing girls and women new possibilities of discourse. Examination of niche and mass media reports, while revealing somewhat predictable responses of fascination and dismissal, has focused on the relationship between reporter and subject. Demonstrating media literacy, riot grrrls involved themselves in the processes of publicity and skilfully managed their own promotion. From its outset riot grrrl challenged not only the authority of journalists, but also that of academia, and began to close the gap between critic and subject.

Notes

1   It should be noted however, that riot grrrl is not confined solely to discussions about music.

2   Sleeve notes to *Cause,* a spoken-word compilation album produced in the US supporting the right of women in the States to a legal abortion (Piece Of Mind, 1992).

3   *'SWIM NOTES', The Strong Women In Music Newsletter* #1, New York, 1993.

4   Sleeve notes to Bikini Kill, *Yeah, Yeah, Yeah, Yeah* / Huggy Bear, *Our Troubled Youth* (Kill Rock Stars/Catcall).

5   Riot grrrl zines are self-published, independent texts that discuss a variety of topics and concerns including music, politics and the personal reflections of those who write them. A further discussion of riot grrrl zines is given in the next chapter.

6   The gendered term 'punkette' is notable here. As Reddington (2004: 244) discusses, in a consideration of the UK punk scene of the late 1970s, the term 'punkette' was often used within the press to refer to women punk musicians as if to communicate that they were 'trespassing on male territory'.

7   Bikini Kill, *Bikini Kill* (Kill Rock Stars).

8   Karren, quoted from a paper, 'Girl Love and Girl Action', presented at the Institute of Contemporary Arts, London, 4 December 1993.

9   For a discussion of gendered behaviour and the absence of women within the front-of-stage area see Krenske and McKay's (2000) study of a heavy metal venue in Brisbane, Australia.

10   Anderson and Jenkins (2001: 321–2) also offer an account of this incident.

11   A published collection of the works of Jamie Reid can be found in Reid and Savage (1987).

12   Karren, quoted from a paper, 'Girl Love and Girl Action', presented at the Institute of Contemporary Arts (ICA), London, 4 December 1993.

13   Tobi Vail, sleeve notes to *Stars Kill Rock* (Kill Rock Stars).

14   *An Introductory Mechanics Guide to Putting Out Records, Cassettes and CDs* (1993) produced by Simple Machines, Arlington, Virginia.

15   See O'Meara (2003) for a discussion of how punk musicians The Raincoats challenged masculine subjectivity in rock.

16   This statement appeared in numerous US zines in the early 1990s. The declaration was also in evidence in the British media – for example, when it was written on a naked woman's body, photographed and included in an article by SUSn Corrigan (1993: 28–31).

17   'Riot Girls', *Daily Star* (18 March 1993), republished in the 'True Stories' section, *Melody Maker* (20 March 1993: 38).

18   Straightedge has developed out of punk music scenes in the US and is based on a lifestyle choice that rejects the practice of promiscuous sex and consumption of illicit drugs, meat and alcohol. For further discussion of straightedge see Wilson and Atkinson (2005).

19   'Rebel Girl' appears on the split LP: Bikini Kill, *Yeah, Yeah, Yeah, Yeah* / Huggy Bear, *Our Troubled Youth* (Kill Rock Stars/Catcall).

20   'Her Jazz', Huggy Bear (Wiiija/Catcall).

21   One could alternatively trace the response to the riot grrrl 'phenomenon' in the US in the publications *Rolling Stone, Spin, Option, Sassy, New Yorker, LA Weekly, US Today, Interview, New York Times, Washington Post, Ms, Newsweek, Seventeen* and *Billboard.*

22   See, for example, the articles published in *LA Weekly* (White, 1992: 20–28), *Spin* (Nasrallah, 1992: 78–80), *Rolling Stone* (France, 1993: 23–4) and *Village Voice* (Aaron, 1993: 63).

23   Riot grrrl articles were published in *Melody Maker*, *NME*, *The Daily Star*, *The Evening Standard*, *The Zine*, *Lime Lizard*, *Elle*, *The Independent Catalogue*, *The Wire*, *Lip 1*, *The Face*, *Ms London*, *The Guardian*, *Vox*, *iD*, *Select*, *Indiecator*, *Shebang*, *Girl About Town* and *The Independent*.

24   See Waugh (1993), Barrowclough (1993) and Matthewman (1993).

25   Another example of this sort of coverage is Miranda Sawyer's article (1993: 24–5).

26   'Her Jazz', Huggy Bear (Wiiija/Catcall).

27   'Bikini Kill', Bikini Kill (Kill Rock Stars).

28   'Her Jazz', Huggy Bear (Wiiija/Catcall).

29   Huggy Bear, live at Harlow Square, 22 March 1994.

Chapter 6

The development of riot grrrl: through zines, the internet and across time

The previous chapter examined the beginnings and spread of the riot grrrl network focusing on activities in the US and the UK. It identified that the realisation of this initiative took several forms. Female audience members began by challenging the traditional division of the gig environment into gendered spaces, where women were largely absent from the front-of-stage area. Other grrrls formed bands, wrote zines, arranged meetings and organised events to introduce girls to music making. Activities were not only music related but concerned themselves with a broad range of issues tackling sexual discrimination. This chapter discusses how riot grrrl developed during the 1990s through extensive (print and electronic) zine networks and dedicated 'grrrl' websites. In particular it considers how zines and the internet have offered a space for girls to discuss issues concerning music, gender and sexuality. Although riot grrrl has spread to other countries, the study chiefly concerns itself with activities, publications and websites produced in the UK and US. Consideration will be given to how print and e-zines described and promoted ideas about riot grrrl, and to what extent they shaped the 'movement' itself.

Chapter 5 argued that traditional interpretations of youth subcultures, which associate youth with delinquency and moral upheaval, are not appropriate frameworks for understanding riot grrrl. Riot grrrl's agenda was targeted specifically at addressing gender inequality within indie rock. The promotion of ideas about riot grrrl through thoUSnds of zines (conventional photocopied publications and online 'e-zines') is also significant. Traditionally (male) youth subcultures have been associated with particular symbolic sites where subcultural activities and meanings are played out. Youth has conventionally been located in 'the street' (see McRobbie, 1990: 77; Corrigan, P., 1993: 103–5) and, as McRobbie has remarked, 'few writers seemed interested in what happened when a mod went home after a weekend on speed. Only what happened out there in the streets mattered' (McRobbie, 1990: 68–9). This chapter chimes with recent studies on communication networks among zine writers (Smith, 1999; Cresser *et al.*, 2001; Schilt, 2003b) and within online music cultures (Hodkinson, 2003; Elliott, 2004; Wilson and Atkinson, 2005; Williams, 2006). It considers how riot grrrl spread not only through face-to-face meetings and organised group activities but also through the production of paper and online texts produced by girls and women in their homes. Thus riot grrrl developed without connection to exterior fetishised locations, and generated a sense of connection and support between participants who met together in the collective space of a club or music venue but were dispersed over a wide geographical area. Riot grrrl is not presented as tied to a locality or structured around an unchanging set of goals, but as a dynamic network that has been adapted by different women in response to their individual and collective concerns.

The latter part of this chapter will focus on how riot grrrl has developed over time. It will consider the rhetoric of inclusion promoted within riot grrrl and balance this with an examination of the extent to which the network attracted a diverse audience. This retrospective will question how far riot grrrl has been effective in challenging gender inequalities within indie rock and empowering young women. It will give a voice to numerous women involved with riot grrrl from the UK, Canada and the US, by presenting a selection of their reflections in their own words. The chapter concludes with a discussion of how a dominant phrase within riot grrrl, that of 'girl power', was used within the marketing and promotion of the multi-million-selling British pop act the Spice Girls. The examination considers to what extent the adoption of this phrase can be understood as the promotion of riot grrrl ideas to a wider audience. In particular it explores the relationship between this girl power message, discourses of feminism and the drive for maximum commercial appeal.

A working definition of zines

Zines are self-published texts devoted to a wide variety of topics including hobbies, music, film and politics. These publications are usually independently produced on a small scale by an individual or small group of people, and are generally non-profit making. Zines are inexpensively produced, often being photocopied rather than printed. As one writer explains: 'The simplest zine is one sheet of legal-sized paper copied on both sides and folded three times, trimmed and stapled to make a 16-page "mini" zine. This can be produced in one night, and part of its appeal is the diminutive size' (*Homegrown*, quoted in Vale, 1996: 4). These texts are also found on the internet in the form of e-zines. However, the option of electronic self-publishing is open only to those with access to a computer, telephone line and scanner.

The word 'zine' is an abbreviation of 'fanzine', which in turn draws its title from an alteration of 'magazine'. Nico Ordway dates the origin of the fanzine to the publications produced by science-fiction enthusiasts in the 1950s, although these texts form part of a lineage of self-published leaflets and newsletters dating from the advent of printing presses (Ordway, 1996: 155). Self-publication has been a method closely associated with several art movements, from the Dada journals to the texts produced by the Surrealists and Situationists. The explosion of fanzines in response to punk rock established these publications as youth culture media. Fanzines could be produced cheaply and quickly on a small scale, articulating the views of music enthusiasts and providing an alternative discourse to that of national magazines and newspapers. The format of punk fanzines, including editorials, interviews with musicians and record reviews, has been reproduced in the fanzines of several subsequent music movements.

Cheap production costs have resulted in a proliferation of zines, allowing those with minimal wealth, such as children, to have a public voice. Writing in 1996 Vale claimed that 'since photocopying became widely available in the 70s, over 50,000 zines have emerged and spread in America alone' (Vale, 1996: 5). The independent character of zines gives them significant value, allowing for discussion topics outside of mainstream fashion to receive coverage. Sara, writer of *Out of the Vortex*, comments: 'Only by controlling the medium do we control the message. We are the medium; we are the message. For this reason zines are extraordinarily unique and powerful political tools' (quoted in Vale, 1996: 168).

Riot grrrl zines

The shortened word 'zine' has greater relevance to riot grrrl publications (Figure 6.1) as the content of zines shows a shift away from the role of the fan in documenting and constructing musical taste cultures. This is not to distance them from music altogether but merely to state that they often had a broader project. This is an important point to emphasise as much of the publicity on riot grrrl in national papers and magazines first defined it as a musical movement and then proceeded to discuss the musical work of a small selection of bands. Yet, although it was initiated by musicians, riot grrrl was important as a more general system of communication among girls and women. Many zines encouraged readers to get involved in music, but writers were also keen to stress that this was not the sole motivation behind the initiative, as Kay and Josie state in their London-based zine *Go Go Girl*: '"Riot Grrrl" is not just about music. It's girl positive energy. Don't feel that you have to be in a band to do something constructive with your time' (*Go Go Girl*: 4). Certainly riot grrrl spawned a considerable number of new bands, but it also resulted in hundreds of publications, emphasising that the network had a larger project.

Figure 6.1   Selection of US riot grrrl zines published between 1991 and 1994

Many grrrl zines included traditional fanzine staples such as record and concert reviews, band interviews and artist profiles. However, they also acted as spaces in which grrrls could share information and voice opinion on issues that affected them. Zines included articles on date rape, abortion rights and discussions of the problems of safety when walking home at night. In addition to being vehicles for the spread of information, zines offered a platform from which girls could share personal experiences. These zines positioned the reader as confidante and included pieces ranging from angry responses to sexism and discussion of broken relationships, to disclosures of sexual abuse. Riot grrrls thus created zines that reflected their thoughts and experiences: '[we] know that we're tired of being written out – out of history, out of the "scene", out of our bodies … for this reason we have created our zine and scene' (*Riot Grrrl!* #3, Massachusetts: 1). As distribution of these publications was limited to small numbers, zines offered the possibility of communicating experiences to a small group of likeminded people. This concept of a grrrl network is clearly apparent in *Hair Pie*, written by two girls in Dyfed, Wales, who subtitle their publication 'The isolated by geography but not attitude zine for girls' (*Hair Pie* #2: title page).

Like other fanzines, the production style of riot grrrl publications confers a tone of intimacy. The text is often handwritten and frequently includes hand-coloured pages or decoration with stickers. The zines share many of the same stylistics as punk fanzines, which, as Hebdige comments, convey a sense of urgency as 'typing errors and grammatical mistakes, misspellings and jumbled pagination were left uncorrected in the final proof' (Hebdige, 1979: 111). Other similarities with earlier self-publications may be noted in the use of collage techniques and detourned magazine images. However, riot grrrl zines are noteworthy as, in both US and UK publications, the selected images usually address the construction of (white, western) femininity. Writers offer a critique of beauty standards and expected feminine behaviour by juxtaposing text and illustrations taken from comics, advertisements, teen magazines and fashion photography.

Although produced on a small scale, each zine contributed to the wider motive of spreading the word of riot grrrl. This attitude is voiced in *Grunge Gerl* #1, a zine written in Los Angeles in the early 1990s: 'I know circulation will start small, maybe 20 copies or so, but with luck, once you all start reading – and contributing to this – we can get the word out that we're girls, we're angry, we're powerful …' (*Grunge Gerl* #1: 1). Most grrrl zines were not sold through retail outlets but were instead distributed at gigs or by mail order. Attendance at a gig at least suggests shared musical tastes but ordering through the post may seem a more distant and impersonal exercise. In practice, however, the reverse seems to hold true. To acquire the addresses of zines one has to tap in to the informal friendship networks active within riot grrrl. Some grrrls produced lists of contacts, while other addresses were printed in review sections of zines or enclosed with the publication in the form of small 'flyers'. Thus lines of connection could be made by writing to zine producers to order copies. Indeed zine writers generally encouraged feedback from readers. In undertaking research into riot grrrl I found that zines despatched by post were always accompanied by a letter or note encouraging the reader to write back with comments:

I want to encourage people not to just order zines like they were any commodity but to write to anyone whose zine you feel inspired by or have a critique of. it would truly bumm me out if this turned into a comodification of 'girl zines' where if you have the cash you can have access to whatever you want. (*Riot Grrrl Press Catalogue*, July 1993)

Kate Eichhorn (2001), in an article discussing her methodological approach to researching zines produced by girls in the mid-1990s, comments on this expectation by zine writers of personal involvement. Eichhorn states that she had been unaware of the etiquette for personal correspondence when ordering zines and so had sent out requests for approximately 100 publications using a laser-printed request form. Her decision not to write personal letters to the zine producers resulted in a poor rate of returned zines as well as expressions of annoyance from some of those who did reply. In a reflection on this response Eichhorn remarks that:

in an attempt to maintain some control over who gains access to their 'zines, many writers use people's letters as a way to determine whether or not they are comfortable sharing their publications. … It appeared as if their goal was not to reach as many people as possible, but to reach people with shared personal and political commitments. (Eichhorn, 2001: 570)

Within my research I found that some zine writers encouraged further grrrl networking by posting out 'friendship books' or 'slam books' with their zines. These 'books' are handmade by stapling several squares of paper together. The front page includes the name and address of the girl who produced the 'book' and the contact details of a friend of hers. Recipients of these books are requested to fill in their name, address and details of their likes and dislikes. When the friendship book becomes full it is sent to the girl whose name appears on the front page. This request for personal interaction is in keeping with the content of the zines. Ella, author of the Sheffield-based zine *Pariah*, emphasised this point in her opening pages: 'It's up to you – this should be a dialogue, so take a pen and paper to continue this conversation' (*Pariah* #1: 2). Zine writers, and other people involved in the network, embraced the idea of 'girl talk' as a means of overcoming isolation and alienation, and as a route through which to better understand oneself. Bands, writers and activists all encouraged girls to involve themselves in this form of female communication. For instance, the writer of the zine *Hotskirt*, published in Little Rock, Arkansas, in the early 1990s, commented on the need for female networks:

Girls, we all need to learn the incredible value and joy to be found in girl friends. It's not just a silly slumber party full of makeup and hair and boyfriend talk. "Girl Talk" is cool, but that's not all it has to be about. It can also be about feelings, about being a girl. (*Hotskirt*: 2)

Articulating space and spaces of articulation

The language of riot grrrl zines conveyed the way in which the network was conceived of spatially by its participants. Contributors involved themselves in a discourse negotiating the ideological location of riot grrrl, exploring notions of public and private space. Within early riot grrrl zines several writers pictured riot grrrl as opening up frontiers and allowing girls and women access to places from which they were previously excluded. One US zine writer characterised the birth of riot grrrl as 'revolution summer, breaking down every wall' (*Quit Whining!* #1: 31), while another declared 'anything that ever was/is exclusive to boystown has had all previous right removed. The world is yours, so do what you want ...' (*Riot Grrrl* #7, Washington, DC: 17). The rhetoric of occupation and conquest was offset by the concern to maintain riot grrrl as a subterranean network. While writers celebrated the multidimensional trajectories of riot grrrl initiatives, many expressed resentment of their documentation in national publications: 'seeing ourselves described by these mainstream writers puts boundaries in our minds. I think this is really dangerous. We can counteract it by keeping alive the "underground" aspect of riot grrrl' (*Riot Grrrl* #8, Washington, DC: 14). Riot grrrl zines in the 1990s thus presented a complex, if not contradictory, concept of riot grrrl as an underground network that rejected public intrusion yet claimed to be open to all: 'every girl is a riot grrrl' (*Riot Grrrl* #8, Washington, DC: front cover). Similarly, the band Huggy Bear exploited a sense of insiderness in their zine while simultaneously refusing to mark out any defining characteristics: 'for a change you can't just blag your way into this "scene" ... all peasy easy by nonchalantly leaning over at the bar and enquiring after its signifiers' (*Reggae Chicken*: 7).

Zine writers thus suggested the notion of 'safe' or private riot grrrl spaces. However, the zines themselves can be understood as 'rhetorical spaces', to employ Lorraine Code's terminology, where individual voices and particular feminist ideas could be articulated (Code, 1995). Zine writers first positioned themselves as gendered subjects within the text, and then proceeded to explore issues and interests relevant to them as women. As the writers of *Hotskirt* argued, 'we want to create a voice, for ourselves and for anyone who is concerned about woman's situation in society today. ... To show that girls can write zines, play in bands, set up shows, live up to their own expectations instead of the medias [*sic*]' (*Hotskirt* #1: 1). Riot grrrls wrote themselves into the text, relating personal experiences and concerns and, in so doing, expanded the discursive parameters of the fanzine. By considering the zine medium as a 'textured location where it matters who is speaking and where and why' (Code, 1995: x), one uncovers a significant aspect of grrrl zines. Fanzines have traditionally been produced within male-dominated music cultures and have concerned themselves with aesthetic judgements about record releases and live performances. While the discussion of feminist concerns was not prohibited, it was none the less absent in these texts as no rhetorical space existed in which it could be articulated. Historically, music fanzines excluded female voices and concerns through their failure to acknowledge the relevance of gender to the music under discussion.

The promotion of riot grrrl through an underground zine network challenges the connection made within early subcultural studies between subcultural practice and the street. The production of these texts necessarily locates youth indoors and, most often, in the private space of the bedroom, which has been theorised as a feminised space of teen consumerism (see Brake, 1980: 143; McRobbie and Garber, 1993: 209–22). As recent ethnographic research by Lincoln has argued, 'contemporary bedroom culture can be understood as an important site in which youth and subcultural activities take place ... [which has] continuing importance as a cultural space in the social life worlds of teenage girls' (Lincoln, 2004: 106). Baker's ethnographic research with pre-teen girls in Adelaide, Australia, concurs that the bedroom is an important 'space for serious play and experimentation, especially in the context of musical engagement' (Baker, 2004: 90). By producing zines, teenage girls demonstrated an active involvement in riot grrrl rather than a passive consumption. Of course other subcultures, such as punk, have also developed through the production of fanzines in the home as well as in public spaces such as live venues and street culture. However, the concept of a private sphere is integral rather than incidental to riot grrrl zines. Whereas music fanzines have historically offered personal responses to an external (street or club) culture, here the culture was produced in the very act of writing. The multiplicitous nature of riot grrrl and the accompanying rhetoric of inclusion – 'ANY GIRL IS A RIOT GRRRL. ANYONE. We are not a club and there are no rules' (*Riot Grrrl* #8, Washington, DC: 14) – encouraged anyone to identify with the network and contribute to its expansion. As one zine writer based in Arlington, Virginia, commented, 'riot grrrl is ... BECAUSE every time we pick up a pen, or an instrument, or get anything done, we are creating the revolution. We ARE the revolution' (*Fantastic Fanzine*, reproduced in *Persephone's Network*: 26).

Zines were a way in which young women could voice their participation in the network from a safe space. This allowed for participation by young women who would be precluded from involvement in a pub or club environment because of licensing laws. As Angela, a British riot grrrl and zine writer based in King's Lynn, commented: 'Unfortunately I never went to any of the gigs, I was very shy the time Riot Grrrl came out and daren't ask any of my London pen-friends to put me up for the nite so I could go and see the bands!' (personal communication, 30 November 1995). A number of teenage women interviewed for this book stated that they often could not attend live performances due to concerns over safety, travel arrangements and access to venues. One zine writer from Hertfordshire explained, 'I was about 15 at the time tho' and couldn't go travelling on the underground on my own' (personal communication, 29 December 1995).

Border control: distribution, scale and publicity

The style of the zines, their scales of production and systems of distribution are critical to notions of riot grrrl as an underground network. The presentation style and small scale of production promotes a sense of alliance with the reader. A remark made by one zine writer from Minneapolis demonstrated how she credited her readership with a level of trustworthiness: 'I print around 200 an issue ... looking at that number scares me because I am really vulnerable in my zine ... Feedback has been amazing though, it's what keeps me going' (personal communication, 26 August 1996). Thus, while these zines may be distributed to people in another country, their content and scale of production gives the impression of a conversation with a group of close friends.

In a very real sense riot grrrl grew, not in spite of its participants being disparately located but because of the freedom and opportunity created by not being bounded within a particular locale. Zines acted as a means of accessing likeminded people who did not live locally. As one 17-year-old zine writer commented, 'none of my friends around me here in Norfolk became involved in riot grrrl at all, they'd never even heard of it' (personal communication, 30 November 1995). Zines became a tool for empowerment, allowing geographically isolated people to correspond with each other and share a common sense of identity. One 16-year-old girl from Liverpool remarked, 'I've made lots of new friends through riot grrl and it's helped me a great deal to feel more accepted and more in control of my life and happier with myself' (personal communication, 6 September 1996).

As discussed in Chapter 5, riot grrrl attracted a considerable amount of press attention.[1] Several writers viewed this public exposure as an invasion, and responded by printing defences against the intrusion. A particular point of debate in US zines was the publicity afforded by teen magazine *Sassy*:

> Let it be known that I … DO NOT like Sassy magazine, and am annoyed at its attempts to infiltrate the underground music scene. Although it is not as bad as, say Teen or Tiger Beat, I do not appreciate Sassy latching on to something they think is hip, then spoonfeeding it to the mainstream. (*Quit Whining!* #1: 22)

Zine writers in the UK expressed a similar indignation at the usurpation of their cultural terrain and argued against such public trespass: 'We're growing, we're underground, and we're denying their power by not talking to them … we don't need the corporate press. We're truly independent, we'll pay our way, we'll use our own channels' (*Ablaze!* #10: 15).

Those involved in riot grrrl repeatedly stressed that no singular viewpoint or cultural product (be it a zine or record) could be taken as representative or even indicative of the whole riot grrrl network. Zine writers repeatedly emphasised that they could offer only personal insights: 'I won't offer a definition because it wouldn't be fair to other grrrls to whom riot grrrl may mean something totally different. I will however offer my insight on what I have seen happen …' (Spirit, *What is a Riot Grrrl Anyway?*). In this sense riot grrrl can be understood as multiplicitous. Elizabeth Grosz's definition of this term is very instructive. She writes: 'A multiplicity is not a pluralised notion of identity (identity multiplied by n locations), but is rather an ever-changing, nontotalisable collectivity, an assemblage defined, not by its abiding identity or principle of sameness over time, but through its capacity to undergo permutations and transformations, that is, its dimensionality' (Grosz, 1994: 192). Those involved in the riot grrrl network delighted in the possibilities opened up by allowing different people to produce their own interpretations of riot grrrl: 'take the ball and run with it' (*Riot Grrrl*, Washington, DC: 2).

Deleuze and Guattari's use of the metaphor of a rhizome is useful to this discussion of the nature of riot grrrl and its network of zines. Deleuze and Guattari reject the recourse to the metaphor of the tree in western thought, with its suggestion of unity, a centralised core and binary thinking ('aborescent pseudomultiplicities') (Deleuze and Guattari, 1988: 8). Instead they propose a celebration of the nature of rhizomes:

the underground stems of plants branching out in different directions without a singular or central trunk. This is a very different concept to 'aborescent' thinking 'which plots a point, fixes an order' (1988: 7). Instead the rhizome 'is composed not of units but of dimensions, or rather directions in motion. It has neither beginning nor end, but always a middle (milieu) from which it grows and which it overspills … The rhizome operates by variation, expansion, conquest, capture, offshoots' (1988: 21). This offers an explanatory model that can be used to present riot grrrl as a rhizomatic network. The image of a root-like structure matches the idea of an underground culture multiplying via lines of connection that are not controlled from a primary location: 'Riot grrrl isn't centralised, it's not organised, we've no leaders, no spokeswomen' (*Ablaze!* #10: 15).

Thus while those involved encouraged grrrl networking and the dissemination of riot grrrl ideas, they did not present these activities as part of a unified process. Although those who identified with the initiative have used this collective name, riot grrrl was conceived as polymorphous. In 1992 Karren, author of the Leeds-based zine *Ablaze!*, speculated gleefully on the way in which this diversity and contradiction would be reflected in the text of zines: 'kids will kick over the news stands and build their revolutionary methods of communication in the form of "fanzines"…We will confuse them by disseminating different pieces of literature under the same name, and there will be no sense in which any is more "authentic" than any other' (Karren, *GirlFrenzy* #3: 31).

Grrrls online

Information about riot spread via paper zines, music events, word of mouth, and through coverage in niche and mass media publications. However, the internet also provided a space where ideas about riot grrrl were promoted, explored and adapted. During the 1990s hundreds of websites appeared that engaged directly with riot grrrl ideas. Details of the activities of riot grrrls and discussions of the development of the initiative were posted on personal web pages, chat forums and within e-zines and websites established to promote the work of individual riot grrrl chapters chiefly in Europe and North America. While many print media journalists declared the 'death' of riot grrrl in the 1990s, and some dismissively characterised it as 'a short-lived upsurge' (Harris, J., 2003: 99), the continuing activities of grrrls online throughout the 1990s and beyond demonstrate that the ideas of the initiative continue to hold significance for many.

Riot grrrl e-zines demonstrated a continuity with the topics and approaches found in paper zines. The mode of address was generally informal and conversational, with typesetting sometimes selected to mimic handwriting rather than echo the formal presentation styles of news media. These online publications covered a range of topics but often included descriptions and personal reflections on riot grrrl, information about bands, and discussions of topics such as feminism, sex, body image and advertising. Just as with paper zines, e-zine writers tended to assume and address an imagined sympathetic female audience. This raises issues of risk and trust on behalf of the writers as an e-zine has the potential to be accessed by anyone, not just a targeted group. As already discussed, those producing paper zines often attempt to police their readership by demanding certain etiquette in postal correspondence. One zine writer commented that there were emotional penalties for circulating a zine in too wide a social sphere: 'I wrote my second zine … when I was 16. It had a lot of personal articles in it and I felt I had a bad response to it. I gave out free copies and the circles that I distributed it to weren't very nice ones, I soon discovered' (personal communication, 2003).

It might be argued that, in mounting their text on a web page, a zine writer abandons, or at least reduces, their ability to act as gatekeeper. While this is somewhat true one should not overlook how the use of 'insider' language in the title of a web page reduces the probability of an 'outsider' accessing the site in a casual search. The decision to use the word 'grrrl' in the titling of websites to some extent filters the audience as it separates the site from the mass of pornographic material accessible online. This point was made by Chrystal Kile in 1996, then publisher of the *Pop Tart* website: 'a very practical reason grrrls/geeks/nerds use these codewords in titles of our site is to make clear that we're not naked and waiting for a hot chat with you!'[2] Moreover, the practice of using pseudonyms and first names within these websites means that writers do not need to disclose too many details about their 'real' identities but are free to explore an online identity of their own design. By this I do not mean to suggest that the identities assumed online are somehow 'false'. Indeed, research has found e-zines 'tend not to be the favoured medium of those wishing to manipulate their real life identities' (Cresser *et al.*, 2001: 466). Instead, my aim is to acknowledge that there is a certain degree of space created by the online medium that allows one to select or consciously present a particular representation of oneself. In many cases an identity produced online is not a censored version of the writer's 'real world' persona but rather a thoughtful articulation of personal dimensions of their offline life. Indeed, as Henderson and Gilding (2004) found in their research into online community discourse, often online communication has a higher level of self-disclosure and intimacy than would be expected of the face-to-face interactions of the same individuals.

One of the possibilities and outcomes of riot grrrl's appearance on the web was that it could engage the interest of a wider number of people and facilitate a greater degree of communication than possible within existing channels. Online zines all contained links pages to other grrrl sites and sometimes formed part of a 'web ring' where visitors could easily click through linked and related pages. Similarly, the web pages of local riot grrrl chapters included hyperlinks to other active national and international chapters, allowing surfers to quickly locate and easily contact those involved. The creation of Riot Grrrl Europe (RGE) in the late 1990s can be taken as illustrative of the aim to involve a wider group of people within the network. RGE acted as an information hub and archive for the activities of riot grrrl chapters across Europe. As Hilde, a founder of the website explained:

> In short, the goal of riot grrrl Europe is providing a place to meet like-minded people in
> your area, and providing information about riot grrrl in Europe, i.e.: tourdates, reviews,
> links, addresses, event dates, and so on. Besides that, we also run a paper zine, simply

called the riot grrrl Europe zine and we have a 'body acceptance' page with rants, stories and links on body image. (personal communication, 21 August 2003)

Hilde explained that RGE had proved effective in providing a way for people who were interested in riot grrrl to find out about others already involved: 'we have 260 members on the mailing list and over 30,000 hits on the website, so you can say that it's pretty successful' (personal communication, 21 August 2003). As the site could be accessed worldwide it publicised the continuing activities of riot grrrl at the turn of the century and perhaps encouraged further participation whether within Europe or beyond. It should be acknowledged that for such sites to continue to be useful resources they need to be actively maintained. While numerous new riot grrrl sites have been created over time others are no longer accessible; for instance, by early 2006 a number of chapter websites along with the RGE website had become inactive.

The appearance of riot grrrl on the web afforded the possibility of immediate and easy communication with likeminded people across the globe. While postal correspondence with zine writers had already established correspondence networks, the use of email and online chat groups allowed for much more rapid communication. Respondents commented on how the internet facilitated the sharing of information and engendered a sense of support and connectivity with an international network. A number of respondents commented on how they placed value and importance on this online communication with other riot grrrls but they also acknowledged that these connections often did not bring in-depth awareness or a real level of engagement with the activities of other chapters. As Clair, a member of riot grrrl London commented: 'We link each other on websites. We join each others' groups to find out what is happening in other chapters/countries. We promote each other and refer people to local chapters if they are unaware of them. ... I don't think we all know exactly what other chapters are doing, but it is important to at least know of their existence' (personal communication, 28 July 2003). Not all participants turned to these web resources in order to network internationally. Often people used internet discussions of riot grrrl as a way to locate and connect with people at a local or national level.

As riot grrrl spread online, its terminology began to be used in new and different contexts. Many websites borrowed the word 'grrrl' in their web pages in order to indicate their concern with female assertiveness while not always positioning themselves in a direct lineage with riot grrrl. As RosieX, writer of the e-zine *geekgirl*, commented in 1996: 'I actually wasn't familiar with [others such as] the Guerrilla Girls or Riot Grrrls, in fact we still ain't made acquaintances. But I guess I've always liked the *grrrowl* in *grrrl* …'.[3] The internet allowed for a migration of the ideas of riot grrrl across new political and ideological terrains. As Amelia DeLoach commented in 'Grrrls Exude Attitude' in 1996, 'Like the Riot Grrrls, the grrrls on the Web don't have a neatly defined central purpose. In many ways, both the online and offline movement are like the web itself – diffuse.'[4] More recently Comstock (2001: 399) has discussed how the 'tough, edgy connotations' of the word grrl/grrrl has made it an attractive point of reference not only for individual riot grrrls or feminist identified non-profit groups but also for more commercial ventures aimed at marketing to young women. She comments that the context of the web is such that 'riotgrrrl' exists not only as an idea to be engaged with but also as a domain name that can be claimed or purchased.

Issues of inclusion

As already discussed, riot grrrl used a rhetoric of inclusion ('every girl is a riot grrrl') so as not to close the network off from different women and girls. However, appraisals of riot grrrl by those involved, including zine writers and musicians, have since questioned the actual inclusivity of the network. One of the criticisms of riot grrrl has been that while ostensibly it is inclusive of all women, in practice it has favoured the concerns of those who are white and middle-class. One person to comment on this was zine writer Mimi Nguyen, who was born in Saigon to Vietnamese parents and whose family moved to the US when she was ten months old. Mimi published the feminist zine *Aim Your Dick* and the personal zine[5] *Slant*. She commented:

> Riot Grrrl is amazing in so many ways: as confrontation, as education, as performance, as aesthetic, as support, as theory, as practice, etc. But it is important to me as a feminist of color to critique Riot Grrrl for the ways in which it has (or hasn't) dealt with differences of race and class. In that aspect, rather than presenting an *alternative*, Riot Grrrl totally parallels 'mainstream' Euro-American feminism. Gender is presumed to be a social category that can be separated from race, class, or even nation. We talk about 'women's issues,' but which women are we talking about? I have a hard time relating to most feminist discourses on body and beauty issues, because they originate from a white middle-class 'American' context, and I didn't grow up that way and don't see myself reflected in that. (quoted in Vale, 1997: 61)

This problem of representation within riot grrrl has parallels with the development of feminist academic work because, while feminist discourse aimed at offering a voice for women, in the early stages of its development all too often the differences within female experience were ignored. This failure to adequately recognise and problematise differences between women has been attributed to the predominance of white, western women within the female academic community. Certainly, subsequent scholarship has highlighted the biases within earlier feminist work and worked towards a better understanding of the diversity of female experience.

However, riot grrrl publications did not simply ignore issues of race and class. Numerous writers stated that a central part of riot grrrl's agenda was to address: 'feminist issues such as rape, abortion rights, bulimia/anorexia, beauty standards, exclusion from popular culture, the sexism of everyday life, double standards, sexuality, self-defence, fat oppression, racism and classism' (*Riot Grrl Guide for the Perplexed*). To take the issue of race first, although riot grrrls discussed a range of issues dealing with equality, it is true that they often seemed to be speaking to an audience of white, feminist women. This is perhaps explicable if one considers riot grrrl within the context of indie rock, a music genre that has generally been performed by white musicians to predominantly white audiences. As Gayle Wald has argued, it is important that issues of race are not forgotten in celebrations of new presentations of gender within indie rock, as: 'the tendency has been to celebrate the gender transgressions of white rock performers in the 1990s without attempting to understand how these transgressions … signal the emergence of new cultural modes of expressing, displaying, and performing whiteness' (Wald, 1997: 152).

The 'whiteness' of the riot grrrl scene was commented on by Sara, a 17-year-old woman who published the zine *Teenage Social Death*. Sara explained that she felt there was a social 'paranoia' among some girls to be seen to conform to particular codes of behaviour and styles of dress, and to support particular bands. She suggested that such people promoted a reductive notion of what riot grrrl and feminism could mean. She remarked:

> I am Iranian. I was at school when I got involved – I was 14. I remember that most of the people involved are white, but maybe that's because riot girl is rock (*Western*) influenced music … BUT WHO SAYS ROCK IS THE ONLY KIND OF MUSIC. I think music is a CUBE with many different faces and we should pick and choose what we like from each side rather than only liking one side. I always thought that the scene was so open, so beautiful, and I wanted to be part of it. But I was rejected by so many people. It turned out to be very exclusive in some ways. (personal communication, 21 August 1996)

In the course of interviews undertaken with riot grrrls for this book, respondents were asked to give a description of themselves, including details such as their age, occupation and ethnicity. The majority of women described themselves as 'white' but some also commented on the problematics of describing their ethnic identity. The comments of zine writer Christine, based in New Hope, Minnesota, can be taken as illustration: 'I'm … a bunch of different ethnic backgrounds and I'm beginning to hate being classified as white 'cos we're still all different, but I am classified a Caucasian to most people's definitions' (personal communication, 26 August 1996). While those interviewed only represent a small sample of views by those involved in riot grrrl, their responses highlight the need for a sensitive understanding of different personal constructions of identity.

A number of respondents questioned the appeal of riot grrrl to people from different socio-economic backgrounds and commented that riot grrrl principally attracted girls and women from the 'middle classes'.[6] Erica, who published the zine *Girlfrenzy*, commented that, in her experience, 'Riot Grrrl was/is a predominantly middle class white revolution (certainly in the UK) – it was NOT the same as Acid House in 1988 where Smiley Face graffiti was scrawled all over Council Estates and every school kid knew what it was all about' (personal communication, 15 December 1995). This comment was echoed by other respondents. Jane, a musician based in Leeds, who attended a number of riot grrrl meetings, reflected that many of the women attracted to riot grrrl were in tertiary education and thus were more likely to come from moderately wealthy backgrounds:

> I am all of 32 now going on 18, white, middle class, British, and bored – most of those I suspect involved in riot grrrl were, certainly most were university students. You didn't get anyone from say [areas of Leeds such as] Chapeltown, Belle Isle, Armley, Halton Moor – people from working class backgrounds and run down areas. (personal communication, 1 May 1995)

Ironically, some women felt excluded by the very assertiveness of the network. One musician and zine writer explained that she felt riot grrrl had set idealistic goals that she felt were personally difficult to live up to. She commented that:

> I was somewhat intimidated by the almost evangelical language used in riot grrrl manifestos and fanzines. It was like 'Change your life NOW! Stop dieting! Don't put up with crap from your boyfriend – dump him' and I felt that I couldn't start living like these women who had it all sussed overnight. Of course, none of the grrrls I eventually met were free from the insecurities I had about weight and attractiveness, etc. It was exciting to read such things but I felt I couldn't live up to them. (personal communication, 6 December 1999)

Further to this she remarked that at the time she was in a relationship with a man who 'wasn't a feminist' and that as a result she began to feel 'like a bit of a fraud'. It is ironic that an appeal for female inclusivity and empowerment should actually have quite the opposite effect on some women. Another woman described how she had produced a zine in order to involve herself in riot grrrl. She commented that she had not enjoyed the process of writing the zine and had since destroyed all copies of it, but also that she had originally decided to produce the zine, 'because the whole subculture was obsessed with women being creative (but in these specific manufactory ways) and you really didn't feel like you belonged properly unless you MADE something. I think this arose from the very best, supportive intentions, but it didn't quite fit with me' (personal communication). If the rhetoric of riot grrrl emphasised self-expression, this comment demonstrates how some of those involved felt guided into particular modes of expression with which they were not comfortable.

In acknowledging the limitations of riot grrrl it is important to consider the context out of which it developed. Riot grrrl engaged with a host of concerns, such as body image, sexuality and domestic violence, but it was none the less grounded within particular indie rock networks and often (at least initially) promoted through various music venues. The way in which riot grrrl developed through underground zine networks, informal meetings and grrrl web pages encouraged female participation by placing an emphasis on personal empowerment and education rather than on a larger goal of outreach and wider social change. As Kay, a riot grrrl and zine writer based in London, observed:

> As a musical genre and as a social, gig-going practice, it had its limiting factors just like any other subculture in that whether you 'got it', or whether you knew where it took place, or could afford to get there was dependent on your economic position, your mobility and your previously established aesthetics. I guess this is one of the key problems of a subculture that wants to attract the disenfranchised, but also wants to keep itself exclusive and protected – some people unfortunately fall by the wayside. (personal communication, 23 August 2000)

It can be argued that riot grrrl's specificity to an indie rock context and underground zine network actually was also one of its strengths. The articulation and prioritisation of feminist ideas and concerns by female indie rock musicians encouraged the participation of women within that music culture. Rachel Holborow, a musician and co-founder of Slampt records, explained that riot grrrl was a big influence on the formation of her independent record label and distribution service. While she acknowledged the shortcomings of the initiative, she emphasised the impact that riot grrrl had on those who were involved:

> Riot girl was a white middle class ghetto inside the white middle class ghetto of punk, and as such couldn't win favour with any but a few. But it did tap into the dis ease [*sic*] among middle class girls who wanted to start dealing with how women were still fucked up and fucked over. ... Oppression is oppression, but you can only start dealing with it in an individual specific way. What is left of Riot Girl now, I note, is diversifying via message and style, and so it is achieving its own ends. (personal communication, 5 November 1999)

The development and impact of riot grrrl

In criticism of the riot grrrl network during the early 1990s numerous journalists asked rhetorically 'What has riot grrrl achieved?' However, the impact of riot grrrl should not be dismissed because indie rock music continues to be male dominated. The importance of the network can be measured in the effect it has had on individuals. Speaking in 1995 Andrea, a musician and founder of the independent record label Garden of Delights, argued that: 'If one teenage girl bought a second hand guitar and expressed her ideas in a song instead of [buying] platform shoes at Miss Selfridge because of riot grrrl "press hype" – then riot grrrl was positive' (personal communication, 28 November 1995). Riot grrrl opened debate concerning the participation of girls and women in creating and performing music. Aisha, a 17-year-old girl living in Sheffield, discussed in 1995 how riot grrrl had given her the motivation to form a band. At the time of interview she was the lead vocalist in a female-centred band called Vampire Scratch. She reflected:

> I was already interested in playing music before I got into riot grrrl, but was under the impression that to be in a band you had to be able to play everything perfectly. Riot grrrl made me realise that you could just start from scratch and that you didn't have to conform to so called 'rules' and other stuff. (personal communication, 5 December 1995)

In 2003 Rowena, a 16-year-old living in Dublin, made a similar comment: 'Riot grrl definitely made me long to start a band who at last had relevant, interesting things to say about all sorts of things, including spreading a grrl positive message' (personal communication, 16 August 2003).

Having been active since 1991, the riot grrrl network has naturally engaged the participation of various musicians at different points in time. While bands such as Bratmobile, Bikini Kill and Huggy Bear were crucial to the promotion of riot grrrl in the early 1990s, many of those who have become involved with the network in recent years have taken inspiration from a wider range of performers. In 1996 Cazz, a zine writer from Stockport, remarked:

> Riot grrrl still exists. The main change is in the bands because a lot of British riot grrrl bands (or bands who identified with it) have split up. Huggy Bear, Mambo Taxi, Pussycat

Thrash all split up within the space of about 6 months last year. But at the same time girls are being inspired by bands like Bis and Kenickie, Lungleg, International Strike Force (formerly Golden Starlet), Pink Kross, etc. Bands who grew out of the riot grrrl scene, yet are not really riot grrrl bands. (personal communication, 30 July 1996)

Four years on from this Louise Hanman, guitarist and lead vocalist in the Liverpool-based punk band Flamingo 50 (Figure 6.2), emphasised the importance and influence of riot grrrl on her music making:

Riot grrrl has definitely influenced what we do as a band, although there are lots of women playing in 'rock/alternative' bands that have inspired us. Riot grrrl as a label I think is useful in describing music and an ideology that has lasted longer than the specific bands that were first described as riot grrrl. When you play somewhere like Liverpool and there are absolutely no female engineers or venue promoters that I know of, and when you play with bands such as Radiohead covers bands, you become very aware that they consider a female based punk band to be the exception to the rule. … I think it inspires us to feel as if what we are doing is important – if simply for diversity's sake. (personal communication, 26 September 2000)

**Figure 6.2	Louise and Karen performing in Flamingo 50**

There is in effect a musical and discursive continuum whereby riot grrrl has remained an influential catalyst for subsequent generations of indie music acts. Over time numerous groups have taken inspiration from riot grrrl and formed bands or developed new initiatives. The next chapter will discuss Ladyfest as one such example. The continuing appeal of riot grrrl has resulted in the successive involvement of different generations of girls, including those who were too young to be involved in the 'first wave' of activities. For instance, in 1996 Christine, a zine writer from New Hope, Minnesota, commented: 'The fact is most of the original riot grrrls are no longer involved. That's going to lead to change no matter what. I can't speak for the movement then, simply 'cos I wasn't there' (personal communication, 26 August 1996). Similarly, in 2003, Sophie, a 19-year-old zine writer and musician from London reflected:

> I first heard about riot grrrl in 1998 (I was 14). I don't know how or why, but somehow I came across a website about it and from then on I was hooked. I loved the fact that it combined feminism with such brilliant music. I then found the Riot Grrrl Europe website, and in 2000 I decided to start Riot Girl London. (personal communication, 23 July 2003)

In recent years new chapters have been formed in Montreal (1999), London (2000), Dublin (2003) and Hasselt, Belgium (2004). This succession of different people has also contributed to a development in the ideas and ideals of the network. Several respondents in 2003 stressed that they were part of a 'second wave' of riot grrrl, which welcomed the involvement of men and 'bois'. As Sophie commented in the *Riot Grrrl London* zine:

> … if you look at the riot grrrl movement now, you will find a hell of a lot of diversity in the members. There is a huge age group involved; a massive range of musical tastes and, apart from a shared feminism, a wide scope of political beliefs. … more and more men [are] getting involved, which can only be a good thing if we're aiming for equality. The new riot grrrl is not restrictive. The new riot grrrl is so much more than we ever thought it could be. The new riot grrrl is evolving. (*Riot Girl London* #3: 1)

The involvement that people have had with riot grrrl is in many respects reflective of a particular stage in their lives. For some teenage girls riot grrrl was their first introduction to feminism; for others it encouraged them to start a band or perhaps establish contact with other likeminded women. As those involved developed their professional careers many dropped out of active involvement in the network, perhaps because they no longer needed it as a support system. Reflecting on the friendships she developed through riot grrrl, zine writer Kay commented:

> At gigs I met a hell of a lot of new friends, both younger than myself (Skinned Teen, say, were 14 then) and older, including mothers and women who'd been involved in other '70s and '80s subcultures like punk. Oh yeah, and there were some men too. Some of these friendships have since dwindled (it's eight years ago now, so I think of that as quite natural), a few turned sour (a large group of volatile, dynamic women, unfortunately, can't maintain unequivocal girl love forever) and some have grown into my sturdiest friends, including people I have shared houses with. (personal communication, 23 August 2000)

However, riot grrrl has had a significant impact in areas beyond those of personal empowerment. The activities of social networking and self-publication, which have formed an integral part of the culture of riot grrrl, have been important in shaping the future careers of many of the women involved. This consequence was anticipated by Erica, publisher of the zine *Girlfrenzy*, in an interview in 1995. She stated that she believed that the effects of riot grrrl:

... will last a long time – just wait 'til all those ex-Riot Grrrls get jobs in The Media and end up on Radio 4! In the same way that some kids will always look to the past subcultures (Beats, Mods, Hippies), some people will look back to Riot Grrrl for inspiration. (personal communication, 15 December 1995)

A number of women involved in riot grrrl have indeed found jobs in the media industries. For example, Bidisha began producing the London-based zine *Girl Pride* at the age of 14 and by the age of 15 was a contributor to the *NME*. In 1993 she assisted her friend SUSn Corrigan (an established music journalist) in organising the riot grrrl day at the Institute of Contemporary Arts (ICA). By 1994 she had published articles in the dance magazine *Trance Europe Express* and the style magazines, *iD* and *Dazed and Confused*. Since then she has published three novels and worked as an arts critic and cultural commentator on numerous radio and television programmes, including those broadcast on Radio 4. Undoubtedly, Bidisha's success is a testament to her talent and ambition, but she is also an example of the sort of motivated young women involved with riot grrrl. A number of people interviewed about riot grrrl for this book have also found work within the popular music and media industries. The occupations that they have taken up have included two record company press and promotions officers, a band manager and promoter, managers of independent record labels, a journalist for a British broadsheet paper and a university Media Studies lecturer. One can trace how through riot grrrl these women became involved in local music initiatives and zine writing, and were able to network with other motivated young women. In stating this, however, I do not mean to overlook the privileges that some of these women had due to their socio-economic backgrounds and how this may have given them particular advantages in accessing education and employment opportunities.

Perhaps a gradual increase in the number of politicised women working within music journalism will help to change the gendered ways in which female musicians are presented in the press. Chapter 3 discussed how the targeting of a male readership by music publications allows for the reproduction of a masculinist discourse within the publication content and has the effect of excluding female readers. While the continuance of a macho or masculinist discourse may be supported by editors on the grounds that music publications are predominantly purchased by men, it is worth considering how the failure to cater to a female readership impacts upon sales figures. The need to actively target female readers was a point raised by a former staff writer for the *Melody Maker* when discussing the fall in circulation figures of the weekly music press in recent years. The journalist had worked for *Melody Maker* during the early 1990s and reflected upon the coverage of riot grrrl within the paper:

I felt missing out on one sex was probably a mistake [laughs]. We noticed that when, say, Sally Margaret Joy was writing for the *Melody Maker*, the figures went up. When she had a cover story, we sold more copies. That can only be that there are certain girls who pick the thing up every week but never buy it. And then one week they go 'Oh, I'm quite interested in Huggy Bear on *The Word*. I'll buy it.' There must be floating voters who will access their music not from a regular source. ... They aren't loyal to one thing every time. And it is those people who are being, actually, left behind I think by the weeklies. They're getting less and less of that floating readership because, as I said, their nets are too narrow. (personal communication, 4 February 1999)

This point certainly connects with the comments of one riot grrrl, who explained to me that she first heard about the network through Sally Margaret Joy's article in *Melody Maker*. She explained that she had originally decided not to buy the paper that week as she was put off by the image on the front cover. In order to symbolise the idea of a riot grrrl 'rebellion', the paper had chosen to put a photograph of two women mud wrestling on the cover. However, a friend at university encouraged her to buy the issue and, she recollects, 'I found the article itself greatly inspiring and it included a handy list of riot grrrl records so, that afternoon, I bunked off a seminar and went shopping' (personal communication, 23 August 2000).

A number of musicians and zine writers commented that they believed that riot grrrl has had an effect on the position of women within the music industry. Corin Tucker, vocalist and guitarist in the highly successful indie rock band Sleater Kinney, based in Portland, Oregon (and former member of Bratmobile), offered her reflections on the impact of the initiative:

> To me, riot grrrl was a group of artists and activists that wanted to change the sexism of the punk rock music scene that they were deeply involved with. I think it did change things, at least in the area where I live, there are a lot more women in bands and working at/running record labels. Fortunately, however, there were always women involved in the Northwest scene. I think having women fronting bands and labels has shifted more power to women. (personal communication, 5 November 1998)

Kathleen Hanna, formerly of Bikini Kill and now performing with Le Tigre, concurred with this view. Reflecting on the changes that had taken place since the emergence of riot grrrl in 1991 she commented:

> I think it [riot grrrl] succeeded. Yeah, being on tour with Le Tigre and stuff. Going to play a show twelve years after I played the same club like with these guys. When I went the first time there were like five people there and four of them were guys and I was singing about rape and stuff like that. … It was pretty powerful even though there were only a couple of people there. Now we go to play and all these women come and all these women have their own bands and their own projects and their own weird things in their head that they are making a reality that they share with us. That's what's changed. I just feel really proud to have been a part of it. (personal communication, 29 November 2000)

The Spice Girls: girl power in the mainstream

Chapter 5 discussed how those involved in riot grrrl devised strategies to avoid the 'dangers' of co-optation by mainstream media sources. They built defences against such an eventuality through press blackouts, misinformation and by challenging those who tried to represent them. However, the feminist message of riot grrrl, promoting female empowerment and rejecting restrictive gender identities, is particularly interesting when considering the notion of co-optation. In this respect, riot grrrl is unlike previous music movements whose fashions and music have been appropriated by high-street fashion designers and major-label clone bands. Riot grrrl could not be reduced to mere spectacle because its core essence was its message. Riot grrrl presented a style of (feminist) politics, rather than a politics of style. However, while to some extent the 'underground' nature of riot grrrl has persevered (as can be evidenced in the number of women still active within the network), some riot grrrl slogans were adopted by the mainstream. In particular, the words 'girl power' were appropriated from riot grrrl and used as the catchphrase of the British pop group, the Spice Girls.

Before discussing the use of this phrase by the Spice Girls, it is worth tracing the prevalence of the slogan within riot grrrl. The words 'girl power' were a repeated phrase that was not promulgated by any one zine or band but was used as a general declaration within the network. For instance, the slogan appeared on the front cover of a US riot grrrl zine (Figure 6.3), on the inner sleeve of a joint record release by Bikini Kill and Huggy Bear, and as the title of a UK zine produced by women in Leeds, Bradford and York (Figure 6.4). Huggy Bear produced a T-shirt design for their 1993 British tour with Bikini Kill, which had the words 'Totally Girl Powered' printed on the reverse. The words also appeared in song lyrics at the time. For instance, the early 1990s single 'Formula One Racing Girls', by Cardiff-based Helen Love, repeated the phrase 'girl power' in its chorus and celebrated a sense of female empowerment borne out of riot grrrl.

Figure 6.3   Front cover of *Riot Grrrl* zine, published in Washington, DC, in the early 1990s

Figure 6.4 *Girl Power!* **zine produced by women in Leeds, Bradford and York in March 1993**

In 1996 the 'girl power' slogan was repeatedly used in the marketing and promotion of the Spice Girls to such an extent that the words actually became synonymous with this pop act. As Jude Davies (1999: 106) observes, the girl power slogan was used to hype the Spice Girls in the lead-up to the launch of their first single, 'Wannabe', in 1996 when a full-page advertisement was placed in the British teen-targeted music magazine *Smash Hits*. The copy of the advertisement read: 'Wanted – anyone with a sense of fun, freedom and adventure. Hold tight, get ready – girl power is comin' at you.'[7] Subsequently, the 'girl power' slogan was incorporated into the merchandising of the band. As Figure 6.5 shows, 'girl power' was printed on a Spice Girls keyring and used as the title of an official book on the band.

Figure 6.5   Spice Girls promotional products and merchandise; the slogan 'girl power' appears on a keyring and as the title of the Spice Girls' book

As a number of critics have pointed out, the message of 'girl power' promoted by the Spice Girls was somewhat contradictory and reductive (Turner, 2001; Lemish, 2003; Schilt, 2003a; Taft, 2004). Their use of the phrase reduced the potential signification of the slogan and curtailed its radicalism. While all of those involved with riot grrrl promoted 'grrrl power', they did so from a diversity of positions. Riot grrrl promoted a form of grrrl power that dealt with the realities of overcoming domestic violence and sexual abuse, promoted the understanding and acceptance of different sexualities, encouraged women to form bands and experiment with music technology and urged girls to resist conventional gender roles. The sloganeering of the Spice Girls is certainly a call to female empowerment, but the band neglected to offer suggestions as to how this might be achieved. To some extent the transformative potential of the words 'girl power' had been replaced by empty sloganeering. The band met queries as to the definition of the phrase with rather vague and all-encompassing replies, but they did offer examples of how girl power could be put into action in their book of the same name:

Girl Power is when …
You help a guy with his bag,
You and your mates reply to wolf whistles by shouting 'Get your arse out!,
You wear high heels *and* think on your feet,
You know you can do it and nothing's going to stop you,
You don't wait around for him to call,

(Spice Girls, 1997: 6)

The version of girl power promoted by the Spice Girls was situated within a discourse of heterosexual romance and seemed to promote churlish point scoring rather than emancipation from constrictive gender roles. The girl power message was re-presented here in a form that diluted its radicalism while offering a catchphrase acceptable for mass-market consumption. It is worth noting here that the Spice Girls were not the first band to copy the slogan 'girl power' for commercial appeal. The British pop act Shampoo, fronted by two vocalists, released a single called 'Girl Power' in 1995. The sleeve art featured the two vocalists: each moodily raising a clenched fist and wearing a knuckleduster emblazoned with the phrase 'girl power'. The image mimicked the marker-pen sloganeering of riot grrrl where some girls had written the phrase r-i-o-t g-r-r-l across their knuckles. The Spice Girls adopted a less confrontational style of gesturality. When uttering the phrase 'girl power' band members would make a peace sign with their hands or often just stretch their hands away from their bodies with the palms facing forward in what appeared as an empty gesture of defiance.

The Spice Girls' message of 'girl power' is certainly problematic, however it might nevertheless be praised for the promotion of an idea of 'empowerment', however diluted, to a young female audience. While acknowledging that the Spice Girls were 'not profound' Whiteley (2000: 227) has argued that the group were important in presenting a message of popular feminism to young fans that was accessible and fun. As Treagus has commented, 'theirs is not a radical subjectivity, but it does mark a shift. … a shift in the battle for hegemony in the representation of females and female subjectivity in popular music, however small a shift it might seem' (Treagus, 1998: 7). Yet, the sassy empowerment that the Spice Girls promoted can not be neatly defined as it both articulated a form of female assertiveness while also centring around traditional feminine concerns such as make-up, clothes and heterosexual love. The ambiguous nature of the Spice Girls' image can be noted across a range of their media productions, from their songs, videos and book *Girl Power!* to their film *Spiceworld*. Dibben's (1999) analysis of the Spice Girls' music video 'Say You'll Be There' points to the polysemic nature of this visual text, where traditional modes of femininity are both confirmed and subverted. As Dibben acknowledges, this ability of the Spice Girls to be interpreted in a number of ways ensures a broad audience appeal and maximum sales potential: 'the traditional signs of femininity are invoked in such a way that popularity is ensured both with a heterosexual male audience, by offering voyeuristic pleasure, and with a female audience, by offering a representation of empowerment which simultaneously retains patriarchal notions of female desireability' (Dibben, 1999: 350).

The relationship between feminism and the Spice Girls' declaration of girl power has been a subject of considerable debate. Within their 1997 book the band presented, in punchy quotes, some statements about feminism that seemed both to acknowledge the importance of the feminist movement to the band members while also distancing them from the history of active political involvement. Emma Bunton ('Baby Spice') is quoted as saying, 'Of course I'm a feminist. But I could never burn my wonderbra. I'm nothing without it!' (Spice Girls, 1997: 15) while a fold-out picture of the band asleep on a king-size bed is accompanied by the statement: 'Feminism has become a dirty word. Girl Power is just a Nineties way of saying it. We can give feminism a kick up the arse' (Spice Girls, 1997: 49). As Taft notes, girl power is presented here as a non-political *alternative* to feminism as the band 'make clear that Girl Power is *not* feminism, but instead is going to be a new way of being girls/women, one that kicks feminism, not embraces or extends it' (Taft, 2004: 71). While the rhetoric of the Spice Girls places emphasis on the supportiveness of the band unit and encourages girls to 'stick with your mates', the presentation of empowerment that they afford is a confidence boost for the individual rather than a call to collective action: 'You believe in yourself and control your own life' (Spice Girls, 1997: 6). In acknowledging this I do not intend to deny the worth of this affirmative message. However, as Taft comments, a message that emphasises individual responsibility and drive oversimplifies and overlooks the ways in which 'gendered, raced, classed, and sexualised identities may give girls privileges or pose challenges' (Taft, 2004: 73). In considering the complexity of identity construction one can note that it is not only in relation to gender politics that the Spice Girls' image is problematic. As Lemish points out, the stylisation and characterisation of Mel B as 'Scary Spice', dressed in animal prints with a pierced tongue, presented a somewhat disturbing portrayal. Lemish comments: 'The literature on the fascination of the white gaze with the black body suggests that framing Melanie B. of all the Spices as the untamed wild creature cannot be dismissed as coincidental' (Lemish, 2003: 27).

A central issue in the debate over the Spice Girls' promotion of girl power is not that a phrase, which has circulated within and held meaning for a particular 'underground' culture, has been co-opted and popularised by the mainstream but that it has been packaged and presented for maximum economic return. As Harris observes: 'the "girlpower" image that highlights young women's sassiness and voice has considerable market value. Young women who attempt to speak up, participate and articulate their experiences have witnessed their words and actions homogenized, commodified and sold back to them in the form of clothing, accessories, toys and popular music' (Harris, A., 2003: 42). Here, then, the exploitation of the 'girl power' message has the effect of reducing it to a series of commercially available consumer products that, although promoting a broadly 'girl positive' message, are very removed from the calls to empowerment and active engagement promoted by riot grrrl. Indeed, as Riordan (2001) points out, the Spice Girls are just one example of the commodification of this pro-girl rhetoric. Considering the marketing of the Spice Girls along with the television series *Buffy the Vampire Slayer* and commercial gURL internet sites, Riordan argues that each of these examples 'point[s] to how a use value, the idea of valuing girls, is changed into an exchange value, commodities intended to "empower" girls' (Riordan, 2001: 290). Similarly, Schilt (2003a) ranks the Spice Girls alongside other recent successful North-American female singer-songwriters as examples of artists who have appropriated and diluted the feminist message of riot grrrl, thereby emptying it of the call to active engagement. In these instances, the radical potential of the girl power message is thus curtailed through its re-presentation as a media product to be consumed.

In offering this critique of the commodification of the girl power message I am not however suggesting that the millions of pre-teen and teenage girls who bought the Spice Girls' records and merchandise should somehow be understood as cultural dupes. As Baker (1999) rightly points out, it is wrong to position young fans of the group as the helpless victims of manipulative marketing. In an active way, young girls could use or reject the different personalities and identities represented by the Spice Girls to work through their own construction of identity. Fritzsche's (2004) research with female fans and former fans of the Spice Girls in Germany shows evidence of this process. Through interviews with these fans, aged between ten and seventeen, Fritzsche found that the girls understood the media image of the Spice Girls as a 'toolbox' that they could use to construct their own identity. The girls drew on different identities within the pop group membership to work out ideas around social expectation. Some playfully trialled different roles by mimicking the behaviours of the band members, while one used the notion of girl power to challenge gender norms. The message and marketing of the Spice Girls may indeed be judged to be a co-optation and watering down of riot grrrl politics, however this is not to deny the significance of the band in the meaning making of their youth audience.

Conclusion

This chapter has explored how riot grrrl operated using different ideological conceptions of public and private space. Grrrls invited involvement by anyone – 'any girls can start gangs anywhere, and you can do stuff by yourself' (*Ablaze!* #10: 15) – while holding fast to the idea of 'the underground'. Zines worked as spaces of articulation, promoting a rhetoric of inclusion: 'This will result in a world-wide society, in which all exist freely and in wonderment, unbounded by old laws of how to live' (*Ablaze!* #10: 17). However, any celebration of riot grrrl needs to be tempered with an acknowledgement of its limitations. The call by riot grrrls to unite with each other resulted in some women feeling that their differences were being denied or ignored. Comments by respondents in this research highlighted how some women felt on the margins of the initiative, perhaps because they did not produce a zine or create music, or because of their class, ethnic or racial identity. Although the zine network connected many women, difficulties in accessing these texts should also be acknowledged. Zines are a transient medium where PO box and email addresses rapidly obsolesce. The small scales of distribution of paper zines mean that they cannot reach a large number of people and access to back issues is often impossible.

The migration of ideas about riot grrrl onto the internet enables an exploration of the different ways in which people engage with and become involved in online cultures. As Williams (2006) has noted, one should not assume that online communities are simply an extension of existing offline cultures. With respect to those involved with straightedge culture he notes that some people use online forums to supplement their involvement within straightedge punk scenes, while other online participants identify themselves as straightedge but are not necessarily interested in punk or hardcore music. For this latter group, the online straightedge community offers a space through which to explore or develop their personal identity. Similarly, the spread of riot grrrl online has opened the network up to different users: from those already involved in local riot grrrl-inspired music scenes to isolated girls who have heard about the initiative and who are using the internet to learn more. While Williams reports conflict between the different members of the straightedge online community no such strong divides are noticeable within riot grrrl. From the outset riot grrrl encouraged the expansion of the network and adaptation of its ideas, which might account for the longevity of the network and the willingness of different generations to take up the idea. Yet, while riot grrrls did not try to establish or maintain boundaries between different participants they did try to 'protect' the initiative from co-optation. The concluding section of this chapter considered how the slogan 'girl power', associated with and reiterated within riot grrrl, moved beyond its circulation within this network to become synonymous with the pop group the Spice Girls. While not wishing to decry the mainstreaming of a call to female empowerment this discussion has revealed how the potentially radical connotations of 'girl power' were emptied out in its translation into a marketable media soundbite.

Notes

1   Riot grrrl articles appeared in a wide variety of publications including *Rolling Stone*, *The New York Times*, *Ms* and *LA Weekly* in the US and the *Daily Star*, *The Wire*, *The Guardian* and *Melody Maker* in the UK.

2   Amelia DeLoach, 'Making Two Negatives a Positive' (http://www.december.com/ cmc/mag/1996/mar/delrec.html), accessed 28 August 1996.

3   RosieX, quoted in DeLoach, ibid.

4   Amelia DeLoach, 'Grrrls Exude Attitude' (http://www.december.com/cmc/mag/1996/ mar/deloach.html), accessed 28 August 1996.

5   A personal zine, or 'perzine', is one that deals with emotional and biographical details of the zine writer's life.

6   This predominance of participation by middle-class girls is noted in Eichhorn's (2001) study of girl-produced zines.

7   The advertisement appeared in *Smash Hits* (4–17 December 1996: 22).

Chapter 7

Ladyfest: online and offline DIY festival promotion

In 2000, nine years after riot grrrl was first promoted, a group of women in Olympia, Washington, organised a week-long festival of music, art, performance and workshops under the name of Ladyfest. The event was organised in commemoration of riot grrrl and reportedly attracted an international audience of approximately 2000 people as well as raising over $30,000 for community-based women's organisations.[1] The event acted as a showcase for artists, a new call to activism and as an example of what could be achieved with DIY spirit. The organisers of the event called for similar festivals to be staged elsewhere using the Ladyfest name. A website was established, which included details of this event and offered advice about festival organisation. The event proved to be an inspiring model and, since then, over 100 Ladyfests have been staged worldwide, each with a dedicated website many of which can be accessed via the original Ladyfest web page. Most festivals have included performances from female-centred acts from the core genres of punk, indie and electronica, along with workshops dealing with a topics ranging from access to employment in the music industry and instrumental tuition to discussions on health, feminism and politics. While all the festivals include musical performance, this sits within a larger programme including other performing and visual arts.

Drawing on comments from those involved, this chapter will trace the growth of Ladyfest and consider the activities and central aims of numerous events held under this banner. It will examine the extent to which Ladyfest continues the work of riot grrrl by operating with a feminist agenda, inspiring women to become involved in creative action and creating a receptive space in which to showcase female musicians and artists. It will consider how these events act as a resource for female performers and audience members, enabling networking and confidence building, but will also discuss the limited reach of these events.

This chapter also examines the spatial dynamics of Ladyfest in order to explore emerging patterns of organisation and mediation within indie music-related networks. As with riot grrrl, networks of zines and websites have been central to the promotion of Ladyfest. Websites have been a key resource for information about these events enabling the formation of new organisational groups and networking between artists and organisers. The 'global' mediation of each event via the web has also meant that each local event has become part of the overall success story of Ladyfest. However Ladyfest cannot be discussed only in relation to these forms of communication as it is clearly grounded on the realisation of 'real world' events. This chapter explores the relationship between online communication and offline meetings, networks and events. As with riot grrrl, women have been encouraged to take the name of

Ladyfest and reinvent it in terms relevant to their own context. However, the focus of Ladyfest on the organisation of a city festival creates a different emphasis to that of riot grrrl. The following discussion considers Ladyfest as a 'public' arts festival, and its relationship with notions of place, community and the public sphere. It will discuss how the location of each festival has influenced the agenda and nature of each event, and how the overall ethos and themes of Ladyfest have been adapted to attend to local specificities.

Parallels can certainly be drawn between the aims and organisation of Ladyfests and other women's music and DIY festivals. For instance, Carson *et al.* (2004: 99) describe how a number of women's music festivals launched in the US in the mid-1970s were 'a wrap-around experience of music, art, workshops, networking, talking, hanging out, sleeping in tents or dormitories, and struggling to find common ground'. A high-profile example of one such event was the Michigan Womyn's Music Festival, which began in 1976 and 'was created from a need for a women-only space in which women could take charge of every aspect of their lives to hear women's music' (Sandstrom, 2000: 293). While it is important to acknowledge the connections between the history of women's music festivals and Ladyfest I also want to emphasise the importance of the particular social and music networks from which Ladyfest developed. The focus of Ladyfest on small, local, DIY events distinguishes it from larger ventures such as Lilith Fair, a commercial touring US festival of women in music, which operated from 1997 to 1999, or the aforementioned Michigan Womyn's Music Festival, which has continued since the 1970s as an annual event. This final chapter focuses on Ladyfest because it sits in a continuum with riot grrrl and is an example of a self-organising network of girls and women drawing inspiration from DIY aesthetics circulating within the punk and post-punk music scenes. While only Ladyfest events will be discussed, it should be noted that these festivals also sit alongside and often share audiences with other DIY feminist and queer identified events. For example, people who attended Ladyfest Manchester 2003 (Figure 7.1) discussed how they had also participated in events such as Sheila Autonomista, an independent, non-profit, women's art, cultural, political, activist festival held in Sydney; Queeruption, a DIY gathering that has taken place in a number of cities internationally since 1998; and Frock On, a series of events including live music and workshops organised by a female collective based in Glasgow.

Background to Ladyfest and links to riot grrrl

The establishment, operation and stated aims of Ladyfest can be placed within a historical continuum stretching back to the post-punk period and following through to the independent music networks of the 1980s and 1990s to include riot grrrl. As Hesmondhalgh (1998) notes, a key discursive and practical thrust of post-punk independent music culture was that of democratisation. For Hesmondhalgh such democratisation was configured around a shift towards easier access to the means of popular music production (in terms of aesthetics, production and distribution), a decentralisation of power in the music industry and a geographical decentralisation of music industry resources (from metropolitan-based major labels to regional independent record labels). This cultural legacy can be felt within many aspects of Ladyfest, not least the use of democratising strategies directly inherited from previous post-punk DIY cultures.

Figure 7.1   Festival programmes and flyers from Ladyfest London 2002 and Ladyfest Manchester 2003

The organisers of the initial Ladyfest made it clear that their intention was not to establish a regular annual event but rather to create a template that others could copy elsewhere. A website[2] was established, which included the minutes from all planning meetings, as well as information and guidelines on how one might stage future festivals. This 'nuts and bolts' highlighting of the processes of cultural production (in this case festival organisation) has been a common feature of DIY cultures since post-punk bands such as The Desperate Bicycles and Scritti Politti included 'how to' guides with 7-inch single releases in the late 1970s (see Laing, 1985; Reynolds, 2005). Throughout the 1980s and 1990s the production of tip sheets, calls to start independent record labels and encouragements to write a zine have been common within indie culture. The widespread use of web-based technologies has allowed this feature of DIY culture to develop further. The nature of the Ladyfest website allows information and new links to be added as events take place. The original Ladyfest website now acts as an archive of information about the aims and approach of the first festival and as a notice board and links page for all the subsequent Ladyfest events that have been staged worldwide. So, while a relatively small number of people attended the first Ladyfest, the posting of information about the event inspired others to take up the challenge of organising similar festivals under the same banner.

In 2001, three Ladyfests were staged in the US (in Bloomington, Indiana, and in Chicago and New York) and the first UK Ladyfest was promoted in Glasgow, Scotland. In 2002, 12 Ladyfests took place: nine of which were in the US and three within European cities. As information about these events was disseminated the number and geographic spread of the festivals increased: 2003 saw the staging of 21 Ladyfests including events in Belgium, Australia, England, Germany and Indonesia; the number of festivals has since grown with 25 festivals organised in 2004 and 31 in 2005. The global spread of Ladyfest has led to events taking place in countries including Austria, Brazil, Poland, Singapore and South Africa. The ideological drive behind these events distinguishes them from other, perhaps more commercially orientated, independent arts festivals. Almost all of the festival organisation teams describe themselves as non-profit organisations. The organisers of Ladyfest Melbourne 2003 were an exception as they registered as a company, but with the express aim of donating any profits to a number of charitable women's causes (personal communication, 19 August 2003). The economic cost and return of festival organisation is certainly something that must be acknowledged. As Stanley Waterman comments, unless an arts festival 'is privately endowed, freeing the organisers to follow their artistic inclinations, it is likely to become caught up in the politics and economics of currying favour with government subsidizers or commercial sponsors' (Waterman, 1998: 61). While some Ladyfest organisers have sought sponsorship there is no evidence so far that commercial interests are dictating or having influence over the agenda and planning of these events. The motivating spirit of DIY activism helps to ensure that Ladyfests are organised on a voluntary basis, running costs kept to a minimum and commercial sponsors do not interfere with the planning of festival programmes.

In many ways the development and ethos of Ladyfest events echo those of riot grrrl. Indeed, there is a considerable crossover between the people involved in the riot grrrl network and those active within Ladyfest. The name itself has a irony that can be seen as companion to the feisty growl of riot grrrl. As the Ladyfest Berlin 2005 website explains 'When the term of »girl« was more and more adopted by the fashion and music industries, the grrrls acquired the tougher and more mature »lady« to create a new subversive term.'[3] The festival title suggests female maturity while simultaneously resisting and satirising notions of gentle, feminine, passivity associated with 'ladylike' behaviour. Just as those involved in riot grrrl encouraged women to claim the name and apply it in a way that was personally meaningful, so Ladyfest can be seen as a way to badge different events that share a common purpose but that do not conform to a standard format. The organisers of the first Ladyfest event did not request that future events should stick to a rigid set of activities. As an organiser of Ladyfest Texas 2003 commented: 'I think web access is great so people can find out this stuff is happening and it's great because you don't have to have permission or anything, you can just take the name and throw one yourself' (personal communication, 2 September 2003). Thus each event, while following the broad aims of the original, offers a different set of activities and core concerns that relate to the interests and agendas of the local organisers. For instance, one of the organisers of Ladyfest Manchester, England, was interested in comics and so the festival included a gallery of comic book art. Organisers of other festivals have been film-makers, community activists and visual artists, and so their emphasis has drawn the festival agenda away from centring chiefly on music.

Ladyfests have typically been staged over three or four days, although there have been a number of one- and two-day festivals as well as more extended programmes, with Ladyfest Berlin 2004 stretching over two weeks. All the festivals feature a mixed programme of events often including music, visual art displays, film screenings and spoken-word performances. Events usually begin around mid-morning and stretch through with a full programme into the night. Workshops form part of the daytime schedule of these festivals, with sessions covering a diverse range of topics and activities from practical sessions on self-defence, music making, car maintenance, crocheting, dancing and cooking to discussions around topics such as racism, surviving sexual abuse, ecology, indie publishing and booking DIY tours. Music has been a central feature in all of the Ladyfests organised so far and often this has included styles of rock associated with riot grrrl. Festival organisers stipulate that the performing acts must be female-centred if not exclusively female. As the website for Ladyfest Spain 2005 explains: 'The goal of Ladyfest is to increase the visibility of women in the indie and underground worlds and this is the reason why women are the main players in this festival.'[4] Some organisers have tried to broaden out the types of music programmed during these events – for example, Ladyfest Texas included an electronica and country showcase and Ladyfest Brisbane 2005 offered a night of hip hop, dancehall, jungle and drum 'n' bass. However, it is notable that the majority of acts fall within the taste formations of the alternative and indie rock cultures from which riot grrrl sprang. African-American musics such as hip hop and R'n'B for instance, while appearing in some festival programmes, have been secondary to a central rock emphasis.

The initiation of Ladyfest, its philosophy and the forms of participation that take place in each event all show a strong level of continuity with the aims of riot grrrl. This lineage was remarked upon by those involved. For example, women involved in Ladyfest Spain 2005 commented that Ladyfest demonstrates an ongoing lineage with and advancement of the ideas of riot grrrl: 'Ladyfest has inherited most of the ideals from the riot grrrl movement. Once the riot grrrl movement was known and accepted, they decided to go a step further and create other means of female involvement and this is how Ladyfest was born' (personal communication, 18 April 2005). Ladyfest has been able to build on the foundations of riot grrrl, attracting the attention of those with an awareness of this network while also tapping in to a new audience who were too young to become involved from the start. As Brea, the music coordinator for Ladyfest Texas 2003, reflected:

> ladyfest couldn't exist without riot grrrl. riot grrrl set up this stage for future ladies to come out and put on a show all about women in d.i.y. atmosphere. ... I liked riot grrrl before I was involved with ladyfest, but I grew up in a real small town and didn't find out about

riot grrrl until the major surge was over with. (personal communication, 2 September 2003)

While the internet presence of Ladyfest sites gives a sense of connected organisation and steady growth, it should be noted that each of these events is largely independent in terms of the development of the programme and the realisation of the festival. Even in a city where a Ladyfest has been staged in successive years there may be no connection or communication between the organisational committees of these events. This point was highlighted by one of my respondents, who was part of an organising team in a city where a Ladyfest event had taken place in a previous year. She commented that the planned festival 'follows the model of earlier Ladyfests, although we do not copy a template. Although we have tried to get information from the previous … [local] organizers, they have not been forthcoming so we do not have the benefit of institutional memory' (personal communication). In this sense Ladyfest has a clear parallel with the development of riot grrrl over time. This has resulted in successions of girls and women setting up urban chapters that have, in some instances, no connection with previous riot grrrls active within the same city. Cateforis and Humphreys (1997) reflect on this process in their consideration of the activities of riot grrrl groups in New York. They comment that the 'rapid decay and growth rate between generations would indicate that Riot Grrrl's communities are not modeled upon stable lineages. Rather, Riot Grrrl is wrested from history, perpetually reinventing its identity in accordance with the goals and concerns of new Grrrls' (Cateforis and Humphreys, 1997: 337). Through interviews with those involved I have found this process of reinvention and renewal to be a facet of both riot grrrl and Ladyfest. Red Chigley, a zine writer and distributor involved in UK riot grrrl chapters and with the organisation of a number of Ladyfests, commented:

> That's the basic vitality of riot grrrl and Ladyfests – girls take something and build on it, transpose it, transform it. And it will be a different thing, unique to all those involved, the country you're at etc. … we don't erase our histories we create them again and again. (personal communication, 2 October 2003)

However, while establishing the links between Ladyfest and riot grrrl, it is also important to recognise that Ladyfest has distinct qualities in part because of its concentration on a single event. As already discussed, people engaged with riot grrrl in a variety of public and private ways: from forming bands and organising music workshops to writing a zine or corresponding with other riot grrrls via postal or online networks. Participation with riot grrrl did not require a coherent, structured framework of organisation as it was made up of people opting in and out of a range of activities in different locations over time. Riot grrrl was *intended* to be open to anyone wishing to identify with its ideas and so did not *require* a prescribed type of participatory behaviour.[5] The organisation of a Ladyfest event sets a timeline for participation and requires face-to-face organisational meetings. Moreover, while many of the riot grrrls that I interviewed did not wish to offer a definition of riot grrrl, the organisation of a festival programme requires those involved to discuss and agree the central objectives of the festival and to work towards achieving these in the final event. In addition to this it should be considered that Ladyfest is intended as a progressive step on from riot grrrl and so, while informed by a similar sensibility, it is attempting to address new issues. As Megan from Ladyfest East commented:

> I think ladyfest was definitely borne of the riot grrl movement. I think it appeals the unapologetically feminist and diy roots of riot grrl. But I don't think of what I am doing with ladyfest as a riot grrl thing. I think that associating ladyfest with riot grrl is rather limiting. I'm interested in making a broader appeal to different women and going outside of a more comfortable space. The comfortable space is nurturing and important in a lot of ways, I feel, but I also think it is time to move past it. (personal communication, 22 January 2004)

Aims of the festivals

While the democratising thrust of Ladyfest has been adapted to suit local specificities this does not preclude the identification of common strategies across the differing festivals. In order to identify the core aims within Ladyfest an analysis of the mission statements and rationale given within the websites of Ladyfests worldwide was undertaken. In keeping with Ladyfest's roots within DIY cultures there was a broad concern with the politics of cultural production. In other words, festival organisers engaged with key concerns over: who controls and has access to the means of cultural production; what the implications of such controls are in relation to what work is promoted; who is represented within the public sphere of artistic works and cultural products. Key motivating factors for the staging of the festivals were a desire to challenge: the continuance of a masculinist culture within indie rock culture; the lack of representation of women within the performing and visual arts; the difficulties encountered by female artists in terms of securing contracts, promotion and distribution. Broadly, the aims of the festivals were articulated in four main ways: facilitation, recognition/promotion, inclusion and support/networking. Each of these aims worked towards counteracting the gendered unevenness of cultural production.

First, Ladyfests were often intended to act as a facilitator of creative action among women within a given cultural field or locality. A number of the organisers commented that in addition to acting as a showcase for established performers Ladyfest could work to inspire women to establish bands. Rina, the communications and sponsorship manager of Ladyfest Melbourne 2003 commented on this by stating that the demand for the event was 'HUGE – it's so wanted and needed. Women have gotten in bands just to perform at Ladyfest' (personal communication, 19 August 2003). Similarly, Nihal, who was planning a Ladyfest in Istanbul, remarked that she hoped that the success of other Ladyfest events might work to inspire women in her country. She commented that the 'only barrier in Turkey is there are not so many women-only music bands. I am hoping that Ladyfest Istanbul will encourage women to be in a band. ... Ladyfest can make women feel the power inside and make them see if they can do we can do it too' (personal communication, 31 March 2005).

Second, organisers often highlighted the supportive and promotional role of Ladyfest as a platform for female artists. Many of the mission statements repeated the core aims of Ladyfest Olympia 2000, which stated that the festival was 'designed by and for women to showcase, celebrate and encourage the artistic, organizational and political work and talents of women'.[6] This rationale clearly fits into a feminist agenda seeking recognition and acclaim for the work of female artists, and an elevation of their status in the professional realm as well as the broader public arena. Here, then, the act of celebration clearly has an ideological and political intent. A parallel might be drawn with the annual Latin American festival in Twin Springs North Carolina documented by Murillo (1997). As Murillo discusses, this festival also adopts the seemingly 'innocent' and 'neutral' aim of being a 'celebration of culture'. While this conception of the festival may not seem at first to be political in nature Murillo notes that 'celebration and culture are not stagnant, rigid, and independent objects; rather, they are public, processual, and ideological responses by the festival organizers that may characterize their interpretations of the changing social context and, by extension, constitute the pedagogical meaning of the festival' (Murillo, 1997: 272). Certainly, there is an educational function in such events as they raise awareness of a diversity of cultural practices and achievements. Indeed Ladyfest is very active in this respect by offering those in attendance workshops, discussion forums, exhibitions, and a showcase of spoken-word and musical performance by female artists.

It is clear that organisers have been motivated not just by a desire to celebrate women's work within the creative arts but by a perceived need to open up new spaces in which to exhibit, perform and display this work. The organisers of Ladyfest Brisbane 2005 commented that, 'women's art is still not given the respect and audience it deserves. ... We are responding to the continued need to carve independent spaces to show our work on our own terms, outside the confines of normatively-defined and approved self-expression.'[7] Thus Ladyfest can be seen to provide a much needed opportunity for the work of women artists to be heard and shown. In this respect the festivals are helping to counteract the barriers that female artists have encountered when dealing with cultural gatekeepers such as record labels, booking agents, venue managers and gallery curators. In the process of doing so they are also validating the work of selected artists. The website for Ladyfest Timisoara 2005 explicitly made this point by stating that the aim was to promote female artists based on the merit of their work and to combat the ghettoisation of women's art.

A third aim of Ladyfests has been to recognise, interrogate and embrace notions of 'difference' and to work towards an inclusionist agenda. An example can be taken of Ladyfest Vienna 2005, whose organisers set out to create a programme that promoted feminist, queer and transgender cultures. Its website stressed an opposition to heteronormativity and a quest to destabilise the neat ways in which gender is categorised, commenting 'a strong transforming opposition should be held against this system that is based on categories of "difference". We want to attack this system by making the functions and mechanisms of creating borders visible.'[8] This drive to deconstruct and challenge particular forms of identity categorisation was in evidence in numerous workshops and discussion sessions within Ladyfests worldwide, which discussed the ways in which constructions of gender inform societal roles.

In addition to challenging the ways in which the construction of gender has operation within society the democratic thrust of Ladyfest has encouraged organisers to consider how they can make each festival an inclusive event. In a variety of ways organisers have tried to identify and remove barriers to participation in their events. For example, an organiser of Ladyfest Philly 2003 reflected that the issue of diversity was one that the organisers had discussed at length. While the key organisers were mostly women from the local indie/punk community, they tried to make the event accessible to others through the music they chose to select for inclusion. The organiser, who sat on the music committee, commented that:

> a mostly white, indie line-up would just not make sense in Philadelphia and it wouldn't accurately represent this city or the people in it. We really tried to diversify at the level of the organizers and were somewhat successful … but where we really had control was at the level of the performers. We tried to include many different genres and mediums, many racial, ethnic and socio-economic backgrounds. (personal communication, 2 September 2003)

She commented that this policy of opening up the types of musics they included in the programme was successful in attracting a diverse audience. Other organisers commented that they had been careful to ensure that they could set an affordable ticket price for their events so that they did not block anyone from attendance on economic grounds. The committee of Ladyfest Ottawa 2005 also expressed awareness of how linguistic bias might act as a barrier to participation and reflected that they were trying to include an increased amount of bilingual/Francophone content within their programme.

Fourth, Ladyfests are intended to have a supportive function and to offer a networking opportunity for participants. As those involved in Ladyfest Timisoara, Romania, commented, the goals of the event stretched beyond a planned music festival as the organisers wished to create a space 'designed for women and their creative, or interactive pieces, and a space to come together and talk, teach one another and discuss'.[9] This drive for communication between women was intended both to foster supportive alliances and to further careers within the arts with the aim that, as stated within the Ladyfest Adelaide 2004 website, 'Participants will expand networks and develop relationships that will offer new pathways and opportunities in music/arts industry involvement.'[10]

Ladyfests are, then, a way of connecting up likeminded people who may be active within existing local, or indeed translocal, music, art or feminist networks, scenes or communities. The comments of Heather, who was involved in the organisation of Ladyfest Halifax 2003 in Canada, suggested that she understood Ladyfest as an opportunity for women to showcase their creative work, support one another and become active within local creative circles. For her, Ladyfest was a way through which participants could gain courage and contacts to work within local communities rather than constituting a community within itself. Heather discussed how she had been afforded the opportunity for travel and networking through an invitation to participate in Ladyfest Los Angeles. Financed by an artist travel grant from the Canadian Government she presented a film she had made at the Los Angeles event and delivered a hands-on animation workshop. She reflected:

> The experience of Ladyfest Los Angeles was completely wonderful. It was dizzyingly glamorous to show my film work in L.A., and yet it was inspiring to see artists joining

forces to showcase underground work. It was a very elegant combination of industry professionals and staunch independents working together to celebrate the achievements of women. Some of the most intelligent, passionate women I've ever met were at that festival. (personal communication, 19 August 2003)

Her reflection on the impact of Ladyfest placed emphasis not on the event as an end in itself but as an enabling device, building the confidence of participants in their daily lives. In relation specifically to Ladyfest Halifax she remarked that the event was an opportunity to build the skills and confidence of those attending. She commented: 'I'm interested in using Ladyfest as a springboard to integrate more women into the arts scene here, rather than treating it like a separatist movement that will replace the existing institutional structures' (personal communication, 19 August 2003). Ladyfest is certainly not unique as a network that intersects and overlaps with other defined and complementary networks and scenes. For example, comparison can be drawn with the investigation by Purdue *et al.* (1997) into DIY culture in the UK. Focusing on case studies of three networks (organic food box schemes, music festivals and local exchange trading systems) the researchers found the DIY culture was made up of 'a family of self-organising networks, with overlapping memberships and values' (Purdue *et al.*, 1997: 647). In this instance, rather like Ladyfest events, the music festivals held importance as an 'expression of marginal identities and novel pleasures' (1997: 647).

Online and offline festival organisation

Having considered the key aims within Ladyfest the discussion will now focus on the planning and production of these events through online communications, such as email and websites, and offline activities such as meetings, fundraisers and indeed the festival event itself. The online and offline presence of Ladyfest function in different ways and allow for different modes of engagement that it is important to understand. As scholars (Nip, 2004; Wilson and Atkinson, 2005) have noted, the relationship between online and offline communities has been somewhat under-theorised. Referring particularly to studies of youth cultures Wilson and Atkinson comment: 'existing research on Internet (youth) cultures tends to focus on either online or offline subcultural experiences, without uncloaking the links between these two subcultural worlds, or interrogating the implications of these links for subcultural members' (Wilson and Atkinson, 2005: 277). Ladyfest presents a good case study through which to examine the links between online and offline worlds.

The promotion of Ladyfest via the web has proved an effective way to disseminate information about festival production by offering information and practical advice on the logistics involved and also providing a way to contact other organisers. The original Ladyfest website can be viewed as a hub or 'nodal point' (Hodkinson, 2003: 290) providing links to other Ladyfest sites past and present. Aside from this original Ladyfest site there is also a European website entitled Ladyfest Europe, which also functions as a hub or node within the Ladyfest network. This site affords an overview of activities happening across this geographic area, acts as a bulletin board and archive, and rallies for the production of further festivals. This sense of electronic connectivity is reinforced by each discrete Ladyfest website, which includes hyperlinks to the two main hub sites as well as to the web pages of other planned festivals taking place in the same country or in neighbouring countries. The documentation of the festivals via each website gives a permanence to these otherwise ephemeral events and is testimony that it is possible to successfully organise a festival without prior experience. Visitors can click through the online pages of past festivals reading message boards, programme details, mission statements, press accounts and even downloading promotional posters. As Elliott (2004: 285) found within his study of the online interactions of enthusiasts of the music genre Goa trance: 'the act of linking between sites should be considered a potentially community-building context (and, thus, a prime ethnographic site) in and of itself'. Similarly, the presence of Ladyfest online creates a supportive virtual network and encourages potential organisers to feel that they are 'part of something'. This function was commented on by Nihal, whom I contacted while she was planning to stage a Ladyfest in Istanbul. She reflected that the 'Ladyfest Europe website is important to someone who has no idea about such things. It makes you feel you can do it and it encourages you in every way. After I mailed them I got mails from all over Europe' (personal communication, 31 March 2005).

Ladyfest websites thus play a key role in disseminating information about festival events and provide an online 'toolbox' enabling women interested in the initiative to organise one themselves. Thus the virtual presence of Ladyfest is instrumental in facilitating the production of local events around the globe using this moniker. It should be acknowledged that those who access this online resource have probably become aware of Ladyfest either through events happening in their area or more likely through awareness of or connections with local or translocal riot grrrl, feminist, queer or music networks or scenes. This has parallels with Atkinson's research into the online and offline interactions of straightedge practitioners where he found that the online promotion of straightedge music events worked as 'a device for bringing people together in real time' (Wilson and Atkinson, 2005: 297).Yet while Ladyfest websites might attract people who have similar or sympathetic interests it is not simply a virtual communication device for people who already know one another or who already exist as a coherent group. Importantly, Ladyfest websites enable the establishment of new connections and contacts, and many of the organising committees are made up of people who have volunteered and come to know one another via email communication. Thus an offline Ladyfest network is established and facilitated by online communication tools.

Academic discussions (Kibby, 2000; Bennett, 2002; Darling-Wolf, 2004) concerned with the characteristics of and participatory engagement within virtual music 'communities' or 'scenes' have resonance with an analysis of the communication systems and forms of interaction found within the websites and chatrooms of Ladyfest organisers and participants. As the term community suggests in this application, certain types of engagement with others via the internet extend beyond temporal, disengaged, disconnected cyber interactions and actually constitute participation within a group of networked individuals sharing similar tastes or concerns. However, while identifying connections between online Ladyfest interactions and theorisations of 'virtual communities', I also want to argue that the concept of networking is key to an understanding of the development of Ladyfest online. As Castells argues, while 'Communities, at least in the tradition of sociological research, were based on the sharing of values and social organization. Networks are built by the choices and strategies of social actors, be it individuals, families, or social groups' (Castells, 2003: 127). Comments from women involved in different Ladyfests around the globe repeatedly used the term network in order to describe involvement in these events both at a local and international level:

> Networking and boosting confidence is something that Ladyfest excels at.
> (Red Chigley, involved in a number of UK Ladyfests as well as contributing to the Ladyfest Europe website, personal communication, 2 October 2003)

> the women's network I think is key here
> (Brea, music organiser Ladyfest Texas 2003, personal communication, 15 August 2003)

> there is a huge network of connected women now … with side projects already started. I think hopefully it at least opened some eyes as to what is possible.
> (organiser for Ladyfest Philly 2003, personal communication, 2 September 2003)

> Through ladyfests amazing networks are already being established, just look at the enormous domino-effect it had in Europe.
> (Hilde, organiser for Ladyfest Amsterdam 2002, personal communication, 21 August 2003)

The use of the term network refers to the active lines of communication and activity between participants and to the facility that has been created for people to establish new working projects or pass on information. This informal organising structure has reflection in the communication channels of riot grrrl and seems in sympathy with the nature of Ladyfest as a feminist project.

While networking, promotion and information about these events is exchanged within cyberspace, the realisation of a public festival raises interesting issues about how these events engage with or respond to the cultures within their locations. In some instances it is easy to trace the relationship between the festivals and existing urban music and art scenes. The first event, for example, was initiated by people who had been active within riot grrrl, and took place in Olympia (Washington), a city central to the growth of the riot grrrl network. The location of the event and the links with riot grrrl enabled it to draw the attention of a large dispersed international audience of riot grrrls. Ladyfest Olympia 2000 also plugged into a local music and arts scene, which has historically drawn international critical acclaim within indie music circles. Thus the festival could draw on an existing local resource of musicians, venues and journalists.

Likewise, a number of other urban festivals, such as those in Seattle, Austin, New York and Timisoara (Romania), had the benefit of drawing on a surrounding pool of people active within well-established local music and arts scenes. Many of those planning a Ladyfest could thus develop a strong organisational network by involving people active within local music, feminist, queer and riot grrrl scenes and networks. For example, Ladyfest Birmingham (UK) 2004 developed contacts with an estimated 150 community groups, businesses, art networks, music establishments and organisations throughout the West Midlands area. The organisers were allowed to promote the event through the mailing lists of some of these organisations, which, they report, allowed them to send 1000 publicity mailouts.[11] Moreover, while each festival may only stretch over three or four days, the long planning period leading up to a Ladyfest allows it to establish a presence within a locale through the staging of numerous fundraising gigs and events in the preceding year.

Crucially, each festival is focused not only on engaging with existing music and art scenes but with affecting change within them. By including the work of local artists within their programmes the events can raise the profile of local female practitioners and showcase artists who may not have much experience of publicly showing or performing their work. Brea, the music organiser for Ladyfest Texas, reflected on this process, commenting, 'we gave priority to local bands since it was our first ladyfest and we were trying to build community here in Austin' (personal communication, 2 September 2003). In response to this she commented that lots of people 'came out of the woodwork' and that the festival had a real impact in both bringing together likeminded people and also in highlighting that there were some strong female bands from the local area. Likewise, Ladyfest Seattle produced a set of aims that were specifically addressed at achieving change at a local level. Their goals included local networking, pooling resources with women's organisations in Seattle, and encouraging local venues and art spaces not directly involved in Ladyfest to show support by booking female artists during the month it took place. In addition to this, some Ladyfests have had an economic impact at a local level through fundraising. Local beneficiaries have included an anti-violence education organisation in New York, Brighton Refuge in the UK and the Girlz Rhythm 'N Rock Camp in Ohio, which is a week-long summer camp led by experienced female musicians offering music workshops and training to young women aged 10–18.

In some instances, organisers used Ladyfest as an opportunity to speak out to and against dominant discourses in the surrounding region or public culture. An illustration of such an engagement with place can be seen in the organisation of Ladyfest Biblebelt 2004. One of the core goals of this event was 'To demonstrate that the definition of grassroots organization must include the acknowledgement that it will manifest itself in forms specific to geography and political history.'[12] In relation to this the organising committee produced a statement that:

> We are doing Ladyfest Biblebelt for everyone who lives in a small southern town and dares to be themselves regardless of the repercussions. We are doing Ladyfest Biblebelt for those who cannot get away from the South and for those who actually want to stay. We are doing Ladyfest Biblebelt to make the south a better place to live. (Ladyfest Biblebelt 2004 website)[13]

Here, organisers viewed the festival as a way to show resistance to what they perceived as the homogenising and constrictive nature of the dominant culture. Ladyfest was an opportunity to celebrate feminist and queer cultures, and to signal both the presence and worth of different constructions of identity. A comparison can be drawn here with Meyer and O'Hara's (2003) study of the National Women's Music Festival (NWMF) when it was staged at Ball State University in Muncie,

Indiana, in 1998. As the study details, this festival (which is an annual event) was organised chiefly by lesbian feminists to promote women's music and so 'provided opportunities for festigoers to escape the constraints of dominant discourse and to engage in teaching and leaning about lesbian feminist politics – a risky activity in most public arenas' (Meyer and O'Hara, 2003: 12). In this instance, as with the various Ladyfests, a temporary space was opened up that allowed those attending the festival to celebrate their identities, as well as providing 'a crucial network for many women who are marginalized in the larger public discourse' (Meyer and O'Hara, 2003: 21).

The mission statement of Ladyfest Biblebelt used an assertive and defiant tone, which some other organisers have purposely avoided. An organiser of Ladyfest Spain discussed the concern of the committee to be sensitive to the ways in which they advertised the festival so as not to alienate their potential audience. She reflected that, while they were keen to follow the central aims of Ladyfest, they needed to adapt their approach in order to reflect the needs and culture of their country. She explained:

> in Spain, it is very difficult to even bring up the idea of transgender issues in any of our publicity because people would completely freak out. Spain just isn't at that point yet where people can have a dialogue about transgender issues because we're still dealing with other basic rights. Needless to say, we would like to keep the component of queer issues in our organizing efforts and transgender issues will be addressed, but just not in the publicity distributed to the open public. Sad … (personal communication, 18 April 2005)

There is thus an important relationship between the aims and organisation of Ladyfest events and the geographic places in which they are staged.

On a smaller scale, one can consider how the festival event itself acts as a transformative space. Spaces that are traditionally male dominated, such as pub bar rooms and live music venues, are transformed during the run of the festival as areas for female performance, empowerment and networking.[14] As an organiser of Ladyfest Amsterdam 2002 commented:

> Being present at Ladyfest, I felt for the first time ever what the real vibe is of women being together in a space, being creative and supportive. It's something I always dreamt of from the day I "became" a riot grrrl and didn't get to experience until 2001, when I visited Ladyfest Glasgow. (personal communication, 21 August 2003)

During the festivals, spaces such as church halls, arts centres and squats are temporarily transformed as venues for feminist discussion groups, music workshops and exhibition spaces for creative work. As Heather, an organiser of Ladyfest Halifax in Canada, explained, 'we're taking on the responsibility of opening up space, especially non-traditional space, to artists. We're also going to try to build the skills and confidence of the women who attend our events, to get them out there being active in the community' (personal communication, 19 August 2003).

As each festival runs over a number of days and includes numerous spaces in which attendees can congregate (by fanzine and merchandise stalls or in bars and café areas) the festival site encourages sociality and networking between those present. Moreover, respondents described how the festival events were powerful in creating a sense of possibility. The realisation of each event acted as a testimony to what could be achieved through collective action and presented an alternative model of behaviour and achievement that indicated possibilities for social change. By this I do not mean to overstate the achievements of Ladyfest but to consider the impact of each event in showcasing creative work and in enacting behavioural patterns that are progressive in terms of gender politics. As Megan, an organiser for Ladyfest East in New York, commented:

> for me, when I think about who ladyfest is going to change things for, I always think of the skills and community that the people involved in the process of putting on a ladyfest will pick up – I'm meaning the organizers, of course, but also all of the volunteers who are going to learn how to cold-call and organize and run technical sound equipment for a show and operate under a lot of stress with a great payoff ... and how revolutionary is it for girls in an incredibly boy-driven scene to participate, even as an audience, in something that was organized and performed entirely by women? (personal communication, 22 January 2004)

Limits

It is difficult to establish to what extent awareness of and involvement in Ladyfest extends to an audience beyond those who are already involved within certain riot grrrl, queer, feminist or Ladyfest networks. While websites are useful promotional tools, perhaps people will only happen to find out about festival details if they search for exact terms such as 'grrrl' and 'Ladyfest'. One respondent from Ladyfest Amsterdam commented that 'one of the biggest limits of Ladyfest: that it's only alive within a certain group, or groups, of people' (personal communication). She commented that this has the benefit of creating an event enjoyed by likeminded people, but it also meant that the ideas around the event were reaching only a small clique of people. The limited 'reach' of Ladyfest, in terms of the interests and taste identifications of those involved, has comparison with Hodkinson's (2003) discussion of internet communication within the goth scene. Despite the *potential* for a heterogeneous group of people to browse and participate in goth websites, Hodkinson's research found that the ways in which people located dedicated websites and discussion groups, and the organisation and links between sites, meant that they were 'relatively exclusive subcultural spaces' (Hodkinson, 2003: 291).

Organisers from a number of other Ladyfests concurred with the summation that generally there is a limited range of people involved, even though organising committees were making efforts to widen participation. One respondent, who was involved in the organisation of Ladyfest Manchester 2003, commented that part of the problem of reach might be accounted for by the modes of communication organisers used. She commented that one limitation was 'relying on emails and existing feminist/rg networks to support the event and not making more inventive and time-consuming links with the communities (e.g. schools, youth clubs, unis, etc etc)' (personal communication, 2 October 2003). It must be noted, however, that the tendency of Ladyfests to reach a distinct and defined audience is not a marker of their particular insularity but a typical feature of festival organisation in general. As Waterman argues, often information about arts festivals 'reaches only those who are already tuned to the right wavelength, i.e., those who already have information about it in the first place' and moreover the 'repertoire can be, and often is, constructed upon a format that favours those with a specific cultural background and/or education' (Waterman, 1998: 67).

As discussed in the previous chapter, one criticism of riot grrrl was that while ostensibly it was inclusive of all women, in practice it tended to favour the concerns of those who are white and middle-class. Ladyfest organisers seem highly aware of issues of inclusion, however a bias towards white, middle-class participation seems to persist. As one organiser from Ladyfest Manchester commented, 'We had all these ideas that we were going to get all these people from ethnic backgrounds involved but as you can see if you look around it is mainly white women … from an age range late teens to early 30s' (personal communication, 6 September 2003). An organiser from Ladyfest Amsterdam commented that perhaps Ladyfest was failing to reach a more diverse range of people because of the approach to feminist issues that the organisers were adopting. So there is somewhat of a contradiction at the heart of Ladyfest. Its rhetoric is about empowerment and inclusion, as the Ladyfest Europe website states the events are about 'encouraging the talents of women and girls but are open to everyone'.[15] Ladyfests thus promote a politics of openness and most of the websites stipulate that the events will not exclude anyone on grounds of age, race, gender, class or sexuality. However, at the same time, the roots of Ladyfest are in the underground indie music scene and so the modes of expression offered within Ladyfest and the types of events staged tend to reflect and appeal to this cultural sphere. Clearly, the events have a palpable impact on those attending, creating for many a sense of empowerment and facilitating the development of new skills. Yet, the appeal of these events, while reaching a transnational audience, still seems to be restricted to a relatively narrow range of people who are already tapped in to alternative and underground taste communities.

Conclusion

One can consider the online communications of Ladyfest, evident in bulletin boards, chat groups, websites and email networks, as indicative of the ways in which new technologies are creatively being put to use within numerous DIY cultures in order to mediate ideas, promote activities or foster new alliances. Within numerous popular music cultures there is evidence of how new communication tools offered by developing media technologies are enabling DIY music promotion, allowing music makers to bypass the gatekeeping function of the music and media industries and to communicate directly with listeners and fans. The ability to communicate through chatrooms, establish electronic mailing lists or network via a global portal like MySpace, illustrates how technologies are facilitating the formation of new networks. But it is important to recognise that these networks are not just being created in the expanse of cyberspace but often have continuity with existing offline cultures and communities. As discussed here, Ladyfest draws its audience from existing music, feminist, queer and riot grrrl networks, but in doing so creates new connections and forges new partnerships. So this is not to present a deterministic argument whereby new technologies determine new relations or impose new social relations but to recognise that these technologies enable new connections and frequently extend the reach of existing interest groups or taste communities.

In terms of the phenomenon of Ladyfest itself, clearly the initiative offers a working model of DIY festival production that has application in a variety of social and geographic contexts. The establishment of so many Ladyfest events has assisted in the promotion of numerous artists who have performed, exhibited or otherwise participated in several Ladyfests worldwide. These festivals provide artists with a ready circuit of venues, sympathetic promoters, and access to new and receptive audiences. They also offer a platform to musicians with little professional experience, thus helping with confidence building and establishing a record of public performance. However, the organisational frame of Ladyfest within any given country is sporadic and discontinuous, involving people for a limited period of time towards the realisation of a local festival who may not continue within event promotion. Thus Ladyfest does not necessarily have a permanent effect on a local music industry or art world in terms of enabling an increased booking of female performers in venues or the availability of gallery spaces for developing artists. What it does seem to provide, however, is inspiration, experience and networking, which have an impact on the lives of those who have contributed, organised and attended Ladyfests.

Notes

1   Information taken from the website of Ladyfest East 2004 (http://www.ladyfesteast. org/about.html), accessed 24 November 2004.

2   See www.ladyfest.org.

3   Ladyfest Berlin 2005 website (http://www.advise-it.de/ladyfest/eng/ladyfest.html), accessed 10 August 2005.

4   Ladyfest Spain 2005 website (http://www.ladyfestspain.org/), accessed 1 August 2005.

5   As already discussed, this egalitarian aim has not truly been realised as people active within riot grrrl have tended to share similar tastes as well as social and cultural backgrounds.

6   Ladyfest Olympia 2000 website (http://www.ladyfest.org/index3.html), accessed 10 August 2005.

7   Ladyfest Brisbane 2005 website (http://www.ladyfestbrisbane.com/about.html), accessed 28 July 2005.

8   Ladyfest Vienna 2005 website (http://www.ladyfestwien.org/ladyfest05_eng.html), accessed 19 August 2005.

9   Ladyfest Timisoara website (http://romania.indymedia.org/en/2005/05/838.shtml), accessed 28 July 2005.

10   Ladyfest Adelaide 2004 website (http://www.adelaiderockladies.net/ladyfestadelaide/), accessed 10 August 2005.

11   Details of the promotion of this event are available at http://www.ladyfestbirmingham. org/support/.

12   Information taken from the website of Ladyfest Biblebelt 2004 (http://ladyfestbiblebelt. org/).

13   http://ladyfestbiblebelt.org/.

14   See Carson *et al.* (2004: 164–8) for a description of the staging of Ladyfest Midwest in 2001, which took place in various venues including an old theatre used as a rock venue and a bar-restaurant.

15   Ladyfest   Europe   website   (http://www.ladyfesteurope.org/old/generalinfo.html), accessed 30 March 2006.

Conclusion

All too often the music industry as a whole has been referenced as 'macho' or 'male' without an investigation into why this might be said to be the case. Using the case study of indie rock, this book has examined how the association of rock with masculinity is produced and maintained within the music industry. I have argued that the heavy weighting of male to female employees in certain sectors of the industry does not in itself explain why particular music genres are understood as male. The association of rock and masculinity is not simply a hangover from the domination of early rock 'n' roll by male performers, nor is it premised solely upon the fact that male performers have been more visible within rock practice. Rock, like all popular music, is not a static form or entity but is continually being performed, listened to and discussed. The creation of new songs, adoption of novel performance techniques, and introduction of unconventional instruments and technologies pushes at and stretches the defining boundaries of the genre. I have argued that the masculinist character of rock practice is not just an inheritance but results from a process of reproduction and continual enactment.

Throughout this book I have discussed the significance of discourses operating within the music industry. These discourses uphold systems of evaluation and aesthetics and produce particular constructions of the nature of the artist. I have considered how different practitioners (including musicians, A&R staff, producers, engineers and journalists) participate in these discourses, which assume a shared conception of the music industry and what it means to work within it. The book has explored, using the example of indie rock, how notions of gender are bound into these discourses. I have argued that rock mythologies, histories and the particular tropes of rock journalism offer a representation of rock that is masculinist. Chapter 1 considered how the notion of rock as masculine is naturalised through the valorisation of male musicians in rock histories, canons and other written documentation, while female rock performers are marginalised as 'other'. Chapter 2 illustrated that even the operations of a supposedly more democratic and egalitarian subgenre such as indie rock are also informed by a masculinist discourse that sustains (albeit differing) models of masculinity as its normative tropes. Chapters 3 and 4 discussed the gendered representation of male and female performers in the written media and the way in which musicians negotiate different constructions of themselves as gendered beings in various performance contexts such as the live gig, photo shoot or promotional video. This approach has begun to unpack the way in which the experience of working as a musician is bound up with gendered discourses.

The detailed analysis of indie rock music is also instructive as it demonstrates the complex discourses operating in the production and mediation of particular music genres. Consideration has been given to different aspects of rock, including its institutions and performance sites, which impact on how female performers experience the rock environment and are in turn understood by a rock audience.

The comments of female musicians highlight that the discourses that confirm rock as masculine operate in diverse and subtle ways. This can be seen in numerous instances such as the heroic language used to describe male musicians in the written media, the emphasis placed on marketing a female band rather than booking them into a studio to write new tracks, or in the bravado and showmanship associated with touring a band. The detailed study of riot grrrl in Chapters 5 and 6 discussed specific challenges that have been made to the masculinist nature of indie rock scenes as well as tracing the reaction of the press to this feminist network. The final chapter examined how DIY festival promotion under the banner of Ladyfest has opened up new performance spaces to women performers and audience members, as well as acting as a way to endorse and encourage the activities of women within the creative arts.

Certainly, the broad findings of the book have application to music practice beyond the parameters of indie rock. The discussion has dealt with the everyday practice of being a musician, from recording songs in a studio to touring, and from signing a deal with a record company to promoting an album. It has examined how these activities involve the negotiation of different gender roles and identities. However, the concentration on a particular music subgenre draws attention to the specific ways in which gender is constructed in music. There is a need for further studies of this nature to be undertaken that examine the importance of gender within other music genres and cultures. I have argued that gender is important not only to how musicians experience the music industry but to the way in which the industry operates. By failing to consider gender, studies of the music industry have missed out on an important dimension of the music business. This book contributes to the developing body of academic material dealing with gender in the context of the music industry.

Appendix 1: Zines

Titles that are italicised are catalogues or listings publications.

Title	Date of issue	Place of publication
Ablaze! #7	(*c*.1991–94)	Leeds, England
Ablaze! #10	(*c*.1991–94)	Leeds, England
Aggamengmong Moggie #14	(1996)	Stockport, England
A Guide to 7 Inch Singles That Give You a Nipple Hardness Factor #3	(Fall 1993)	Los Angeles, California
Amp #6	(1999)	London, England
Amp #12	(2000)	London, England
Angel #3	(1995)	Mablethorpe, England
Baby Pop #1	(1999)	Leeds, England
Ball and Chain #1	(1995)	Birmingham, England
Ball and Chain #2	(1996)	Birmingham, England
Bamboo Girl #8	(1999)	New York, New York
Betsy #1	(2003)	UK
Bulldozer #1	(*c*.1991–94)	Oberlin, Ohio
Chica #1	(*c*.2001)	Glasgow, Scotland
Chica #2	(*c*.2002)	Glasgow, Scotland
Cocksucker Blues #3	(Summer 1993)	Newport, Wales
Cream #3	(*c*.1996)	London, England

Creplochian Fairy Tales	(*c.*1993–96)	England
Crumpy #1	(1992)	Little Rock, Arkansas
Demirep #4	(*c.*1996)	New Hope, Minnesota
Discharge #2	(*c.*1991–94)	Richmond, Virginia
Discharge #3	(*c.*1991–94)	Richmond, Virginia
Destroy All Music #3	(1993)	Cardiff, Wales
Dyke Dreams #2	(*c.*1995–96)	Mablethorpe, England
Electra #4	(Spring/Summer 2002)	Conwy, Wales
Fake #0	(1992)	Potomac, Maryland
Fantastic Fanzine #2	(*c.*1991–94)	Arlington, Virginia
Fantastic Fanzine #3½	(*c.*1991–94)	Arlington, Virginia
Fantasy Bus Queue #1½	(1996)	Leicester, England
Female Perversions #1	(February 2001)	Helsinki, Finland
Firecraquer #1	(July 1992)	Chicago, Illinois
Fragrance	(1994)	Leicester, England
Fragrance, vol. 3, issue 10	(*c.*1994)	Leicester, England
Freak #4	(*c.*1996)	Winchester, England
Future is a Dare	(2002)	London, England
Galactic #2	(1996)	York, England
Galactic #4	(1996–98)	York, England
Girlfrenzy #3	(*c.*1991–94)	London, England
Girlfrenzy #6	(*c.*1996)	Hove, England
Girl Friend #5	(*c.*1991–94)	Amerherst, Massachusetts

Girlfriend #1	(*c*.1991–94)	North Salem, New York
Girl Pride #6	(*c*.1991 – 94)	London, England
Girl Power!	(March 1993)	Leeds/Bradford/York, England
Girl's Annual	(*c*.1994)	London, England
Go Go Girl	(*c*.1991–94)	London, England
Grrrl Trouble	(*c*.1991–94)	Washington, DC
Grunge Gerl #1	(*c*.1991–94)	Los Angeles, California
Hair Pie #2	(*c*.1991–94)	Dyfed, Wales
Hate and Hope	(1993)	Newcastle-upon-Tyne, England
Head Shaved Smooth	(*c*.1993)	Newcastle-upon-Tyne, England
Hip Mama: The Parenting Zine #18	(1999)	Oakland, California
Hot Lava Monster	(1992)	Daly City, California
Hotskirt	(*c*.1991–94)	Little Rock, Arkansas
Intermission #2	(1991)	Wakefield, USA
Intimate Wipe	(*c*.1991–94)	London, England
Jaded #1	(*c*.1991–94)	Arlington, Virginia
Juicy #6	(2002)	Roydon, England
Just How Far Should Baby Go?	(1994)	Beckenham, England
Kill the Robot	(*c*.1991–94)	Yellow Springs, Ohio
Kingfish #2	(1992)	Berkeley, California
Kookie Monster's Free Peach Thingy	(*c*.1991–94)	Cardiff, Wales

Koo Koo	(*c*.1991–94)	USA
Ladyfest Manchester Programme	(September 2003)	Manchester, England
Ladyfest London Programme	(2002)	London, England
Let Me Live #1	(*c*.1991–94)	Columbus, Ohio
Literal Stimulation #1	(1993)	Coventry, England
Literal Stimulation #2	(1993)	Coventry, England
Literal Stimulation #3	(1993)	Coventry, England
Literal Stimulation #5	(1993)	Coventry, England
Love and Desire and Hate	(1993)	London, England
Madwoman #3	(Spring 1992)	Chicago, Illinois
Malefice #1	(Summer 1992)	Chicago, Illinois
Man Overboard	(*c*.1991–94)	Rockville, Maryland
Milly Tint #7	(November 1997)	England
Moseisley #1	(*c*.1993–95)	Co. Antrim, N. Ireland
My Little Fanzine #9	(1995)	Loughton, England
My Little Fanzine #10	(1995)	Loughton, England
My Little Fanzine #11	(1995)	Loughton, England
Nausea	(1993)	Brentwood, England
No!	(1993)	Leeds, England
Notta Babe! #1	(Summer 1992)	Arlington, Virginia
Not Your Bitch #6	(Spring 1996)	Denver, Colorado
Off Kilter Coffee Filter #1	(*c*.1993)	Rugby, England

Order A New World #2	(*c.*1991–94)	Olympia, Washington
Pariah #1	(*c.*1991–94)	Sheffield, England
Pariah #2	(*c.*1991–94)	Sheffield, England
Pearshaped #3	(1999)	Yamagata, Japan
Pearshaped #4	(2000)	Yamagata, Japan
Persephone's Network	(April 1993)	Cleveland, Ohio
Phone Fuck	(1992)	Massachusetts
Plague Your Eyes	(*c.*1991–94)	London, England
Playground Lies #2¼	(*c.*1994–95)	King's Lynn, England
POF	(1993)	Lansdale, PA
Pop Girls #2	(1999)	Glasgow, Scotland
Pungk is the Theory Slampt is the Practise	(*c.*1992–94)	Newcastle-upon-Tyne, England
Quit Whining #1	(*c.*1991–94)	South Hadley, Massachusetts
Radical Tampax (spoof zine produced by a journalist writing for the UK publication *Select*)	(1994)	London, England
Rape	(*c.*1992–1993)	Washington, DC
Real Girls	(2001)	Stockport, England
Rebel Grrrl Punk #6	(2001)	Wilmslow, England
Red Roses For Me #6	(*c.*1993)	Fareham, England
Red Rover #1	(Summer 1992)	Washington, DC
Reggae Chicken	(*c.*1991–94)	London, England
Riotcats #1	(*c.*1993)	Gloucestershire, England

Riot Gear #3	(March 1992)	San Francisco, California
Riot Grrrl (collaborative flyer)	(*c.*1991–94)	Minnesota, Washington, Massachusetts, New York, Ohio, New York City
Riot Grrrl	(July 1991)	Washington, DC
Riot Grrrl #3	(*c.*1991–94)	Washington, DC
Riot Grrrl #7	(1992)	Washington, DC
Riot Grrrl #7½	(*c.*1991–94)	Washington, DC
Riot Grrrl #8	(*c.*1991–94)	Washington, DC
Riot Grrrl	(*c.*1992)	Washington, DC
Riot Grrrl #6	(*c.*1991–94)	Arlington, Virginia
Riot Grrrl #5	(March 1993)	New York City
Riot Grrrl #2	(March 1992)	Amherst, Massachusetts
Riot Grrrl #3	(1992)	Massachusetts
Riot Grrrl!	(1993)	Leeds and Bradford, England
Riot Grrrl Belgium presents Flappergathering #1	(Summer 2002)	Maasmechelen, Belgium
Riot Grrrl Essex Zine	(2002)	Essex, England
Riot Girl London #2	(2002)	London, England
Riot Girl London #3	(January 2003)	London, England
Riot Grrrl! New England	(February 1992)	South Hadley, Massachusetts
Riot Grrrl Outer Space – Cool Stuff Catalogue	(*c.*1993)	San Jose, California

Riot Grrrl Press Catalogue	(July 1993)	Arlington, Virginia
Riot Grrrl Review *#1*	(*c.*1994–95)	Fort Myers, Florida
Riot Grrrl Review *#3*	(1996)	Fort Myers, Florida
Sawtooth #1	(*c.*1993)	Leeds, England
Second Skin #4	(*c.*1991–94)	New York, New York
Second Skin #5	(*c.*1991–94)	New York, New York
Simba	(*c.*1993–95)	Brighton, England
Skin Swing Feel	(July1993)	Newcastle-upon-Tyne, England
Skit On You!#1	(*c.*1991–94)	Leeds, England
Soda Jerk #1	(1993)	Near Stroud, England
Soda Jerk #2	(1993)	Near Stroud, England
Sparkle #2	(*c.*1996)	Leeds, England
Sticky Fingers #1	(1993)	Birmingham, England
Sweet Tart	(1993)	Decatur, Georgia
Tennis and Violins	(1996)	Fort Myers, Florida
The ABC of Linus and Bone Records	(June 1993)	London, England
The Birth of Naughty Word	(1994)	West Sussex, England
The Melody Haunts My Reverie #3	(1993)	Tiverton, England
The Nerve: Central England Riot Grrrl Zine	(*c.*2001)	England
The Pamzine #3	(June–July 2000)	London, England
The Pamzine #4	(January–February 2001)	London, England

The Pamzine: The 'Pamnibus' Edition	(2002)	London, England
The Root of Twinkle, vol. 2, issue 2	(June 1992)	Connecticut
The Scream: A Situationist Manifesto for the 1990s #1	(March 1993)	Liverpool, England
The Scream: A Situationist Manifesto for the 1990s #2	(May 1993)	Liverpool, England
The Scream: A Situationist Manifesto for the 1990s #3	(September 1993)	Stockport, England
The Scream: A Situationist Manifesto for the 1990s #4	(January 1994)	Stockport, England
The Scream: A Situationist Manifesto for the 1990s #5	(May 1994)	Liverpool, England
The Vegg Issue	(*c*.1992–95)	London, England
This is! #Ø½	(2002)	London, England
Throbbing Organ #33	(1993)	London, England
Throbbing Organ #35	(1993)	London, England
Twat! #2	(*c*.1996)	Denver, Colorado
Waaah #1	(1995)	Leicester, England
What is Riot Grrrl?	(*c*.1991–94)	Washington, DC
What's This Generation Coming To?	(1993)	Newcastle-upon-Tyne, England
Who's That Bitch?	(2001)	Wigan, England
Who's That Bitch? #3	(February 2003)	Wigan, England
Wicked, Good, Everything! #1	(1993)	Saltash, England

Appendix 2: Interviews

Ablaze, Karren Zine writer who was involved in the Leeds riot grrrl chapter. She produced a zine called *Ablaze!*, co-organised riot grrrl events and was a guest speaker at the 'Grrrlstyle Revolution Day' at the Institute of Contemporary Arts (ICA), London. At time of interview she was lead vocalist in the female-centred band Coping Saw and had worked as a press officer in the music industry in London. Taped interview by post, 6 October 1994.

Aisha Sheffield-based woman involved in riot grrrl. At time of interview she was lead vocalist in the female-centred band Vampire Scratch. Postal interview, 5 December 1995.

Ali At time of interview bass player in the all-female band Bêtty Noire, based in Liverpool. Former member of a Liverpool band called Barbel. Personal interview in Liverpool, 4 March 1999.

Alice At time of interview drummer in all-female band Bêtty Noire, based in Liverpool. Personal interview in Liverpool, 4 March 1999.

Amy Musician living in Winchester, Hants. At time of interview she was a guitarist in a band called Candy Flesh and had produced zines titled *Squishy Fishy* and *Freak*. Postal interview, 25 July 1996.

Andrea American woman who was resident in Birmingham, England. At time of interview she ran an independent record label called Garden of Delights. She has recorded and released her own records and is a vocalist, guitarist and bass player. Postal interview, 28 December 1995.

Angela Woman involved in riot grrrl living in King's Lynn, Norfolk. She produced the zine *Playground Lies*. Postal interview, 30 November 1995.

Anna Woman involved in riot grrrl living in Wirral, Merseyside. In the process of writing a zine when interviewed. Postal interview, 6 September 1996.

Anne A founder of the riot grrrl Montreal chapter established in 1999. At the time of interview she was the drummer in a band called The Frenetics and a contributor to a Montreal riot grrrl zine. Interview conducted by email, January 2000.

Ashley Drummer in the four-piece female-centred band We Start Fires based in Darlington, England. Personal interview at the Masque, Liverpool, 10 September 2003.

Barbero, Lori At time of interview drummer with the Minneapolis-based all-female band Babes In Toyland. Interview conducted at the Dour Music Festival, Belgium, 10 July 1994.

Becky Lead vocalist and guitarist in the four-piece female-centred band We Start Fires based in Darlington, England. Personal interview at the Masque, Liverpool, 10 September 2003.

Bela Woman living in York who was involved with riot grrrl and contributed to riot grrrl zines. She played bass in the female-centred band Coping Saw. Taped interview by post, 9 February 1995.

Berenyi, Miki At time of interview she was vocalist and guitarist in the female-centred British indie band Lush. Interview conducted at Warwick University, Coventry, 20 January 1996.

Brea Musician and member of the organising committee of Ladyfest Texas 2003. She has performed in two bands, one of which had an all-female membership. Interview by email, 2 September 2003.

Cafritz, Julie Former member of the US band Pussy Galore. At time of interview she was member of the female-centred band Free Kitten. Interview conducted at the Princess Charlotte, Leicester, 9 January 1995.

Cazz Zine writer based in Stockport, Cheshire, who was involved in riot grrrl. Postal interview, 30 July 1996.

Chidgey, Red Involved with Ladyfest Europe and in the organisation of Ladyfest Amsterdam 2002, Ladyfest Manchester 2003 and Ladyfest Brighton 2005. She has also been involved with Riot Grrrl Europe and with various chapters of riot grrrl in the UK. She was a founder member of the Riot Grrrl Essex chapter in 2001. She has produced a number of zines and at time of interview was operating a distro called 'Fingerbang'. Interview by email, 2 October 2003.

Christine A woman based in Denver, Colorado. Having been inspired by riot grrrl she produced a zine called *Not Your Bitch* and a girl zine catalogue. Postal interview, 4 July 1996.

Christine Zine writer from New Hope, Minnesota. She produced a zine called *Demirep* and was involved in riot grrrl. Postal interview, 26 August 1996.

Clair Founder member of riot girl London. She is a zine writer who has produced a number of publications including *Button Moon*, *Hairspray Queen* and *Sister-Disco*. Interview by email, 28 July 2003.

Corrigan, Suzy American journalist based in London at time of interview. She has written for numerous publications including the *NME, ID* and *The Guardian*. She curated the 'Grrrlstyle Revolution Day' at the ICA, London, and edited the anthology *Typical Girls: New Stories by Smart Women* (1997). Postal interview, November 1995.

Dale, Pete Zine writer and co-founder of Slampt! Underground Organisation (a British record label and distribution network). Member of the indie bands Avocado Baby, Milky Whimpshake and the female-centred band Red Monkey, and a former member of Spraydog. Based in Newcastle-upon-Tyne. Interview conducted by email, 10 November 1999.

Deal, Kim Vocalist and guitarist from Dayton, Ohio. She was a founder member of the commercially successful and highly influential indie rock group The Pixies (1986–92) who reformed in 2004 for a series of live dates. In 1990 she formed the female-centred band The Breeders. At time of interview she was touring with The Amps. Interview conducted at the Clinton Rooms, Nottingham, 5 September 1995.

du Santiago, Marie At time of interview she was guitarist with the female-centred band Kenickie who were based in Sunderland. Following the break up of Kenickie in 1998, du Santiago formed the female-centred band Rosita with former Kenickie bass player, Emmy-Kate Montrose. Interview conducted at Aston University, Birmingham, 9 May 1997.

Erica A zine writer, involved in riot grrrl, based in Mablethorpe, Lincolnshire. She produced the queercore zines *Angel* and *Dyke Dreams*. Postal interview, December 1995.

Erica Zine editor living in Hove, East Sussex. She began producing the zine *Girlfrenzy* in 1990. Postal interview, 15 December 1995.

Eriksson, Lisa Swedish singer, guitarist and songwriter in female-centred band Schulte/Eriksson. The band formed in Liverpool in late 1997. Personal interview in Liverpool, 20 March 1999.

Fateman, Joanne Member of the US band Le Tigre. Personal interview conducted at Le Bateau, Liverpool, 29 November 2000.

Frischmann, Justine At time of interview she was the lead vocalist in the female-centred band Elastica, based in London. Interview conducted at Edwards No. 8, Birmingham, 13 February 1994.

Frendo, Josephine At time of interview vocalist in the Swedish female-centred band Girlfrendo. Interview conducted at Brian's Diner, Liverpool, 19 June 1998.

Gordon, Kim Bass guitarist in the highly influential New York indie rock group Sonic Youth, formed in 1981. Member of the female-centred band Free Kitten. She co-produced Hole's debut album *Pretty On The Inside*. Interview conducted at the Princess Charlotte, Leicester, 9 January 1995.

Gwen Drummer involved in riot grrrl living in Evenley, Northamptonshire. She produced a number of zines inspired by riot grrrl. Postal interview, 24 December 1995.

Hanman, Louise Musician based in Liverpool. Lead vocalist and guitarist in the punk band Flamingo 50 and drummer in the band Three Minute Margin. Interview conducted by email, 26 September 2000.

Hanna, Kathleen Founder member of the female-centred band Bikini Kill (1991–98) from Olympia, Washington. After the break-up of Bikini Kill she released a solo record under the name of Julie Ruin. She is lead vocalist of the all-female band Le Tigre. Personal interview conducted at Le Bateau, Liverpool, 29 November 2000.

Harrison, Gayl At time of interview bass guitarist in the all-female three-piece band Sidi Bou Said, based in London. Interview conducted at Warwick University, Coventry, 13 May 1995.

Hartling, Eve At time of interview member of the all-female four-piece band Jale (1993–96), based in Halifax, Nova Scotia. Interview conducted at the Princess Charlotte, Leicester, 23 June 1994.

Heather Independent film-maker and member of the film committee for Ladyfest Halifax, Canada 2003. She participated in Ladyfest Los Angeles 2002 as a workshop leader. Interview by email, 19 August 2003.

Helen At time of interview vocalist in all-female band Bêtty Noire, based in Liverpool. Personal interview in Liverpool, 4 March 1999.

Helen Participant in Ladyfest Manchester who had also attended fundraising events for Ladyfest Glasgow. She is a singer-songwriter. Personal interview in Manchester, 6 September 2003.

Hilde An organiser of Ladyfest Amsterdam 2002 who was also responsible for designing the website for Ladyfest Europe. She founded the Riot Grrrl Europe mailing list and website. At time of interview she was living in Rotterdam and a member of an all-female metal-punk band. Interview conducted by email, 21 August 2003.

Holborow, Rachel Musician and co-founder of Slampt! Underground Organisation, comprising a record label and distribution network. Member of the indie bands Avocado Baby, Red Monkey and Pussycat Thrash. She performed with Huggy Bear while on a Japanese tour as an additional bass player. Based in Newcastle-upon-Tyne. Interview conducted by email, 10 November 1999.

Holland, Annie At time of interview bass guitarist in the female-centred band Elastica. Interview conducted at Edwards No. 8, Birmingham, 13 February 1994.

Jae At time of interview keyboard and saxophone player in all-female band Bêtty Noire, based in Liverpool. Personal interview in Liverpool, 4 March 1999.

Karla Independent music publisher and business manager of Ladyfest Melbourne 2003. Interview by email, 8 September 2003.

Kay London-based woman who became involved with riot grrrl in 1992. She co-wrote the zines *Intimate Wipe* and *Go Go Girl*. Interview conducted by email, 14 August 2000.

Kirsty Musician and zine writer from Fort Myers, Florida, who was involved in riot grrrl. Postal interview, 13 February 1997.

Ladyfest Manchester organiser Woman involved in the organisation of Ladyfest Manchester 2003. Personal interview in Manchester, 6 September 2003.

Ladyfest Philly organiser Woman living in Philadelphia who was part of the organising committee for Ladyfest Philly 2003. Interview by email, 2 September 2003.

Ladyfest Spain organisers Joint interview with two organisers of Ladyfest Spain 2005. Interview by email, 19 April 2005.

Ladyfest Texas organiser and musician. Interview by email, 5 November 2003.

Laverne, Lauren At time of interview she was vocalist with the female-centred band Kenickie who were based in Sunderland. Following the break-up of Kenickie in 1998, Laverne developed a solo career, which included a top ten hit in collaboration with the dance act Mint Royale. Since 1999 she has worked as a presenter on a number of television music programmes for Channel 4, BBC Choice and ITV. She currently presents a radio show for Xfm. Interview conducted at Aston University, Birmingham, 9 May 1997.

Lemmon, Claire At time of interview vocalist and guitarist in the all-female three-piece band Sidi Bou Said, based in London. Interview conducted at Warwick University, Coventry, 13 May 1995.

Lisa Cardiff-based musician involved in riot grrrl. She has written and recorded songs under the name of Cupcake. Taped interview by post, 15 November 1995.

Luecking, Juliana A spoken-word artist based in Brooklyn, New York. She was part of the 1980s hardcore scene in Washington, DC, where she performed monologues between band performances. She has delivered her material at numerous indie rock shows and riot grrrl events, and has released a number of CD recordings. Le Tigre have featured her voiceovers on their releases. Taped interview by post, 20 August 1994.

MacLeod, Alyson At time of interview drummer in the all-female four-piece band Jale (1993–96), based in Halifax, Nova Scotia. Interview conducted at the Princess Charlotte, Leicester, 23 June 1994.

Maddy A woman from Leicester who was involved in riot grrrl. She produced a number of zines under the titles *Fragrance*, *Sheep* and *Waaah*. At time of interview she was the bass player in a band. Postal interview, 20 January 1996.

Marion A member of the organising team for Ladyfest Manchester. She has produced a number of zines. Personal interview in Manchester, 6 September 2003.

Megan Ladyfest organiser living in New York. She attended Ladyfest Amsterdam in 2002 and was inspired to organise a similar event on her return to the US. At time of interview she was one of the 12 organisers of Ladyfest East 2004. Interview by email, 22 January 2004.

Melissa Keyboard player and vocalist in the four-piece female-centred band We Start Fires based in Darlington, England. Personal interview at the Masque, Liverpool, 10 September 2003.

Montrose, Emmy-Kate At time of interview she was bass guitarist with the female-centred band Kenickie who were based in Sunderland. Following the break-up of Kenickie in 1998, Montrose formed the female-centred band Rosita with former Kenickie bass player, Marie du Santiago. Interview conducted at Aston University, Birmingham, 9 May 1997.

Music journalist Male journalist and former staff writer for *Melody Maker*. Interviewed in London, 4 February 1999.

Natasha At time of interview vocalist, guitarist and songwriter in female-centred band Pooka. She has since collaborated with a number of musicians and is working on her own material. Interview conducted at the Lomax, Liverpool. 9 October 1997.

Nicole Woman living in Southbury, Connecticut. She was in the process of starting a distribution service for riot grrrl and 'gurl' personal zines when interviewed. Interview conducted by email, 28 November 1999.

Nihal Woman living in Istanbul, Turkey. At the time of interview she was planning a Ladyfest in Istanbul. Interview by email, 31 March 2005.

Nikki Bass player and vocalist in the four-piece female-centred band We Start Fires based in Darlington, England. Personal interview at the Masque, Liverpool, 10 September 2003.

Paula Contributor to a number of zines, she also produced her own publication under the title *Agaba*. She was involved in riot grrrl and played guitar in a number of bands. At time of interview she worked as a press/promotions officer for a London record label. Taped interview by post, 26 September 1995.

Peel, John BBC broadcaster and taste-maker whose long-running Radio 1 show played an important role in promoting new music. Personal interview at 'Peel Acres', Suffolk, 17 February 1994.

Pierce, Jennifer At time of interview member of the all-female four-piece band Jale (1993–96), based in Halifax, Nova Scotia. Interview conducted at the live music venue the Princess Charlotte, Leicester, 23 June 1994.

Richmond, Jane Woman based in Leeds who was involved in riot grrrl. Vocalist and rhythm guitarist in The Postcards. Postal interview, 1 May 1995.

Rina Musician and former member of female-centred band My Two Stomach Poles, based in Toronto. She ran a radio show named 'Ovary Evolution' while at university in Montreal, Canada. Director Ladyfest Pty Ltd, and communications and sponsorship manager of Ladyfest Melbourne 2003. Interview by email, August 2003.

Rowena Bass player and vocalist living in Dublin. She was a founder member of Riot Grrl Dublin. Interview by email, 16 August 2003.

Safari At time of interview vocalist in the Swedish female-centred band Girlfrendo. Interview conducted at Brian's Diner, Liverpool, 19 June 1998.

Samson, JD Member of US band Le Tigre. Personal interview conducted at Le Bateau, Liverpool, 29 November 2000.

Sara Woman based in Surbiton, Surrey. At time of interview she was a zine writer and vocalist in a riot grrrl-influenced band called Lucrezia. Postal interview, 21 August 1996.

Sarah Woman living in Northfield, Birmingham. She was involved in riot grrrl and produced a zine called *Ball and Chain*. Postal interview, 29 December 1995.

Scarlet, Sophie Founder member of Riot Girl London, which was set up in 2000. She is a musician who has performed in a band called Tar Baby. She is also a zine writer whose publications include *Antisocial Scarlet*. Interview conducted by email, 23 July 2003.

Schulte, Anna German singer, guitarist and songwriter. At time of interview she was a member of the female-centred band Schulte/Eriksson, which formed in Liverpool in late 1997. Personal interview in Liverpool, 20 March 1999.

Sharon At time of interview vocalist, guitarist and songwriter in female-centred band Pooka. She is now producing music as a solo artist. Interview conducted at the Lomax, Liverpool, 9 October 1997.

Simone Musician living in York who was involved with riot grrrl. At time of interview she was a vocalist in the female-centred band Coping Saw in which she also played drums and recorder. She worked as a gig promoter and managed the Leeds-based band Bewilderness. She wrote for a number of riot grrrl zines and was involved in the Leeds/Bradford riot grrrl group. Taped interview by post, 9 February 1995.

Stein, Laura At time of interview member of the all-female four-piece band Jale (1993–96), based in Halifax, Nova Scotia. Interview conducted at the Princess Charlotte, Leicester, 23 June 1994.

Sue At time of interview guitar player in all-female band Bêtty Noire, based in Liverpool. Personal interview in Liverpool, 4 March 1999.

Tucker, Corin Former member of US band Bratmobile. Vocalist and guitarist in the highly successful all-female band Sleater Kinney and Cadillaca, based in Portland, Oregon. Interview conducted by email, 5 November 1998.

Van Der Vlugt, Marijne At time of interview lead vocalist in the indie pop band Salad, based in London. She previously worked as a presenter on the music television channel, MTV. Interview conducted at the Lomax, Liverpool, 18 April 1997.

Victoria Woman living in Montreal, Canada. Along with four others, she founded a riot grrrl Montreal chapter in 1999 and established a web page. At time of interview she was vocalist and guitarist in a female-centred band and also performed in a female folk duo called I Am, She Is. She was a contributor to a Montreal riot grrrl zine. Interview conducted by email, 28 January 2000.

Woods, Melanie At time of interview drummer and vocalist in the all-female three-piece band Sidi Bou Said, based in London. Interview conducted at Warwick University, Coventry, 13 May 1995.

Zine writer British guitarist involved in riot grrrl. She performed in a number of bands, playing bass and drums. She became involved in riot grrrl in 1993. At time of interview she was working as a PA. Interview conducted by post, 6 December 1999.

Select discography

Cassette-only releases

Avocado Baby   *A Million and Nine* (Slampt: SLAMPT 002)

Bikini Kill/Huggy Bear   *Riot Grrrls* (live recording), Brighton Pavilion, 18 March 1993

Various Artists   *Skinless Wonder: Slampt City Punk Soul Explosion* (Slampt)

Various Artists   *Schism Fix: Plankton, Lo-fi, Junk, Compilation Tape* (Plankton, Lo-fi, Junk: CONF 1/PLANK 2)

Singles

Bikini Kill   'Peel Sessions' (Peel-1)
'New Radio' (Kill Rock Stars: KRS 212)
'The Anti-Pleasure Dissertation' (Kill Rock Stars: KRS 250)
'I Like Fucking/I Hate Danger' (Kill Rock Stars: KRS 253)

Bikini Kill/Tribe 8/ Lucy Stoners/7 Year Bitch   'There's a Dyke in the Pit' (Outpunk: OUT 5)

Bratmobile   'Kiss & Ride' (Homestead: HMS 178-7) 1992

Breeders   'Head To Toe' (4AD: BAD D4012)
'Canonball' (4AD: Breed 1) 1993

Chia Pet   'Hey Baby' (Koko pop: Koko 4)

Crunt   'Swine/Sexy' (Insipid Vinyl: IV-31) 1993

Flamingo 50   'Sodastream Selector Volume 1' split-single with Fabiola (Sodastream Politics) 2000
'Go Betsy Go!' (No Concessions Records) 2001

Free Kitten	'Lick!' (In The Red: ITR 015) 1993 'Oh Bondage Up Yours!' (Sympathy For The Record Industry: SFIRI 256) 1992 'Punks Suing Punks' (Kill Rock Stars: KRS 257)
Frumpies	'Babies and Bunnies' (Kill Rock Stars: KRS 213) 'Safety First' (Wiiija: WIJ 31V) 1993 'Frumpies Forever' (Kill Rock Stars: KRS 366)
Girlfrendo	'Girlfrendo Anthem' (Where It's At Is Where You Are: WIAIWYA 1) 'Get Ready To Be Heartbroken' (Piao!: Piao! 9) 1998 'Air' (Piao!: Piao! 13) 1998
God Is My Co-Pilot	'Gender Is As Gender Does' (Funky Mushroom: FM 008)
Hanna, Kathleen/ Slim Moon	'Rockstar/Mean: Wordcore Volume 1' (Kill Rock Stars: KRS 101)
Heavens To Betsy	'These Monsters Are Real' (Kill Rock Stars: KRS 212)
Heavens To Betsy/ Bratmobile	'My Secret/Cool Schmool' (K: PUNK 1)
Helen Love	'Formula One Racing Girls' (Damaged Goods: damgood 18) 'Beat Him Up' (Damaged Goods: damgood 89)
Hole	'Dicknail' (Sub Pop: SP 93) 1990 'Retard Girl' (Sympathy For The Record Industry: SFTRI 53) 'Beautiful Son' (City Slang: EFA 04916-02MS) 1993 'Malibu' (Geffen: GFS 22369) 1998
Huggy Bear	'Her Jazz' (Wiiija/Catcall: TROUBLE 001) 'Long Distance Lovers' (Gravity: Gravity 9) 'Rubbing The Impossible To Burst' (Wiiija: WIJ 16V) 'Don't Die' (Wiiija: WIJ 23)
Jale	'Cut' (Sub Pop: SP 126/309) 1994

Kenickie	'Nightlife' (EMIDisc: DISC 006) 1997 'Punka' (EMIDisc: DISC 007) 1997 'Stay In The Sun' (EMI: EMI 20) 1998
Linus	'Driven Thing' (Bone: BUD 1)
Linus/Pussycat Trash Comet Gain/Skinned Teen	'Some Hearts Paid To Lie' (Wiiija: WIJ 25)
Luecking, Juliana	'She's Good People: Wordcore Volume 5' (Kill Rock Stars: KRS 105) 1992
Lush/Ivy/Solar Race Splendora/Jale/Fuzzy	'From Greer To Eternity' (Fierce Panda: NING 05) 1994
Mambo Taxi	'Poems on the Underground' (Clawfist: HUNKA 19)
Marine Research	'Queen B' (Where It's At Is Where You Are: WIAIWYA 7)
Period Pains	'Spice Girls (Who Do You Think You Are?)' (Damaged Goods: damgood 135) 'BBC Sessions' (Damaged Goods: damgood 158)
Pooka	'The Insect' (Rough Trade: r 4077) 1996 'Mean Girl' (Trade2: TRDS 009/ 854 978-7) 1997
Schulte/Eriksson	'For the Sake of Clarity' (Org: Org 054)
Sidi Bou Said	'Three Sides' (Ultimate: Topp 017) 1993
Sing-Sing	'Feels Like Summer' (Aerial: AEROV002) 2000
Sleater Kinney	'Little Babies' (Matador: OLE 326-7) 1998 'One More Hour' (Matador: OLE 321-7) 1998
We Start Fires	'Strut' (Marquis Cha Cha) 2006 'Hot Metal' (Marquis Cha Cha) 2006 'Magazine' (Hot Noise) 2007
Voodoo Queens	'Kenuwee Head' (Too Pure: Pures 24)

Albums

7 Year Bitch	*7 Year Bitch* (Kill Rock Stars: KRS 201)

Amps	*Pacer* (4AD: CAD 5016) 1995
Babes In Toyland	*Spanking Machine* (Twin Tone: EFA 26-89183-2) 1990 *To Mother* (Twin Tone: TTR89208) 1991 *Fontanelle* (Southern: 185012) 1992 *Painkillers* (Southern: 18512-2) 1993 *Nemesisters* (Warner Brothers) 1995 *Minneapolism: Live – The Last Tour* (Cherry Red) 2001
Bikini Kill/ **Huggy Bear**	*Yeah, Yeah, Yeah, Yeah/Our Troubled Youth* (Kill Rock Stars/Catcall: PUSS 001LP) 1993
Bikini Kill	*Pussy Whipped* (Wiiija: WIJ 028CD) 1993 *Reject All American* (Kill Rock Stars: KRS 260CD) 1996
Björk	*Debut* (One Little Indian: TPLP 31) 1993 *Post* (One Little Indian: TPLP 51) 1995 *Homogenic* (One Little Indian: TPLP 71) 1997 *Selmasongs* (One Little Indian: TPLP 151) 2000 *Vespertine* (One Little Indian: TPLP 101) 2001 *Greatest Hits* (One Little Indian: TPLP 359) 2002 *Medúlla* (One Little Indian: TPLP 358) 2004 *Volta* (One Little Indian: TPLP 460) 2007
Bratmobile	*Pottymouth* (Kill Rock Stars: KRS 208) 1992 *The Real Janelle* (Kill Rock Stars: KRS 219) 1994
Breeders	*Pod* (4AD: CAD 0006) 1990 *Last Splash* (4AD: CAD 3014) 1993 *Title TK* (4AD: CAD 2205) 2002
Coping Saw	*Outside, Now* (Paroxysm)
Crunt	*Crunt* (Trance: TR-19) 1994
Elastica	*Elastica* (Deceptive: BLUFF 014LP) 1995 *The Menace* (Deceptive: BLUFF 075CD) 2000
Flamingo 50	*Flamingo 50/Lack of Reason A Split CD* (Prehisto) 2003 *Tear It Up* (Spank) 2006
Free Kitten	*Unboxed* (Wiiija: WIJ 036CD) 1994

Nice Ass (Wiiija: WIJ 041CD) 1995
Sentimental Education (Wiiija: WIJCD 1076) 1997

Frumpies   *Frumpies One-Piece* (Kill Rock Stars: KRS 335)

Heaven's To Betsy   *Calculated* (Kill Rock Stars: KRS 222)

Hersh, Kristin   *Hips And Makers* (4AD: GAD 4002CD) 1998
Strange Angels (4AD: CAD 8003CD) 1998
Sky Motel (4AD: CAD9008CD) 2001
Sunny Border Blue (4AD: CAD2102CD) 2001
The Grotto (4AD: 5230220615) (2003)

Hole   *Pretty On The Inside* (City Slang: EFA 040712)
1991
Live Through This (City Slang: EFA 049351X)
1994
Celebrity Skin (Universal: GED 25164) 1998

Huggy Bear   *Taking The Rough With The Smooch*
(Wiiija: BOMB 015) 1993
Weaponry Listens To Love (Wiiija: WIJ 037) 1994

Jale   *Dreamcake* (Sub Pop: SP 137/317/ EFA LP 08317-
12)
So Wound (Sub Pop: SP 350) 1996

Julie Ruin   *Julie Ruin* (Kill Rock Stars: KRS297) 2000

Kenickie   *At The Club* (EMIDisc: 7243 8 561471 2) 1997
Get In (EMI) 1998
The John Peel Sessions (Strange Fruit) 1999

Le Tigre   *Le Tigre* (Wiiija: WIJCD 11080) 1999
Feminist Sweepstakes (COS, Mr. Lady, Touch &
Go) 2001
This Island (Universal, Touch & Go, Strummer/
Universal) 2004
After Dark (Universal) 2005
TKO (Universal International) 2005

Lois   *Butterfly Kiss* (K: KLP 15)
Strumpet (K: KLP 21)
Bet The Sky (K: KLP 36) 1995
Infinity Plus (K: KLP 58) 1996

Lord, Mary Lou   *Real* (Deep Music: DM 011) 1992
         Mary Lou Lord (Kill Rock Stars: KRS 238) 1995
         Got No Shadow (Work: OK 67574) 1998
         Live City Sounds (Rubric Records: RUB30) 2002
         Baby Blue (Rubric Records: RUB56) 2004

Love, Courtney   *America's Sweetheart* (Virgin: CDVUS249) 2004

Lush   *Lovelife* (4AD: CAD 6004)
         Spooky (4AD: GAD 2002)
         Split (4AD: GAD 4011)

Luecking, Juliana   *Big Broad* (Kill Rock Stars: KRS 228) 1994

Marine Research   *Sounds From The Gulf Stream* (K: KLP 100) 1999

PJ Harvey   *Dry* (Too Pure: PURE D10) 1992
         4-Track Demos (Island: ILPN 2079) 1993
         Rid Of Me (Island: ILPS 8002/ 514 696-1) 1993
         To Bring You My Love (Island: ILPS 8035) 1995
         Strychnine Ballroom: Live At Louse Point (Silver Wolf) 1996
         Is This Desire? (Island: ILPS 8076/ 524 563 1) 1998
         Stories From The City, Stories From The Sea (Island: 548144) 2000
         Uh Huh Her (ISL, Island: ILPS8143) 2004

Pooka   *Pooka* (WEA: 4509935152) 1993
         Spinning (Trade 2: TRDCD 1003/ 524 426-2) 1997
         Fools Give Birth To Angels (Pooka CD 04) 2001
         Shift (Rough Trade: RTRADECD012) 2001

Pussycat Thrash   *Non Stop Hip Action* (Slampt Underground: SLAMPT 25) 1994

Red Monkey   *Make The Moment* (Slampt Underground: SLAMPT 50) 1997
         Gunpowder, Treason And Plot (Troubleman) 2001

Sidi Bou Said   *Broooch* (Ultimate: TOPPLP 005)
         Bodies (Ultimate: TOPPCD 034) 1995
         Obsessive (Ultimate: TOPPCD 053) 1997

Skinned Teen/   *Bazooka Smooth/Jail Bait* (Lookout: Lookout 88)
Raooul   1994

Sleater Kinney

Call The Doctor (Chainsaw: CHSW 13CD) 1996
Dig Me Out (Matador: OLE 2692) 1997
Sleater Kinney (Matador: OLE 2672) 1998
The Hot Rock (BEG, Kill Rock Stars) 1999
All Hands On The Bad One (Matador: OLE 440-2) 2000
One Beat (Kill Rock Stars: KRS387) 2002
The Woods (Sub Pop: SPCD670) 2005

Throwing Muses

Throwing Muses (4AD: CAD 607) 1986
The Fat Skier (4AD: CAD 706) 1987
House Tornado (4AD: CAD 802) 1988
Hunkpapa (4AD: CAD 901) 1989
The Real Ramona (4AD: CAD 1002) 1991
Red Heaven (4AD: CAD 2013) 1992
The Curse (4AD: TAD 2019CD)
University (4AD: CAD 5002) 1995
Limbo (4AD: CAD 6014) 1996
In A Doghouse (4AD: DAD 607CD) 1998
Live in Providence (Throwing Music) 2003

Tribe 8

By the Time We Get To Colorado (Outpunk: OUT 7V) 1993
Snarkism (Alternative Tentacles: VIRUS 181) 1997
Role Models For Amerika (Alternative Tentacles: VIRUS 212) 1998

Tsunami

Deep End (Simple Machines: SMR 13CD)
Heart's Tremolo (Simple Machines: SMR 25CD)
World Tour and Other Destinations (Simple Machines: SMR 33CD) 1995
A Brilliant Mistake (Simple Machines: SMR 53) 1997

Wack Cat

That's What My Girlfriend Says (Paroxysm)

We Start Fires

How To Be A Lady (Head Girl Records: WSFCD001) 2001

Various Artists

International Pop Underground Convention (K: KLP 11) 1992

Various Artists

Internal/External Featuring ... (K: KLP 106)

Various Artists

Julep – Another Yoyo Studio Compilation (Yoyo Recordings: Yoyo LP2) 1993

Various Artists   *Ladyfest UK 2003* (Bearos Records: Bearos 037
                                            CD) 2003

Various Artists   *Outpunk Dance Party: A Queer Punk Compilation*
                                            (Outpunk: Out 12V)

Various Artists   *Seek Refuge ...* (Garden of Delights: Garden 3)

Various Artists   *Cause: Rock For Choice* (Piece of Mind: Piece 31)

Various Artists   *Jackson's Jukebox* (Kill Rock Stars: KRS 354)

Various Artists   *Taking A Chance On Chances: Troubleman/*
                                            Slampt Compilation From The Last Few Years of
                                            the 1990's (Troubleman/Slampt: TMU 035/
                                            SLAMPT 55) 1999

Various Artists   *Kill Rock Stars Compilation* (Kill Rock Stars: KRS
                                            201)

Various Artists   *Stars Kill Rock Compilation* (Kill Rock Stars: KRS
                                            207)

Various Artists   *Rock Stars Kill Compilation* (Kill Rock Stars: KRS
                                            221)

References

Aaron, Charles (1993) 'A Riot of the Mind', *Village Voice*, 27 January–2 February, p. 63.

Aldridge, Meryl (1998) 'The Tentative Hell-Raisers: Identity and Mythology in Contemporary UK Press Journalism', *Media, Culture and Society*, 20, pp. 109–27.

Aldridge, Meryl (2001) 'Lost Expectations? Women Journalists and the Fall-out from the "Toronto Newspaper War"', *Media, Culture and Society*, 23(5), pp. 607–24.

Ali, Lorraine (1994) 'He Screamed Out Our Angst', in Holly George-Warren and Shawn Dahl (eds) *Cobain: By the Editors of Rolling Stone*. New York: Little, Brown & Company (originally published in *Rolling Stone*, 16 April 1992), pp. 97–8.

Andersen, Mark and Jenkins, Mark (2001) *Dance of Days: Two Decades of Punk in the Nation's Capital*. New York: Soft Skull Press.

Andsager, Julie L. and Roe, Kimberly (1999) 'Country Music Video in Country's Year of the Woman', *Journal of Communication*, Winter, pp. 69–82.

Archer, Robyn and Simmonds, Diana (1986) *A Star is Torn*. London: Guild Publishing.

Arnold, Gina (1992) 'Revolution Grrrl-Style', *Option*, 44, May/June, pp. 44–6.

Arnold, Gina (1998) *Kiss This: Punk in the Present Tense*. New York: Pan.

Arnold, Gina (2004) 'Ten Years On, Courtney Still Loves to Shock and Roll', *Independent*, Foreign News section, 20 March, pp. 22, 23.

Arthur, Nicole (1995) 'Rock Women', in Nathaniel Wice and Steven Daly (eds) *Alt.Culture: An A-to-Z Guide to the '90s – Underground, Online, and Over-the-counter*. New York: Harper Perennial, pp. 208–9.

Auslander, Philip (1999) *Liveness: Performance in a Mediatized Culture*. London: Routledge.

Auslander, Philip (2004) 'I Wanna Be Your Man: Suzi Quatro's Musical Androgyny', *Popular Music*, 23 (1), pp. 1–16.

Azerrad, Michael (1994) 'Inside the Heart and Mind of Nirvana', in Holly George-Warren and Shawn Dahl (eds) *Cobain: By the Editors of Rolling Stone*. Toronto: Little, Brown & Company (originally published in *Rolling Stone*, 16 April 1992), pp. 32–9.

Baker, Lindsay (1997) 'Norse Code', *Guardian Weekend*, 27 November, pp. 12–18.

Baker, Sarah Louise (1999) 'Selling the Spice Girls', in Rob White (ed.) *Australian Youth Subcultures: On the Margins and in the Mainstream*. Australian Clearinghouse for Youth Studies: Hobart, pp. 74–82.

Baker, Sarah Louise (2004) 'Pop in(to) the Bedroom: Popular Music in Pre-teen Girls' Bedroom Culture', *European Journal of Cultural Studies*, 7 (1), pp. 75–93.

Bangs, Lester (1991) *Psychotic Reactions and Carburettor Dung: Literature as Rock 'n' Roll, Rock 'n' Roll as Literature* (ed. Greil Marcus). London: Minerva.

Banks, Jack (1998) 'Video in the Machine: The Incorporation of Music Video into the Recording Industry', *Popular Music*, 16 (3), pp. 293–309.

Barber, Lynn (1998) 'Interview: Bjork: Speaking in Tongues' *Observer*, Life section, 18 October, p. 4.

Barnes, Anthony (2005) 'Move Over, Boys. Girls with Guitars are Leading the New Rock Revolution', *Independent on Sunday*, News section, 30 January, p. 13.

Barrowclough, Anne (1993) 'Save The World? Not A Hope Grrrls', *Mail on Saturday*, 27 March, p. 27.

Bath Chronicle (2004) 'Kurt Off in his Prime', 9 April, p. 10.

Bayton, Mavis Mary (1989) *How Women Become Rock Musicians*. Unpublished PhD thesis, University of Warwick.

Bayton, Mavis (1997) 'Women and the Electric Guitar', in Sheila Whiteley (ed.) *Sexing the Groove: Popular Music and Gender*. London: Routledge, pp. 37–49.

Bayton, Mavis (1998) *Frock Rock: Women Performing Popular Music*. Oxford: Oxford University Press.

Becker, Scott (1998) *We Rock So You Don't Have To: The Option Reader #1*. San Diego: Incommunicado Press.

Bennett, Andy (2001) '"Plug in and Play!" UK "Indie-Guitar" Culture', in Andy Bennett and Kevin Dawe (eds) *Guitar Cultures*. Oxford: Berg, pp. 45–61.

Bennett, Andy (2002) 'Music, Media and Urban Mythscapes: a study of the "Canterbury Sound"', *Media, Culture and Society*, 24 (1), pp. 87–100.

Bennett, Andy and Kahn-Harris, Keith (2004) *After Subculture: Critical Studies in Contemporary Youth Culture*. Basingstoke: Palgrave Macmillan.

Bennett, H. Stith (1980) *On Becoming a Rock Musician*. Amherst: University of Massachusetts Press.

Berger, Harris M. (1999) *Metal, Rock and Jazz: Perception and the Phenomenology of Musical Experience*. Hanover, New Hampshire: Wesleyan University Press.

Berry, Venise T. (1994) 'Feminine or Masculine: The Conflicting Nature of Female Images in Rap Music', in Susan C. Cook and Judy S. Tsou (eds) *Cecilia Reclaimed: Feminist Perspectives on Gender and Music*. Urbana: University of Illinois Press, pp. 183–201.

Bicknell, Gareth (2004) 'Still Giving Teens Spirit; On the Tenth Anniversary of Kurt Cobain's Suicide', *Daily Post* (North Wales edition), 2 April, pp. 4–5.

Billen, Andrew (1995) 'The Billen Interview', *Observer*, Life section, 8 October, p. 8.

Billen, Andrew (2001) 'Stalkers, Demented Fans and a Letter Bomb: The Life of Bjork', *Evening Standard*, 15 August, p. 23.

Blackman, Shane J. (1998) 'The School: "Poxy Cupid", an Ethnographic and Feminist Account of a Resistant Female Youth Culture: The New Wave Girls', in Tracey Skelton and Gill Valentine (eds) *Cool Places: Geographies of Youth Cultures*. London: Routledge, pp. 207–28.

Blackstock, Russell (1994) 'Bjonkers!: Bjork Surprises Fans at Festival in Iceland', *Sunday Mail*, 10 July, p. 35.

Blécourt, Willem De (July 2000) 'The Making of the Female Witch: Reflections on Witchcraft and Gender in the Early Modern Period', *Gender and History*, 12 (2), pp. 287–309.

Bowler, Dave and Dray, Bryan (1996) *Iron Maiden: Infinite Dreams*. London: Boxtree.

Bradby, Barbara (1990) 'Do-Talk and Don't-Talk: The Division of the Subject in Girl-Group Music', in Simon Frith and Andrew Goodwin (eds) *On Record: Rock, Pop, and the Written Word*. New York: Pantheon Books, pp. 341–68.

Bradby, Barbara (1993) 'Lesbians and Popular Music: Does it Matter Who is Singing?', in Gabriele Griffin (ed.) *Outwrite: Lesbianism and Popular Culture*. London: Pluto Press, pp. 148–71.

Brake, Mike (1980) *The Sociology of Youth Culture and Youth Subcultures: Sex and Drugs and Rock 'n' Roll?* London: Routledge & Kegan Paul.

Breen, Marcus (1987) 'Rock Journalism: Betrayal of the Impulse', in Marcus Breen (ed.) *Missing in Action: Australian Popular Music in Perspective*. Victoria: Verbal Graphics Pty Ltd, pp. 202–27.

Brett, Philip, Wood, Elizabeth and Thomas, Gary (eds) (1994) *Queering The Pitch: The New Gay and Lesbian Musicology*. London: Routledge.

Brite, Poppy Z. (1998) *Courtney Love: The Real Story*. London: Orion.

Brown, Glyn (1997) 'The Ice Melts', *Independent*, Eye on Monday (Media section), 17 November, p. 4.

Brown, Paul (1993) 'Riot Squad', *The Zine*, 1, July, p. 27.

Bruzzi, Stella (1997) 'Mannish Girl: k.d. lang – from Cowpunk to Androgyny', in Sheila Whiteley (ed.) *Sexing the Groove: Popular Music and Gender*. London: Routledge, pp. 191–206.

Burns, Lori and Lafrance, Mélisse (2002) *Disruptive Divas: Feminism, Identity and Popular Music*. London: Routledge.

Butler, Judith (1990) *Gender Trouble: Feminism and the Subversion of Identity*. London: Routledge.

Cairns, Dan (2000) 'On Record', *Sunday Times*, Features section, 17 September.

Callan, Jessica, Simpson, Eva and Callan, Suzanne (2002) '3am: It's More Baby Talk For Bjork', *Mirror*, 2 May, p. 13.

Cameron, Sam (2003) 'The Political Economy of Gender Disparity in Musical Markets', *Cambridge Journal of Economics*, 27 (6), pp. 905–17.

Carby, Hazel V. (1990) '"It Jus Be's Dat Way Sometime" The Sexual Politics of Women's Blues', in Ellen Carol DuBois and Vicki L. Ruiz (eds) *Unequal Sisters: A Multicultural Reader in US Women's History*. London: Routledge, pp. 238–49.

Carey, Tanith (1996) 'She's Bjorking Mad', *Daily Mirror*, Features section, 29 February, pp. 24–5.

Carson, Mina, Lewis, Tisa and Shaw, Susan M. (2004) *Girls Rock! Fifty Years of Women Making Music*. Lexington: University Press of Kentucky.

Castells, Manuel (2003) *The Internet Galaxy: Reflections on the Internet, Business, and Society*. Oxford: Oxford University Press.

Cateforis, Theo and Humphreys, Elena (1997) 'Constructing Communities and Identities: Riot Grrrl New York City', in Kip Lornell and Anne K. Rasmussen (eds) *Musics of Multicultural America: A Study of Twelve Musical Communities*. New York: Schirmer, pp. 317–42.

Cavanagh, David (1993) 'PJ Harvey: *Rid Of Me*' review, *Select*, 85, May, p. 85.

Cavanagh, David (1995) 'Nemesis in a Scarlet Dress', *Independent*, Magazine section, 25 February, p. 30.

Chapple, Steve and Garofalo, Reebee (1978) *Rock 'n' Roll is Here to Pay: The History and Politics of the Music Industry*. Chicago: Nelson-Hall.

Chick, Stevie (1999) 'Venini/Brassy/Marine Research', *NME*, 14 August, p. 29.

Chick, Stevie (2004) 'Voice from the Grave', *The Times*, The Eye, 27 November, p. 16.

Chideya, Farai, Rossi, Melissa and Hannah, Dogen (1992) 'Revolution, Girl Style', *Newsweek*, 23 November, p. 84.

Citron, Marcia J. (1993) *Gender and the Musical Canon*. Cambridge: Cambridge University Press.

Clarke, Betty (2003) 'Gus Gus: Scala. London', *Guardian*, 29 January, p. 22.

Clawson, Mary Ann (1999a) 'Masculinity and Skill Acquisition in the Adolescent Rock Band', *Popular Music*, 18 (1), pp. 99–114.

Clawson, Mary Ann (1999b) 'When Women Play the Bass: Instrument Specialization and Gender Interpretation in Alternative Rock Music', *Gender and Society*, 13 (2), pp. 193–210.

Coates, Norma (1998) 'Can't We Just Talk About Music? Rock and Gender on the Internet', in Thomas Swiss, John Sloop and Andrew Herman (eds) *Mapping the Beat: Popular Music and Contemporary Theory*. Massachusetts: Blackwell, pp. 77–99.

Code, Lorraine (1995) *Rhetorical Spaces: Essays on Gendered Locations*. London: Routledge.

Cohen, Sara (1991) *Rock Culture in Liverpool: Popular Music in the Making*. Oxford: Oxford University Press.

Cohen, Sara (1997) 'Men Making a Scene: Rock Music and the Production of Gender, in Sheila Whiteley (ed.) *Sexing the Groove: Popular Music and Gender*. London: Routledge, pp. 17–36.

Cohen, Stanley (1980) *Folk Devils and Moral Panics: The Creation of the Mods and Rockers*. Oxford: Martin Robertson.

Comstock, Michelle (2001) 'Grrrl Zine Networks: Re-composing Spaces of Authority, Gender and Culture', *JAC: A Journal of Compositional Theory*, 21 (2), pp. 383–409.

Connolly, Paul (2001) 'Off The Wall?', *The Times*, 18 August.

Cooper, Sarah (1995) *Girls! Girls! Girls! Essays on Women and Music*. London: Cassell.

Cornwell, Jane (1995) 'The World According to Bjork', *The Guardian*, Features, 2 June, p. T16.

Corrigan, Paul (1993) 'Doing Nothing', in Stuart Hall and Tony Jefferson (eds) *Resistance Through Rituals: Youth Subcultures in Post-war Britain*. London: Routledge, pp. 103–5.

Corrigan, Susan (1993) 'Who are the Riot Grrrls?', *ID*, 115, April, pp. 28–31.

Corrigan, Susan (ed.) (1997) *Typical Girls: New Stories By Smart Women*. London: Sceptre.

Cresser, Francis, Gunn, Lesley and Balme, Helen (2001) 'Women's Experiences of On-Line Publication', *Media, Culture and Society*, 23 (4), pp. 457–73.

Cross, Alan (1995) *The Alternative Music Almanac, V1.0*. Ontario: Collectors Guide Publishing Inc.

Culshaw, Peter (2005) 'Elves, Hay Wagons and Jumping into Puddles', *Daily Telegraph*, 8 September, p. 25.

Dahl, Linda (1984) *Stormy Weather: The Music and Lives of a Century of Jazzwomen*. London: Quartet Books.

Daily Star (1993) 'Riot Girls', 18 March, republished in *Melody Maker*, True Stories section, 20 March 1993, p. 38.

Daly, Steven and Wice, Nathaniel (1995) *Alt.Culture: An A-to-Z Guide to the '90s – Underground, Online, and Over-the-counter*. New York: HarperCollins.

Darling-Wolf, Fabienne (2004) 'Virtually Multicultural: Trans-Asian Identity and Gender in an International Fan Community of a Japanese Star', *New Media and Society*, 6 (4), pp. 507–28.

Darrington, Ian (2000) '"What Do You Play?": Trumpet Mouthpieces in the Jazz Scene'. Unpublished paper presented at the Institute of Popular Music, University of Liverpool.

Davies, Helen (2001) 'All Rock and Roll is Homosocial: The Representation of Women in the British Rock Music Press', *Popular Music*, 20 (3), pp. 301–19.

Davies, Jude (1999) '"It's Like Feminism But You Don't Have to Burn Your Bra": Girl Power and the Spice Girls Breakthrough 1996–7', in Andrew Blake (ed.) *Living Through Pop*. London: Routledge, pp. 159–73.

Davies, Laura Lee (1993) 'Princess of Wails', *Time Out*, 22–29 December, p. 20.

Davies, Laura Lee (1995) 'Velocity Girls: Indie, New Lads, Old Values', in Sarah Cooper (ed.) *Girls! Girls! Girls! Essays on Women and Music*. London: Cassell, pp. 124–34.

De Beauvoir, Simone (1952) *The Second Sex*. New York: Bantam.

Dee, Johnny (1993) 'Princess of Wails', *NME*, 3 July, p. 35.

Deleuze, Gilles and Guattari, Felix (1988) *A Thousand Plateaus: Capitalism and Schizophrenia* (trans. Brian Massumi). London: Athlone Press.

Dellar, Fred (ed.) (1995) *Excess All Areas: A Who's Who of Rock Depravity*. London: IPC Magazines (free with *Vox*, 56, May/June 1995).

Denselow, Anthony (1980) Article on The Pretenders, *Observer Magazine*, 20 January.

Denselow, Robin (1980a) 'Pat Benatar', *The Guardian*, 22 February.

Denselow, Robin (1980b) 'Suzi Quatro', *The Guardian*, 26 January.

Dibben, Nicola (1999) 'Representations of Femininity in Popular Music', *Popular Music*, 18 (3), pp. 331–55.

Dibben, Nicola (2002) 'Construction of Femininity in 1990s Girl-group Music', *Feminism and Psychology*, 12 (2), pp. 168–75.

Dickerson, James (1998) *Women on Top: The Quiet Revolution that's Rocking the American Music Industry*. New York: Billboard Books.

Dingwall, John (1996a) 'Going Off Her Rocker All Over the World', *Daily Record*, 25 July, p. 26.

Dingwall, John (1996b) 'Record Women: My Love Drug', *Daily Record*, 31 January, p. 21.

Dingwall, John and Oxley, Ken (1996) 'Snap, Crack and Pop', *Daily Record*, 22 February, p. 12.

Dreyfus, Kay (1999) *Sweethearts of Rhythm: The Story of Australia's All-girl Bands and Orchestras to the end of the Second World War*. Strawberry Hills, New South Wales: Currency Press.

Driscoll, Catherine (1999) 'Girl Culture, Revenge and Global Capitalism: Cybergirls, Riot Grrls, Spice Girls', *Australian Feminist Studies*, 14 (29), pp. 173–93.

Duncombe, Stephen (1997) *Notes From Underground: Zines and the Politics of Alternative Culture*. London: Verso.

Du Plessis, Michael and Chapman, Kathleen (1997) 'Queercore: The Distinct Identities of Subculture', *College Literature*, 24 (1), February, pp. 45–58.

Edmands, Bob (1980) Inga Rumpf review, *NME*, 26 April.

Eichhorn, Kate (2001) 'Sites Unseen: Ethnographic Research in a Textual Community', *Qualitative Studies in Education*, 14 (4), pp. 565–78.

Elliott, Luther (2004) 'Goa Trance and the Practice of Community in the Age of the Internet', *Television and New Media*, 5 (3), pp. 272–88.

Empire, Kitty (2003) 'Bjork to the Future' *The Observer*, Observer Review Pages, 1 June, p. 11.

Evans, Liz (1993a) 'Here Comes Trouble', *Elle*, January, pp. 12–15.

Evans, Liz (1993b) 'Rebel Yell', *Elle*, July, pp. 35–41.

Evans, Liz (1994) *Women, Sex and Rock 'n' Roll: In Their Own Words*. London: Pandora.

Evans, Liz (1995) 'Rock 'n' Roll Madonna', *Kerrang!*, 543, 29 April, p. 38.

Evans, Liz (ed.) (1997) *Girls Will Be Boys: Women Report on Rock*. London: Pandora.

Fairchild, Charles (1995) '"Alternative" Music and the Politics of Cultural Autonomy: The Case of Fugazi and the DC Scene', *Popular Music and Society*, 19 (1), pp. 17–36.

Feigenbaum, Anna (2005) '"Some Guy Designed This Room I'm Standing In": Marking Gender in Press Coverage of Ani DiFranco', *Popular Music*, 24 (1), pp. 37–56.

Felder, Rachel (1993) *Manic Pop Thrill*. Hopewell, New Jersey: Ecco Press.

Fenster, Mark (1993) 'Genre and Form: The Development of the Country Music Video', in Simon Frith, Andrew Goodwin and Lawrence Grossberg (eds) *Sound and Vision: The Music Video Reader*. London: Routledge, pp. 109–28.

Finnegan, Ruth (1989) *The Hidden Musicians: Making Music in an English Town*. Cambridge: Cambridge University Press.

Flynn, Bob (2005) 'Hot Flushes at the Coolest Show in Town', *The Sunday Times*, 24 April, p. 6.

Fonarow, Wendy (1997) 'The Spatial Organisation of the Indie Music Gig', in Ken Gelder and Sarah Thornton (eds) *The Subcultures Reader*. London: Routledge, pp. 361–9.

Forde, Eamonn (2001) 'From Polyglottism to Branding: On the Decline of Personality Journalism in the British Music Press', *Journalism*, 2 (1), pp. 23–43.

Fornas, Johan (1995) 'The Future of Rock: Discourses that Struggle to Define a Genre', *Popular Music*, 14 (1), pp. 111–25.

Foucault, Michel (1990) *The History of Sexuality Volume 1: An Introduction*. London: Penguin.

Fouz-Hernández, Santiago and Jarman-Ivens, Freya (2004) *Madonna's Drowned Worlds: New Approaches to her Cultural Transformations, 1983–2003*. Aldershot: Ashgate.

Fowler, Simon (1995) 'Tea and Sympathy with the Devil', *Select*, 58, April, p. 80.

France, Kim (1993) 'Grrrls At War', *Rolling Stone*, 8–22 July, pp. 23–4.

Franks, Tom (1995) 'Alternative to What?', in Ron Sakolsky and Fred Wei-Han Ho (eds) *Sounding Off: Music as Subversion/Resistance/Revolution*. New York: Autonomedia, pp. 109–20.

Fricke, David (1994) 'Blood on the Tracks', *Melody Maker*, 29 October, p. 29.

Fricke, David (1995) 'Live!', *Melody Maker*, 2 September, p. 25.

Frith, Simon (1978) *The Sociology of Rock*. London: Constable.

Frith, Simon (1981) *Sound Effects: Youth, Leisure, and the Politics of Rock 'n' Roll*. New York: Pantheon.

Frith, Simon (1990) 'Afterthoughts', in Simon Frith and Andrew Goodwin (eds) *On Record: Rock, Pop and the Written Word*. New York: Pantheon Books, pp. 419–24.

Frith, Simon (1996) *Performing Rites: Evaluating Popular Music*. Oxford: Oxford University Press.

Frith, Simon (1998) *Performing Rites: Evaluating Popular Music*. Oxford: Oxford University Press.

Frith, Simon and McRobbie, Angela (1990) 'Rock and Sexuality', in Simon Frith and Andrew Goodwin (eds) *On Record: Rock, Pop and the Written Word*. New York: Pantheon Books (reprinted from Screen Education, 29, 1978), pp. 371–89.

Fritzsche, Bettina (2004) 'Spicy Strategies: Pop Feminist and Other Empowerments in Girl Culture', in Anita Harris (ed.) *All About the Girl: Culture, Power and Identity*. London: Routledge, pp. 155–62.

Fuchs, Cynthia (1998) 'If I had a Dick: Queers, Punks and Alternative Acts', in Thomas Swiss, John Sloop and Andrew Herman (eds) *Mapping the Beat: Popular Music and Contemporary Theory*. Oxford: Blackwell, pp. 101–18.

Fulton, Rick (1997) 'Nothing Can Go Wrong if You Fall in Love With Your Best Mate', *Daily Record*, 12 September, p. 56.

Gaar, Gillian G. (1993) *She's A Rebel: The History of Women in Rock & Roll*. London: Blandford.

Gaines, Donna (1994) 'Suicidal Tendencies', in Holly George-Warren and Shawn Dahl (eds) *Cobain: By the Editors of Rolling Stone*. New York: Little, Brown & Company, pp. 128–32.

Garratt, Sheryl (1985) 'Crushed By the Wheels of Industry', in Sue Steward and Sheryl Garratt (eds) *Signed, Sealed and Delivered: True Life Stories of Women in Pop*. London: Pluto, pp. 60–81.

Garratt, Sheryl (1990) 'Teenage Dreams', in Simon Frith and Andrew Goodwin (eds) *On Record: Rock, Pop and the Written Word*. New York: Pantheon Books, pp. 399–409.

Gelder, Ken and Thornton, Sarah (1997) *The Subcultures Reader*. London: Routledge.

George-Warren, Holly and Dahl, Shawn (eds) (1994) *Cobain: By the Editors of Rolling Stone*. New York: Little, Brown & Company.

George-Warren, Holly and Romanowski, Patricia (2001) *The Rolling Stone Encyclopedia of Rock and Roll* (3rd edn). New York: Fireside.

Gill, Andy (1997) 'On Record: Bjork Homogenic', *The Independent*, 19 September, p. 19.

Gill, Andy (2003) 'Einar Orn: Life's Rich Pageant', *The Independent*, 28 November, pp. 18–19.

Gill, John (1995) *Queer Noises: Male and Female Homosexuality in Twentieth-century Music*. London: Cassell.

Gisbourne, Mark (1996) *Beyond Reason: Art and Psychosis – Works from the Prinzhorn Collection* (exhibition guide). London: Hayward Gallery.

Glamour (1993) 'Grrrl Talk', May, p. 134.

Goad, D. (1994) 'Riot Grrrls Rrreally Borrring', *Your Flesh* #29: 10 Year Anniversary 1984–94, p. 22.

Goodwin, Andrew (1992) *Dancing in the Distraction Factory: Music Television and Popular Culture*. London: Routledge.

Gordon, Bryony (2002) 'I'm Glad You Think of me as a Nutter', *Daily Telegraph*, 9 September, p. 13.

Gorman, Clem (1978) *Back Stage Rock: Behind the Scenes with the Bands*. London: Pan.

Gottlieb, Joanne and Wald, Gayle (1994) 'Smells Like Teen Spirit: Riot Grrrls, Revolution and Women in Independent Rock', in Andrew Ross and Tricia Rose (eds) *Microphone Fiends: Youth Music and Youth Culture*. London: Routledge, pp. 250–74.

Gourse, Leslie (1995) *Madame Jazz: Contemporary Women Instrumentalists*. Oxford: Oxford University Press.

Gracyk, Theodore (1996) *Rhythm and Noise: An Aesthetics of Rock*. London: IB Tauris and VO Ltd.

Grad, David (1992) 'The Hole Truth', *Puncture*, 24, May, pp. 5–6.

Grajeda, Tony (2002) 'The "Feminization" of Rock', in Roger Beebe, Denise Fulbrook and Ben Saunders (eds) *Rock Over the Edge: Transformations in Popular Music Culture*. Durham, NC: Duke University Press.

Gray, Louise (1994) 'From Beauty to the Beat', *The Times*, 1 March.

Green, Karen and Taormino, Tristan (eds) (1997) *A Girl's Guide to Taking Over the World: Writings From the Girl Zine Revolution*. New York: St Martin's Griffin.

Green, Lucy (1997) *Music, Gender, Education*. Cambridge: Cambridge University Press.

Greene, Jo-Ann, Harrison, Andrew and Waller, Johnny (1994) 'The Shot Heard Around The World', *Select*, 48, June, pp. 71, 74–81.

Greig, Charlotte (1989) *Will You Still Love Me Tomorrow? Girl Groups from the 50s On...*. London: Virago.

Groce, Stephen and Cooper, Margaret (1990) 'Just Me and the Boys? Women in Local-level Rock and Roll, *Gender and Society*, 4 (2), June, pp. 220–9.

Grogan, Siobhan (1999) 'Llama Farmers/Twist', *NME*, 9 October, p. 34.

Grosz, Elizabeth (1994) 'A Thousand Tiny Sexes: Feminism and Rhizomatics', in Constantin V. Boundas and Dorothea Olkowski (eds) *Gilles Deleuze and the Theater of Philosophy*. New York: Routledge.

Guardian (1999) 'Every Dead Rock Star has a Silver Lining', 5 April, p. 11.

Halberstam, Judith (2003) 'What's that Smell? Queer Temporalities and Subcultural Lives', *International Journal of Cultural Studies*, 6 (3), pp. 313–33.

Hallam, Susan, Rogers, Lynne and Creech, Andrea (2005) *Survey of Local Authority Services 2005*, Research Report RR700. Nottingham: Department for Education and Skills.

Hallissy, Margaret (1987) *Venomous Woman: Fear of the Female in Literature*. Westport, CN: Greenwood Press.

Harding, Deborah and Nett, Emily (1984) 'Women and Rock Music', *Atlantis*, 10 (1), Fall/Autumn, pp. 61–76.

Hardy, Phil and Laing, Dave (1976a) *The Encyclopedia of Rock Volume One: The Age of Rock 'n' Roll*. St Albans: Panther.

Hardy, Phil and Laing, Dave (1976b) *The Encyclopedia of Rock Volume Two: From Liverpool to San Francisco*. St Albans: Panther.

Hardy, Phil and Laing, Dave (1976c) *The Encyclopedia of Rock Volume Three: The Sounds of the Seventies*. St Albans: Panther.

Hardy, Phil and Laing, Dave (1995) *The Faber Companion to 20th-century Popular Music*. London: Faber & Faber.

Harker, Dave (1980) *One For The Money: Politics and Popular Song*. London: Hutchinson.

Harris, Anita (2003) 'gURL Scenes and Grrrl Zines: The Regulation and Resistance of Girls in Late Modernity', *Feminist Review*, 75, pp. 38–56.

Harris, John (1995) 'From Despair to Where?', *NME*, 25 February, p. 5.

Harris, John (2003) 'Girl Fight', *Q*, 207, October, p. 99.

Harris, John (2004) 'Mr Kurt, He Dead', *The Times*, Weekend Review, 3 April, p. 18.

Harron, Mary (1990) 'McRock: Pop as Commodity' in Simon Frith (ed.) *Facing the Music: Essays on Pop, Rock and Culture*. London: Mandarin.

Hebdige, Dick (1979) *Subculture: The Meaning of Style*. London: Methuen.

Henderson, Dave and Johnson, Howard (1999) *Leaving the 20th Century: The Last Rites of Rock n Roll*. Pewsey: Black Book Company.

Henderson, Samantha and Gilding, Michael (2004) '"I've Never Clicked This Much With Anyone in My Life": Trust and Hyperpersonal Communication in Online Friendships', *New Media and Society*, 6 (4), pp. 487–506.

Hersh, Kristen (1997) 'The Snowballing of Alt. Rock', in Susan Corrigan (ed.) *Typical Girls: New Stories By Smart Women*. London: Sceptre, pp. 61–6.

Hesmondhalgh, David (1996) *Independent Record Companies and Democratisation in the Popular Music Industry*. Unpublished PhD thesis, Goldsmiths College, London.

Hesmondhalgh, David, (1998) 'Post-punk's Attempt to Democratise the Music Industry: The Success and Failure of Rough Trade', *Popular Music,* 16 (3) pp. 255–74.

Hesmondhalgh, David (1999) 'Indie: The Institutional Politics and Aesthetics of a Popular Music Genre', *Cultural Studies,* 13 (1), pp. 34–61.

Heylin, Clinton (ed.) (1993) *The Penguin Book of Rock and Roll Writing.* London: Penguin.

Hibbett, Ryan (2005) 'What Is Indie Rock?', *Popular Music and Society,* 28 (1), pp. 55–77.

Hillburn, Robert (1994) 'In Seattle, a Mood of Teen Dispirit', *LA Times,* F1, 12 April, pp. 8–9.

Hirsh, Paul M. (1990) 'Processing Fads and Fashions: An Organization-set Analysis of Cultural Industry Systems', in Simon Frith and Andrew Goodwin (eds) *On Record: Rock, Pop, and the Written Word.* New York: Pantheon Books, pp. 127–39.

Hirshey, Gerri (2001) *We Gotta Get Out of This Place: The True, Tough Story of Women in Rock.* New York: Grove Press.

Hodkinson, Paul (2003) '"Net.Goth": Internet Communication and (Sub)Cultural Boundaries', in David Muggleton and Rupert Weinzierl (eds) *The Post-Subcultures Reader.* Oxford: Berg, pp: 285–98.

Hodkinson, Paul (2005) '"Insider Research" in the Study of Youth Cultures', *Journal of Youth Studies,* 8 (2), pp. 131–49.

Home, Stewart (1991a) 'Towards Nothing: Notes From the Generation Positive on the Nature of Conspiracy', in Stewart Home (ed.) *Neoist Manifestos,* collected in the double volume *Neoist Manifestos/The Art Strike Papers.* Stirling: AK Press.

Home, Stewart (1991b) 'About the Art Strike', in Stewart Home (ed.) *Neoist Manifestos,* collected in the double volume *Neoist Manifestos/The Art Strike Papers.* Stirling: AK Press.

hooks, bell (1995) 'Madonna: Plantation Mistress or Soul Sister?', in Evelyn McDonnell and Ann Powers (eds) *Rock She Wrote: Women Write About Rock, Pop, and Rap.* London: Plexus, pp. 318–25.

Hopkins, Susan (1999) 'The Art of "Girl Power": Femininity, Feminism and Youth Culture in the 1990s', in Rob White (ed.) *Australian Youth Subcultures: On the Margins and in the Mainstream.* Hobart: Australian Clearinghouse for Youth Studies, pp. 94–101.

Hopper, Jessica (1997) 'Lost TV', *Grand Royal,* 5, p. 66.

Hornburg, Michael (1995) *Bongwater.* London: Quartet Books.

Hornby, Nick (1995) *High Fidelity.* London: Indigo.

Hornby, Nick and Schafer, Ben (eds) (2001) *Da Capo Best Music Writing 2001: The Year's Finest Writing on Rock, Pop, Jazz, Country and More.* Cambridge, MA: Da Capo Press.

Hoskyns, Barney (ed.) (2003) *The Sound and the Fury: A Rock's Backpages Reader – 40 Years of Classic Rock Journalism.* London: Bloomsbury.

Hotten, Jon (1995) 'Celebrity Fabulousness', *Raw,* 10–23 May, p. 44.

Hoye, Jacob (ed.) (2003) *VH1's 100 Greatest Albums.* New York: MTV/Pocket Books.

Huxley, Ros and English, Sue (1998) *Women and Jazz: Research Project Report*, commissioned by South West Jazz, Exeter, in partnership with Chard Festival of Women in Music, Somerset.

Jacques, Alison (2001) 'You Can Run But You Can't Hide: The Incorporation of Riot Grrrl into Mainstream Culture', *Canadian Woman Studies/Les Cahiers de la Femme,* Special Issue: Young Women – Feminists, Activists, Grrrls, 20/21 (4/1), pp. 46–50.

Japenga, Ann (1992) 'Punk's Girl Groups Are Putting the Self Back in Self-Esteem', *New York Times*, Section 2: Arts and Leisure, 15 November, p. 30.

Jensen, Joli (1993) 'Patsy Cline, Musical Negotiation, and the Nashville Sound', in George H. Lewis (ed.) *All That Glitters: Country Music in America.* Bowling Green, OH: Bowling Green State University Popular Press, pp. 38–50.

Johnson, Bruce (2000) *The Inaudible Music: Jazz, Gender and Australian Modernity.* Sydney: Currency Press.

Johnson-Grau, Brenda (2002) 'Sweet Nothings: Presentation of Women Musicians in Pop Journalism', in Steve Jones (ed.) *Pop Music and the Press.* Philadelphia: Temple University Press, pp. 202–18.

Jones, Dylan (ed.) (1996) *Meaty, Beaty, Big and Bouncy! Classic Rock and Pop Writing from Elvis to Oasis.* London: Hodder & Stoughton.

Jones, Michael Lewis (1997) *Organising Pop: Why So Few Pop Acts Make Pop Music.* Unpublished PhD, University of Liverpool.

Jones, Steve (1995) 'Covering Cobain: Narrative Patterns in Journalism and Rock Criticism', *Popular Music and Society*, 19 (2), pp. 103–18.

Joy, Sally Margaret (1992) 'Revolution Grrrl Style Now!', *Melody Maker*, 10 October, pp. 30–32.

Joy, Sally Margaret, Lester, Paul, Arundel, Jim and True, Everett (1992) 'Busting Out of Bimbo Hell?', *Melody Maker*, 19 September, pp. 44–6.

Juno, Andrea (1996) *Angry Women in Rock: Volume One.* New York: Juno Books.

Kaplan, E. Ann (1987) *Rocking Around the Clock: Music Television, Postmodernism, and Consumer Culture.* London: Routledge.

Katz, Susan (1978) *Superwomen of Rock.* New York: Tempo Books.

Kavaler-Adler, Susan (1993) *The Compulsion to Create: A Psychoanalytic Study of Women Artists.* London: Routledge.

Kearney, Mary Celeste (1997) 'The Missing Links: Riot Grrrl – Feminism – Lesbian Culture', in Sheila Whiteley (ed.) *Sexing the Groove: Popular Music and Gender.* London: Routledge, pp. 207–29.

Keightley, Keir (1996) '"Turn it Down!" She Shrieked: Gender, Domestic Space, and High Fidelity, 1948–59', *Popular Music*, 15 (2), pp. 149–77.

Kellner, Douglas (1995) *Media Culture: Cultural Studies, Identity and Politics Between the Modern and the Postmodern.* London: Routledge.

Kennedy, Kathleen (2002) 'Results of a Misspent Youth: Joan Jett's Performance of Female Masculinity', *Women's History Review*, 11 (1), pp. 89–114.

Kent, Greta (1983) *A View From the Bandstand.* London: Sheba.

Kent, Nick (1994) *The Dark Stuff: Selected Writings on Rock Music 1972–1993.* London: Penguin.

Kessler, Ted (1995) 'Thin White Kook', *NME*, 28 January, pp. 32–4.

Kibby, Majorie D. (2000) 'Home on the Page: A Virtual Place of Music Community', *Popular Music*, 19 (1), pp. 91–100.

Kitts, Jeff and Tolinski, Brad (2002) *The 100 Greatest Guitarists of All Time*. Milwaukee: Hal Leonard.

Knowles, Ben (1998) 'Unbelievable Truth', *Melody Maker*, 10 January, p. 21.

Kofman, Veronica (1997) 'Helen Love: The Backwards Approach to Moving Ahead', *Rockrgrl*, 14, March, p. 17.

Krenske, Leigh and McKay, Jim (2000) '"Hard and Heavy": Gender and Power in a Heavy Metal Music Subculture', *Gender, Place and Culture*, 7 (3), pp. 287–304.

Kruse, Holly (1993) 'Subcultural Identity in Alternative Music Culture', *Popular Music*, 12 (1), pp. 33–41.

Kruse, Holly (1999) 'Gender', in Bruce Horner and Thomas Swiss (eds) *Key Terms in Popular Music and Culture*. Oxford: Blackwell, pp. 85–100.

Kruse, Holly (2002) 'Abandoning the Absolute: Transcendence and Gender in Popular Music Discourse', in Steve Jones (ed.) *Pop Music and the Press*, Philadelphia: Temple University Press, pp. 134–55.

Kureishi, Hanif and Savage, Jon (1995) *The Faber Book of Pop*. London: Faber & Faber.

Laing, Dave (1985) *One Chord Wonders: Power and Meaning in Punk Rock*. Milton Keynes: Open University Press.

Lamacq, Steve (2000) *Going Deaf for a Living: A DJ's Story*. London: BBC Worldwide Ltd.

Larkin, Colin (1992) *The Guinness Who's Who of Indie and New Wave Music*. Enfield, Middlesex: Guinness.

Larkin, Colin (ed.) (1995) *The Guinness Who's Who of Jazz* (2nd edn). London: Guinness.

Larkin, Colin (ed.) (2000) *The Virgin Encyclopedia of Nineties Music*. London: Virgin Books.

Lavie, Aliza and Lehman-Wilzig, Sam (2003) 'Whose News? Does Gender Determine Editorial Product?', *European Journal of Communication*, 18 (1), pp. 5–29.

Leblanc, Lauraine (1999) *Pretty in Punk: Girls' Gender Resistance in a Boys' Subculture*. New Brunswick, New Jersey: Rutgers University Press.

LeClaire, Sarah (1995) 'Live!', *Melody Maker*, 25 February, p. 17.

Leigh, Spencer (1999) 'What's it All About, Alfie?'. Paper presented at Robert Shelton Memorial Conference, Institute of Popular Music, University of Liverpool.

Leith, Sam (2004) 'Kurt Cobain: Self-hating Icon of the Inarticulate Generation', *Daily Telegraph*, 10 April, p. 7.

Lemish, Dafna (2003) 'Spice World: Constructing Femininity the Popular Way', *Popular Music and Society*, 26 (1), pp. 17–29.

Leonard, Marion (1997) '"Rebel Girl, You Are the Queen of My World": Feminism, "Subculture" and Grrrl Power', in Sheila Whiteley (ed.) *Sexing the Groove: Popular Music and Gender*. London: Routledge, pp. 230–55.

Leonard, Marion (1998) 'Paper Planes: Travelling the New Grrrl Geographies', in Tracey Skelton and Gill Valentine (eds) *Cool Places: Geographies of Youth Cultures*. London: Routledge, pp. 101–18.

Leonard, Marion and Strachan, Rob (with Gwen Ansell, Steve Jones, Olivier Julien, Claire Levy, Christian Mörken and Masahiro Yasuda) (2003) 'Music Press', in John Shepherd, David Horn, Dave Laing, Paul Oliver and Peter Wicke (eds) *Continuum Encyclopedia of Popular Music of the World Volume I: Media, Industry and Society*. London: Continuum, pp. 38–42.

Lester, Paul (1994) 'Bejewelled!', *Melody Maker*, 10 September, p. 24.

Lewis, Lisa A (ed.) (1992) *The Adoring Audience*. London: Routledge.

Lincoln, Sian (2004) 'Teenage Girls' "Bedroom Culture": Codes versus Zones', in Andy Bennett and Keith Kahn-Harris (eds) *After Subculture: Critical Studies in Contemporary Youth Culture*, Basingstoke: Palgrave Macmillan, pp. 94–106.

Lindberg, Ulf, Guðmundsson, Gestur, Michelsen, Morten and Weisethaunet, Hans (2000) *Amusers, Bruisers and Cool-headed Cruisers: The Fields of Anglo-Saxon and Nordic Rock Criticism*. Århus: Institute for Scandinavian Studies.

Logan, Nick and Woofinden, Bob (eds) (1977) *The New Musical Express Book of Rock, No. 2*. London: W.H. Allen & Co. Limited.

Logan, Nick and Woofinden, Bob (1982) *The Illustrated Encyclopedia of Rock*. London: Salamander Books Limited.

Lull, James (1987) 'Thrashing in the Pit: An Ethnography of San Francisco Punk Subculture', in Thomas R. Lindlof (ed.) *Natural Audiences: Qualitative Research of Media Uses and Effects*. Norwood, NJ: Ablex, pp. 225–52.

Lynskey, Dorian (2005) 'Strange? Us?', *The Guardian*, 26 August, p. 6.

Mair, Avril (1994) 'Love and Hate', *ID*, 127, April, p. 39.

Mäki-Kulmala, Airi (1995) 'Subculture, Rock Music and Gender', in Will Straw, Stacey Johnson, Rebecca Sullivan and Paul Friedlander (with Gary Kennedy) (eds) *Popular Music: Style and Identity* (International Association for the Study of Popular Music Seventh International Conference on Popular Music Studies). Montreal: The Centre for Research on Canadian Cultural Industries and Institutions, pp.. 205–7.

Manaugh, Sara (1993) 'Purge-ama Party', *Puncture*, 27, Summer, p. 39.

Manning, Sarra (1994) 'Viewpoint', *Melody Maker*, 29 January, p. 35.

Manning, Sarra (1998) 'Rock Star: From Kinderwhore to Queen of Couture', *Minx Magazine*, 18, April, pp. 72–76.

Marks, Craig (1995) 'Endless Love', *Spin*, 10 (11), February, pp. 42–51, 88.

Martin, Piers (1999) 'Cred Whippersnapper', *NME*, 23 January, p. 10.

Matthewman, Hester (1993) 'Rock Against Men is Music to the Riot Grrrls' Ears', *Independent on Sunday*, 14 March, p. 7.

Mazzarella, Sharon R. and Muto, Jan (eds) (1995) 'Special Issue: Ripped Jeans and Faded Flannel: Grunge, Youth and Communities of Alienation', *Popular Music and Society*, 19 (2).

Mazzarella, Sharon R. (1995) '"The Voice of a Generation"? Media Coverage of the Suicide of Kurt Cobain', *Popular Music and Society*, 19 (2), pp. 49–68.

Mcbeth, Jim (2000) 'Bjorking Mad', *Scotsman*, 25 May, p. 6.

McClary, Susan (1991) *Feminine Endings: Music, Gender, and Sexuality*. Minnesota: University of Minnesota Press.

Mcdonald, Peter (1994) 'Grunge Rock Idol Wanted to Burn Out, Not Fade Away', *Evening Standard,* 11 April, p. 20.

McDonnell, Evelyn (1995) 'The Feminine Critique: The Secret History of Women and Rock Journalism', in Evelyn McDonnell and Ann Powers (eds) *Rock She Wrote: Women Write About Rock, Pop, and Rap*. London: Plexus, pp. 15–23.

McDonnell, Evelyn (1997) 'Rebel Grrrls', in Barbara O'Dair (ed.) *Trouble Girls: The Rolling Stone Book of Women in Rock*. New York: Random House, pp. 453–63.

McDonnell, Evelyn and Powers, Ann (eds) (1995*) Rock She Wrote: Women Write About Rock, Pop, and Rap*. London: Plexus.

McLeod, Kembrew (2001) '"*½": A Critique of Rock Journalism in North America', *Popular Music*, 20 (1), pp. 47–60.

McLeod, Kembrew (2002) 'Between Rock and a Hard Place: Gender and Rock Criticism', in Steve Jones (ed.) *Pop Music and the Press*. Philadelphia: Temple University Press, pp. 93–113.

McNair, James (2001) 'Songs in the Key of Ice', *The Independent*, 30 March, p. 13.

McRobbie, Angela (1989) 'Second-hand Dresses and the Role of the Ragmarket', in Angela McRobbie (ed.) *Zoot Suits and Second-hand Dresses: An Anthology of Fashion and Music*. Hampshire: Macmillan, pp. 23–49.

McRobbie, Angela (1990) 'Settling Accounts With Subcultures: A Feminist Critique', in Simon Frith and Andrew Goodwin (eds) *On Record: Rock, Pop, and the Written Word*. New York: Pantheon Books, pp. 66–80.

McRobbie, Angela (1994) *Postmodernism and Popular Culture*. London: Routledge.

McRobbie, Angela and Garber, Jenny (1993) 'Girls and Subcultures', in Stuart Hall and Tony Jefferson (eds) *Resistance Through Rituals: Youth Subcultures in Post-war Britain*. London: Routledge, pp. 209–22.

Melody Maker (1992a) 'Grrrls! Grrrls! Grrrls!' (transcription of Women in Rock debate), 26 September, pp. 26–7.

Melody Maker (1992b) 'Only Love Can Break Your Heart', 19–26 December, p. 46.

Meyer, Marcy and O'Hara, Laura Shue (2003) 'When They Know Who We Are: The National Women's Music Festival comes to Ball State University', in Patrice M. Buzzanell, Helen Sterk and Lynn H. Turner (eds) *Gender in Applied Communication Contexts*. Thousand Oaks, CA: Sage, pp. 3–23.

Middleton, Richard (1993) *Studying Popular Music*. Milton Keynes: Open University Press.

Milano, Brett (2003) *Vinyl Junkies: Adventures in Record Collecting*. New York: St Martin's Griffin.

Milioto, Jennifer (1998) 'Women in Japanese Popular Music: Setting the Subcultural Scene', in Tôru Mitsui (ed.) *Popular Music: Intercultural Interpretations*, Graduate Program in Music, Kanazawa University: Kanazawa, pp. 485–97.

Miller, Bonny H. (1994) 'Ladies' Companion, Ladies' Canon? Women Composers in American Magazines from *Godley's* to the *Ladies' Home Journal*', in Susan C. Cook and Judy S. Tsou (eds) *Cecilia Reclaimed: Feminist Perspectives on Gender and Music*. Urbana and Chicago: University of Illinois Press, pp. 156–82.

Mills, Fred (1992) 'Pretty on the Inside' review, *Puncture*, 23, January, p. 43.

Mohan, Dominic (2004) 'Last Great Rock Hero', *The Sun*, 3 April.

Mojo (1995) 'The 100 Greatest Albums Ever Made', *Mojo*, 21, August, pp. 50–88.

Mojo (1996) '100 Greatest Albums Ever Made', *Mojo*, 26, January, pp. 50–88.

Mojo (1996) '100 Greatest Guitarists of All Time', *Mojo*, 31, June, pp. 54–103.

Mojo (1997) '100 Greatest Singles of All Time', *Mojo*, 45, August, pp. 42–88.

Moran, Caitlin (1994) 'Hole in One', *Melody Maker*, 19 February, pp. 12–13.

Moran, Caitlin (1999) 'Cat Woman', *Observer Life* (Sunday supplement magazine), 17 January, pp. 10–15.

Morris, Gina (1993a) 'Bjork on the Child Side', *NME*, 3 July, pp. 12–13.

Morris, Gina (1993b) 'Single of the Week – PJ Harvey: "50 Ft Queenie"' review, *NME*, 12 April, p. 18.

Morris, Gina (1997) 'Straight to Hell … Yeah!', in Liz Evans (ed.) *Girls Will Be Boys: Women Report on Rock* (republished from *Select*, November 1995). London: Pandora, pp. 147–60.

Morton, Roger (1992) 'Midwife Crisis', *NME*, 22 August, p. 5.

Morton, Roger (1996) 'Godmother of Grunge', *Observer Preview*, 14 April, p. 5.

Morton, Roger (1999) 'Funfair for the Common Man', *NME*, 19 June, pp. 22–3.

Muggleton, David and Weinzierl, Rupert (2003) *The Post-subcultures Reader*. Oxford: Berg.

Mulvey, John (1994) 'The Nightmare Before Christmas', *NME*, 24–31 December, pp. 14–15.

Mundy, John (1999) *Popular Music on Screen*. Manchester: Manchester University Press.

Mungham, Geoff and Pearson, Geoff (eds) (1976) *Working Class Youth Culture*. London: Routledge & Kegan Paul.

Murillo Jr, Enrique G. (1997) 'Pedagogy of a Latin American Festival', *Urban Review*, 29 (4), pp. 263–81.

Murray, Colin (1997) 'Head North for an Ice Time, Bjork!', *The People*, 23 November, p. 15.

Myers, Ben (1998) 'The Crocketts: Freaky, Folky, Drunken Punk', *Melody Maker*, 14 March, p. 10.

Myers, Caren (1993) 'Heart and Hole', *Melody Maker*, 3 April, p. 16.

Nasrallah, Dana (1992) 'Teenage Riot', *Spin*, 8 (8), November, pp. 78–80.

Negus, Keith (1992) *Producing Pop: Culture and Conflict in the Popular Music Industry*. London: Edward Arnold.

Nehring, Neil (1997) *Popular Music, Gender, and Postmodernism: Anger is an Energy*. London: Sage.

Nicholson, Geoff (1991) *Big Noises: Rock Guitar in the 1990s*. London: Quartet Books.

Nip, Joyce Y.M. (2004) 'The Relationship Between Online and Offline Communities: The Case of the Queer Sisters', *Media, Culture and Society*, 26 (3), pp. 409–28.

NME (2006) '100 Greatest British Albums Ever!', 28 January, pp. 24–9.

O'Brien, Karen (1995) *Hymn To Her: Women Musicians Talk*. London: Virago.

O'Brien, Lucy (1994) 'Ship Shape', *Vox*, 47, August, p. 127.

O'Brien, Lucy (1995a) 'Babes in Boyland', *Everywoman*, August, 117, pp. 10–13.

O'Brien, Lucy (1995b) *She Bop: The Definitive History of Women in Rock, Pop and Soul*. London: Penguin.

O'Brien, Lucy (1998) 'Important Women Pop and Rock Artists Ignored in Music of the Millennium Chart', *Women in Music*, April/May, p. 1.

O'Connell, Sharon (1998) 'Black Box Recorder: Singing in the Wreckage', *Melody Maker*, 2 May, p. 10.

O'Dair, Barbara (ed.) (1997) *Trouble Girls: The Rolling Stone Book of Women in Rock*. New York: Random House.

O'Hagan, Sean (2004) 'Death and Glory', *Observer Music Magazine*, 1 February, p. 39.

O'Meara, Caroline (2003) 'The Raincoats: Breaking Down Punk Rock's Masculinities', *Popular Music*, 22 (3), pp. 299–313.

Odintz, Andrea (1997) 'Technophilia: Women at the Control Board', in Barbara O'Dair (ed.) *Trouble Girls: The Rolling Stone Book of Women in Rock*. New York: Random House, pp. 211–17.

Ordway, Nico (1996) 'History of Zines', in V. Vale (ed.) *Zines! Volume One*. San Francisco: V/Search.

Padel, Ruth (2000) *I'm A Man: Sex, Gods and Rock 'n' Roll*. London: Faber & Faber.

Page, Betty (1993) 'Welcome to the Haemorrhage', *NME*, 24 April, p. 29.

Paglia, Camille (1992) *Sex, Art, and American Culture: Essays*. London: Penguin.

Parkes, Taylor (1994) 'Manic Depression', *Melody Maker*, 20 August, p. 12.

Partridge, Robert (1973) '*Melody Maker* Special on Women in Rock', *Melody Maker*, 10 November, pp. 1, 36.

Pearson, Deanne (1980) 'Women in Rock', *NME*, 29 March, pp. 1, 27–30, 51.

Peel, John (1994) 'Love Sends Postcards From Edge of Chaos', *The Guardian*, 30 August.

Peterson, Richard A. and David G. Berger (1975) 'Cycles in Symbol Production: The Case of Popular Music', *American Sociological Review*, 40, April, pp. 158–73.

Pinterics, Natasha (2001) 'Riding the Feminist Waves: In with the Third?', in 'Young Women: Feminists, Activists, Grrrls', *Canadian Women's Studies* (Special Issue), 20/21 (4/1), pp. 15–21.

Placksin, Sally (1985) *Jazz Women 1900 to the Present: Their Words, Lives and Music*. London: Pluto Press.

Plant, Sadie (1991) 'When Blowing the Strike is Striking the Blow', in Stewart Home (ed.) *The Art Strike Papers*, collected in the double volume *Neoist Manifestos/The Art Strike Papers*. Stirling: AK Press.

Porcello, Thomas (2004) 'Speaking of Sound: Language and the Professionalization of Sound-Recording Engineers', *Social Studies of Science*, 34 (5), pp. 733–58.

Porter, Charlie (1998) 'Chilled Out', *The Times*, Features section, 26 September.

Post, Laura (1997) *Backstage Pass: Interviews with Women in Music*. Norwich, Victoria: New Victoria Publishers.

Powlson, Nigel (2000) 'Slightly Mad', *Derby Evening Telegraph*, 27 October, p. 4.

Press, Joy (1997) 'Shouting Out Loud: Women in UK Punk', in Barbara O'Dair (ed.) *Trouble Girls: The Rolling Stone Book of Women in Rock*. New York: Random House.

Price, Simon (1996) 'The Return of the Manics', *Melody Maker*, 13 January, p. 25.

Pringle, Gill (1994) 'A Hole Lot of Love', *Daily Mirror*, 22 April, p. 19.

Purdue, Derrick, Dürrschmidt, Jörg, Jowers, Peter and O'Doherty, Richard (1997) 'DIY Culture and Extended Milieux: LETS, Veggie Boxes and Festivals', *Sociological Review*, 45 (4), pp. 645–67.

Rabinow, Paul (ed.) (1991) *Foucault Reader: An Introduction to Foucault's Thought*. London: Penguin.

Railton, Diane (2001) 'The Gendered Carnival of Pop', *Popular Music*, 20 (3), pp. 321–31.

Raphael, Amy (1993) 'Hole Lotta Love', *The Face*, 53, February, pp. 35–42.

Raphael, Amy (1995) *Never Mind The Bollocks: Women Rewrite Rock*. London: Virago.

Reddington, Helen (2003) 'Lady Punks in Bands: A Subculturette?', in David Muggleton and Rupert Weinzierl (eds) *The Post-subcultures Reader*. Oxford: Berg, pp. 239–51.

Reid, Jamie and Savage, Jon (1987) *Up They Rise: The Incomplete Works of Jamie Reid*. London: Faber & Faber.

Reynolds, Simon (1989) 'Against Health and Efficiency: Independent Music in the 1980s', in Angela McRobbie (ed.) *Zoot Suits and Second Hand Dresses: An Anthology of Fashion and Music*. Basingstoke: Macmillan, pp. 245–55.

Reynolds, Simon (1992) 'Belting Out that Most Unfeminine Emotion'. *New York Times* (Arts and Leisure: Section 2), 2 September, p. 27.

Reynolds, Simon (2005) *Rip it Up and Start Again: Postpunk 1978–1984*. London: Faber & Faber.

Reynolds, Simon and Press, Joy (1995) *The Sex Revolts: Gender, Rebellion and Rock 'n' Roll*. London: Serpents Tail.

Rhodes, Colin (2000) *Outsider Art: Spontaneous Alternatives*. London: Thames & Hudson.

Riordan, Ellen (2001) 'Commodified Agents and Empowered Girls: Consuming and Producing Feminism', *Journal of Communication Inquiry*, 25 (3), pp. 279–97.

Robbins, Trina (1999) *From Girls to Grrrlz: A History of Women's Comics from Teens to Zines*. San Francisco: Chronicle Books.

Roberts, Chris (ed.) (1994) *Idle Worship: How Pop Empowers the Weak, Rewards the Faithful and Succours the Needy*. London: HarperCollins.

Roberts, David, McFall, Sally, Bennett, Mark and MacDonald, Bruno (eds) (1998) *Guinness Rockopedia: The Ultimate A–Z of Rock and Pop*. London: Guinness.

Roberts, Robin (1990) '"Sex as a Weapon": Feminist Rock Music Videos', *NWSA Journal*, 2 (1), Winter, pp. 1–15.

Robinson, John (2004) 'Curt Answers', *The Guardian*, Guide, 10 April, p. 23.

Rodnitzky, Jerome L. (1975) 'Songs of Sisterhood: The Music of Women's Liberation', *Popular Music and Society*, 4, pp. 77–85.

Rolling Stone (1997) '30th Anniversary Issue: Women of Rock', *Rolling Stone*, 773, 13 November.

Rolling Stone (2005) 'The 50th Anniversary of Rock: The Immortals – The 100 Greatest Artists of All Time', *Rolling Stone*, 972, 21 April.

Roman, Leslie G. (1988) 'Intimacy, Labor, and Class: Ideologies of Feminine Sexuality in the Punk Slam Dance', in Leslie G. Roman and Linda K. Christian-

Smith (with Elizabeth Ellsworth) (ed.) *Becoming Feminine: The Politics of Popular Culture*. London: Falmer Press, pp. 143–84.

Romney, Jonathon (1995) 'Access All Areas: The Real Space of Rock Documentary', in Jonathon Romney and Adrian Wootton (eds) *Celluloid Jukebox: Popular Music and the Movies Since the 50s*. London: BFI Publishing, pp. 82–93.

Rosenberg, Jessica and Garofalo, Gitana (1998) 'Riot Grrrl: Revolutions from Within', *Signs: Journal of Women in Culture and Society*, 23 (3), pp. 809–41.

Ross-Trevor, Mike (1980) 'The Recording Engineer', in Peter Gammond and Raymond Horricks (eds) *The Music Goes Round and Round: A Cool Look at the Music Industry*. London: Quartet Books, pp. 117–34.

RT (2005) 'Mugison: Mugimama', *The Sun*, 22 April.

Rush, Ramona R., Oukrop, Carol E. and Sarikakis, Katharine (2005) 'A Global Hypothesis for Women in Journalism and Mass Communications: The Ratio of Recurrent and Reinforced Residuum', *Gazette: The International Journal for Communication Studies,* 67 (3), pp. 239–53.

Sandall, Robert (1994) 'Grunge King Unable to Deal With Stardom', *The Sunday Times*, 10 April, p. 19.

Sandall, Robert (1999) 'Crucial Cuts', *The Sunday Times*, Features section, 31 October.

Sandstrom, Boden (2000) 'Women Mix Engineers and the Power of Sound', in Pirkko Moisala and Beverley Diamond (eds) *Music and Gender*. Urbana and Chicago: University of Illinois Press, pp. 289–305.

Sawyer, Miranda (1993) 'Life's a Riot With Grrrlvsboy!', *Select,* May, pp. 24–5.

Schilt, Kristen (2003a) '"A Little Too Ironic": The Appropriation and Packaging of Riot Grrrl Politics by Mainstream Female Musicians', *Popular Music and Society*, 26 (1), pp. 5–16.

Schilt, Kristen (2003b) '"I'll Resist With Every Inch and Every Breath": Girls and Zine Making as a Form of Resistance', *Youth and Society*, 35 (1), pp. 71–97.

Schippers, Mimi (2002) *Rockin' Out of the Box: Gender Maneuvering in Alternative Rock*. New Brunswick, New Jersey: Rutgers University Press.

Schinder, Scott and the editors of Rolling Stone Press (1996) *Rolling Stone's Alt-Rock-a-Rama*. New York: Delta.

Select (1994) Issue 48, June, p. 13.

Select (1997) 'The Future is Female', 87, October, pp. 66–90.

Shank, Barry (1994) *Dissonant Identities: The Rock 'n' Roll Scene in Austin, Texas*. London: Wesleyan University Press.

Sheinwold, Patricia (1980) *Too Young To Die: The Stars the World Tragically Lost*. London: Cathay Books.

Shepherd, John (1991) *Music as Social Text*. Cambridge: Polity Press.

Shuker, Roy (1998) *Key Concepts in Popular Music*. London: Routledge.

Shuker, Roy (2004) 'Beyond the "High Fidelity" Stereotype: Defining the (Contemporary) Record Collector', *Popular Music*, 23 (3), pp. 311–30.

Sinclair, David (1997) 'Depression Moving in from Iceland', *The Times*, 19 September.

Skelton, Tracey and Valentine, Gill (eds) (1998) *Cool Places: Geographies of Youth Culture*. London: Routledge.

Skeggs, Beverley (1993) 'Two Minute Brother: Contestation through Gender, "Race" and Sexuality', *Innovation,* 6 (3), pp. 299–322.

Sky, Rick (1980) 'How Wendy Wu Became a Pop Star', *Observer Magazine,* 27 April.

Smaill, Adele (2005) *Challenging Gender Segregation in Music Technology: Findings and Recommendations for Music Education and Training Providers in the North-west.* A report for the Regional Equality in Music Project, University of Salford.

Smith, Giles (1995) *Lost in Music: A Pop Odyssey.* London: Picador.

Smith, Joan (1994) 'Kinderwhoring', *The Guardian Weekend,* 24 September, pp. 52–4.

Smith, Matthew J. (1999) 'Strands in the Web: Community-building Strategies in Online Fanzines', *Journal of Popular Culture,* 33 (2), pp. 87–99.

Smith, Richard (1995) *Seduced and Abandoned: Essays on Gay Men and Popular Music.* London: Cassell.

Snead, Elizabeth (1992) 'Feminist Riot Grrrls Don't Just Wanna Have Fun', *USA Today,* 7 August, p. 5D.

Solonas, Valerie (1983) *SCUM Manifesto.* London: AIM and Phoenix Press (originally published 1968).

Spencer, Neil (1996) 'Nordic But Nice', *Observer Review,* 28 January, p. 13.

Spice Girls (1997) *Girl Power!* London: Zone/Chameleon.

Stambler, Irwin (1989) *The Encyclopedia of Pop, Rock and Soul* (revised edn). London: Macmillan.

Steward, Sue and Garratt, Sheryl (1985) *Signed, Sealed and Delivered: True Life Stories of Women in Pop.* London: Pluto Press.

Strachan, Rob (2006) 'Music Video and Video and Genre: Structure, Context and Commerce' in Steven Brown and Ulrik Volgsten (eds) *Music and Manipulation: On the Social Uses and Social Control of Music.* Oxford: Berghahn.

Strachan, Rob and Leonard, Marion (2003) 'Singer-songwriter', in John Shepherd, David Horn, Dave Laing, Paul Oliver and Peter Wicke (eds) *Continuum Encyclopedia of Popular Music of the World Volume II: Performance and Production.* London: Continuum, pp. 198–202.

Strachan, Robert (2003) *Do-it-Yourself: Industry, Ideology, Aesthetics and Micro Independent Record labels in the UK.* Unpublished PhD thesis, University of Liverpool.

Stratton, Jon (1982) 'Between Two Worlds: Art and Commercialism in the Record Industry', *Sociological Review,* 30, pp. 267–85.

Straw, Will (1991) 'Systems of Articulation, Logics of Change: Communities and Scenes in Popular Music', *Cultural Studies,* 5 (3), October, pp. 368–88.

Straw, Will (1997) 'Sizing Up Record Collections: Gender and Connoisseurship in Rock Music Culture', in Sheila Whiteley (ed.) *Sexing The Groove: Popular Music and Gender.* London: Routledge, pp. 3–16.

Sullivan, Caroline (1993a) 'Good Golly, Ms Polly', *The Guardian,* 1 October, p. 8.

Sullivan, Caroline (1993b) 'PJ Harvey: Rid Of Me', *The Guardian,* 23 April, pp. 2, 14.

Sullivan, Caroline (1994a) 'Brixton Academy: Bjork; Pop', The *Guardian,* 28 February, p. 7.

Sullivan, Caroline (1994b) 'Epitaph for Generation X', *The Guardian*, 12 April, p. 19.

Sullivan, Caroline (1995) 'The Joy of Hacking: Women Rock Critics' in Sarah Cooper (ed.) *Girls! Girls! Girls! Essays on Women and Music*. London: Cassell, pp. 138–45.

Sullivan, Caroline (1996) Live Review: Bjork, Sheffield, *The Guardian*, 22 January, p. 41.

Sullivan, Caroline (1997a) 'Pop CD of the Week: Iceland Cometh', *The Guardian*, 19 September, p. T20.

Sullivan, Caroline (1997b) 'Sending Out an SOS', *The Guardian*, 15 November, p. 7.

Sullivan, Caroline (1998) 'Don't Call Me Pixie', *The Guardian*, 30 November, p. 12.

Sutherland, Steve (1993) 'Love Resurrection', *NME*, 17 April, p. 26.

Sutherland, Steve (1998) 'Just an Angster's Poll', *Uncut*, November, p. 94.

Szasz, Thomas S. MD (1971) *The Manufacture of Madness: A Comparative Study of the Inquisition and the Mental Health Movement*. London: Routledge & Kegan Paul.

Taft, Jessica K. (2004) 'Girl Power Politics: Pop-culture Barriers and Organisational Resistance', in Anita Harris (ed.) *All About the Girl: Culture, Power and Identity*. London: Routledge, pp. 69–78.

Tagg, Philip (1989) 'An Anthropology of Stereotypes in TV Music?', *Svensk tidskrift för musikforskning [Swedish Musicological Journal]*, Göteborg, pp. 19–42.

Taylor, Lori (1993) 'Riot Grrls Respond To Fame'. Unpublished paper presented to American Folklore Society, Eugene, Oregon, 30 October.

Taylor, Richie (2001) 'Ireland's Top Stars Have Made their Mark on Bjork', *The Sun*, 24 August.

Terry, N. (September 1993) 'Linus', *Lime Lizard*, p. 14.

Théberge, Paul (1991) 'Musicians' Magazines in the 1980s: The Creation of a Community and a Consumer Market', *Cultural Studies*, 5 (3), pp. 270–93.

Théberge, Paul (1997) *Any Sound You Can Imagine: Making Music/Consuming Technology*. Hanover, NH: Wesleyan University Press.

Thicknesse, Robert (2004) 'The Legacy: How *Times* Music Critics See Him', *The Times,* Times2, 5 April, p. 8.

Thompson, Dave (2000) *Alternative Rock*. San Francisco: Miller Freeman Books.

Thomson, Liz (ed.) (1982) *New Women in Rock*. London: Omnibus Press.

Thomson, Neil (1999) 'On Band Two: TV One', *NME*, 29 May, p. 14.

Thorncroft, Antony (1994) 'The Bjork Saga', *Financial Times*, Arts, 26 February, p. xxiv.

Thornton, Sarah (1990) 'Strategies for Reconstructing the Popular Past', *Popular Music*, 9 (1), pp. 87–95.

Thornton, Sarah (1994) 'Moral Panic, the Media and British Rave Culture', in Andrew Ross and Tricia Rose (eds) *Microphone Fiends: Youth Music and Youth Culture*. London: Routledge, pp. 176–92.

Thornton, Sarah (1995) *Club Cultures: Music, Media and Subcultural Capital*. Cambridge: Polity Press.

Toynbee, Jason (1993) 'Policing Bohemia, Pinning Up Grunge: the Music Press and Generic Change in British Pop and Rock', *Popular Music*, 12 (3), pp. 289–300.

Toynbee, Jason (2000) *Making Popular Music: Musicians, Creativity and Institutions*. London: Arnold.

Treagus, Mandy (1998) 'Gazing at the Spice Girls: Audience, Power and Visual Representation', *Outskirts: Feminisms Along the Edge*, 3 (online journal: http://www.chloe.uwa.edu.au/outskirts/archive/volume3/treagus), November.

Tredre, Roger and Vulliamy, Ed (1994) 'Lost Generation's Leader finds his Place in Nirvana', *Observer*, 10 April, p. 3.

True, Everett (1992) 'Why Women Can't Rock', *Melody Maker*, 19 September, p. 46.

Tucker, Sherrie (2000) *Swing Shift: "All-Girl" Bands of the 1940s*. London: Duke University Press.

Turner, Chérie (2001) *The Riot Grrrl Movement: The Feminism of a New Generation*. New York: Rosen Publishing Group.

Upton, Sam (1996) 'The Hills Are Alive', *Select*, 78, December, p. 55.

Ussher, Jane (1991) *Women's Madness: Misogyny or Mental Illness*. London: Harvester Wheatsheaf.

Vale, V. (ed.) (1996) *Zines! Volume One*. San Francisco: V/Search.

Vale, V. (ed.) (1997) *Zines! Volume Two*, San Francisco: V/Search.

Van Poznak, Elissa (1993) 'Angry Young Women', *The Guardian*, 24 March, p. 8.

Vaughan, Bonnie (1994) 'Addicted to Love', *The Guardian, Guide*, 9 April, p. 14.

Vernallis, Carol (1998) 'The Aesthetics of Music Video: an analysis of Madonna's "Cherish"', *Popular Music*, 17 (2), pp. 153–85.

Verrico, Lisa (2004) 'Singalong? Not Bjork', *The Times*, Times2 section, 20 August, p. 18.

Wade, Michael (1972) *Voxpop: Profiles of the Pop Industry*. London: Harrap.

Waksman, Steve (1999) *Instruments of Desire: The Electric Guitar and the Shaping of Musical Experience*. London: Harvard University Press.

Wald, Gayle (1997) 'One of the Boys? Whiteness, Gender, and Popular Music Studies', in Mike Hill (ed.) *Whiteness: A Critical Reader*. New York: New York University Press, pp. 151–67.

Wald, Gayle (2002) 'Just a Girl? Rock Music, Feminism, and the Cultural Construction of Female Youth', in Roger Beebe, Denise Fulbrook and Ben Saunders (eds) *Rock Over The Edge: Transformations in Popular Music Culture*. Durham: Duke University Press, pp. 191–215.

Wallace, Richard (1994) 'End of a Legend', *Daily Mirror*, 11 April, pp. 8–9.

Walser, Robert (1993) *Running With the Devil: Power, Gender, and Madness in Heavy Metal Music*. Hanover, NH: Wesleyan University Press.

Waterman, Stanley (1998) 'Carnivals for Elites? The Cultural Politics of Arts Festivals', *Progress in Human Geography*, 22 (1), pp. 54–74.

Waugh, Daisy (1993) 'Don't Mess With the Girls Who Just Wanna Be Grrls', *Evening Standard*, 16 August, p. 10.

Weisbard, Eric and Marks, Craig (1995) *Spin Alternative Record Guide*. New York: Vintage.

Wells, Steven (1993) 'Ready, Teddy, Go!', *NME*, 6 March, p. 13.

Wener, Louise (2005) 'For the Briefest of Moments the Genie was Out of the Bottle', *Observer* (Review section), 6 February, p. 6.

White, Emily (1992) 'Revolution Grrrl Style Now', *LA Weekly*, 14 (32), 10–16 July, pp. 20–28.

Whiteley, Sheila (ed.) (1997) *Sexing the Groove: Popular Music and Gender*. London: Routledge.

Whiteley, Sheila (2000) *Women and Popular Music: Sexuality, Identity and Subjectivity*. London: Routledge.

Wilkins, Amy C. (2004) '"So Full of Myself as a Chick": Goth Women, Sexual Independence, and Gender Egalitarianism', *Gender & Society*, 18 (3), pp. 328–49.

Williams, J. Patrick (2006) 'Authentic Identities: Straightedge Subculture, Music, and the Internet', *Journal of Contemporary Ethnography*, 35 (2), pp. 173–200.

Willis, Paul (1990) 'The Golden Age', in Simon Frith and Andrew Goodwin (eds) *On Record: Rock, Pop, and the Written Word*. New York: Pantheon Books, pp. 43–55.

Wilson, Brian and Atkinson, Michael (2005) 'Rave and Straightedge, the Virtual and the Real: Exploring Online and Offline Experiences in Canadian Youth Subcultures', *Youth and Society*, 36 (3), pp. 276–311.

Wilson, Elizabeth (1993) 'Is Transgression Transgressive?' in Joseph Bristow and Angela R. Wilson (eds) *Activating Theory: Lesbian, Gay and Bisexual Politics*. London: Lawrence & Wishart, pp. 107–17.

Wise, Nick (1995) *Courtney Love*. London: Omnibus Press.

Wise, Sue (1990) 'Sexing Elvis', in Simon Frith and Andrew Goodwin (eds) *On Record: Rock, Pop, and the Written Word. New York*: Pantheon Books, pp. 390–98.

Woodworth, Marc (ed.) (1998) *Solo: Women Singer-songwriters in Their Own Words*. New York: Delta.

Films and documentaries

Blur: Starshaped (1993) Dir. PMI Video

The Doors (1991) Dir. Oliver Stone

Kurt and Courtney (1998) Dir. Nick Broomfield

Reeling with PJ Harvey (1994) Dir. Pinko and Maria Mochnaz

The Rose (1979) Dir. Mark Rydell

Spiceworld: The Movie (1997)

Spinal Tap (1984) Dir. Rob Reiner

Stardust (1974) Dir. Michael Apted

Velvet Goldmine (1998) Dir. Todd Haynes

Index

The definite article is ignored in the alphabetical arrangement but is not inverted. For example 'The Beach Boys' will be found under 'B'. References to illustrations are in bold